D0429282

WILLIAMS-SONOMA

THE WINE GUIDE

TIME-LIFE BOOKS
Time-Life Books is a division of Time Life Inc.
Time Life is a trademark of Time Warner Inc. U.S.A.

TIME-LIFE CUSTOM PUBLISHING
Vice President and Publisher: Terry Newell
Vice President of Sales and Marketing: Neil Levin
Director of Financial Operations: J. Brian Birky
Director of Acquisitions and Editorial Resources: Jennifer L. Pearce

WILLIAMS-SONOMA
Founder and Vice-Chairman: Chuck Williams
Associate Book Buyer: Cecilia Michaelis

WELDON OWEN INC.
Chief Executive Officer: John Owen
Chief Operating Officer: Larry Partington
Vice President International Sales: Stuart Laurence
Vice President and Publisher: Roger S. Shaw

Managing Editor: Claire Ellerton
Series Editor: Janet Goldenberg
Contributing Editor: Norman Kolpas
Copy Editors: Carole Clements, Ingrid Karikari, Gail Nelson
Indexer: Naomi Good
Proofreader: Alicia Eckley

Art Director: Emma Forge
Senior Designer: Alison Shackleton
Series Designer: Diane Dempsey
Production Director: Stephanie Sherman
Production Manager: Lisa Cowart-Mayor

Photographs: All supplied by Cephas Picture Library.
All photographs by Mick Rock except:
Wine Magazine, 6; Diana Mewes, 259.

The Williams-Sonoma Guides
conceived and produced by Weldon Owen Inc.
814 Montgomery Street, San Francisco, CA 94133

In collaboration with Williams-Sonoma
3250 Van Ness Avenue, San Francisco, CA 94109

Separations by Bright Arts Graphics (S) Pte. Ltd.
Printed in Singapore by Tien Wah Press (Pte.) Ltd.

A WELDON OWEN PRODUCTION

First printed in 1999.

10 9 8 7 6 5 4 3 2

Library of Congress Cataloging-in-Publication Data
The wine guide / contributing editors, Larry Walker
& Wink Lorch; illustrations by Trevor Lawrence.
p. cm. -- (Williams-Sonoma guides)
Includes index.
ISBN 0-7370-0063-5 (hc.)
1. Wine and winemaking. I. Walker, Larry, 1936– .
II. Lorch, Wink. III. Series.
TP548.W763 1999
641.2'2--dc21 99-33472
CIP

A NOTE ON WEIGHTS AND MEASURES

All recipes include customary U.S. and metric measurements. Metric conversions are based on a standard developed for these books and have been rounded off. Actual measurements may vary.

WILLIAMS-SONOMA

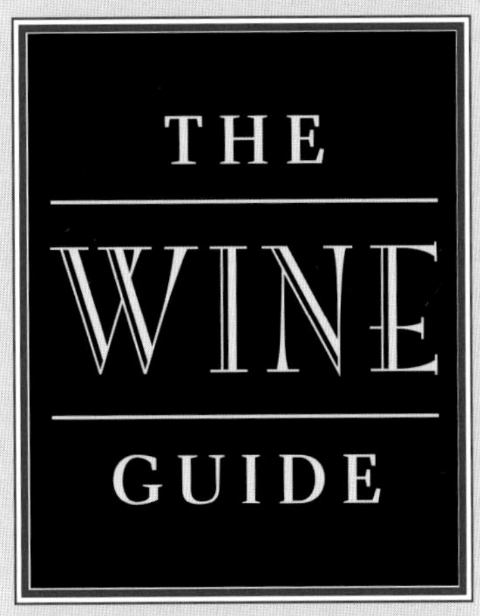

THE WINE GUIDE

CONTRIBUTING EDITORS / LARRY WALKER AND WINK LORCH

ILLUSTRATOR / TREVOR LAWRENCE

CARTOGRAPHER / ANDREW THOMPSON

FOREWORD BY CHUCK WILLIAMS

CONTENTS

la récolte 1986 a produit
291.800 bordelaises et demies
7.250 magnums et jéroboams
tout en bouteilles au Château

Foreword

"Red or White?"

It's hard to believe that not long ago, this was the most commonly asked wine question. Today it sometimes seems as if you need to study full time to keep up with everything there is to know about wine.

That's why I'm particularly pleased with this comprehensive, easy-to-use guide to wine. Logically organized, it explains anything you might need to know about, from grape varieties and wine regions to the shapes of bottles and glassware, from buying and storing wine to opening, pouring, and tasting it. You'll also find advice on cooking with wine and matching wine with food.

Whether you're trying to decide which wine to buy or what to order, how much to serve at a party or how long to store a special bottle, you'll quickly find the answer here.

Or you can sit back and learn at your leisure. Like good wine, this book is designed to be enjoyed and savored.

CHAPTER 1

Wine Basics

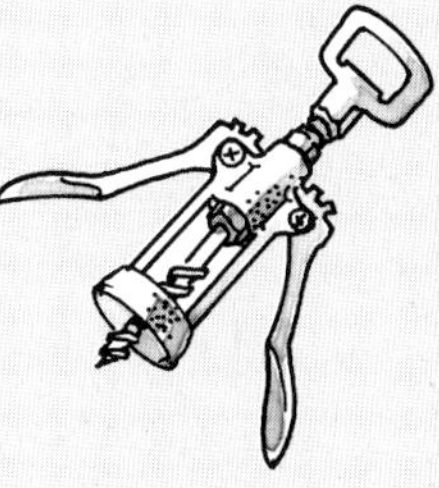

Information on how to open, taste, and serve wine, along with an introduction to key wine styles and grape varieties.

Evolution of Wine

For all its richness and complexity, wine is essentially fermented grape juice. However, much of the pleasure of wine lies in its seemingly infinite variety. The five basic types of wine are red, white, rosé, sparkling, and fortified wine. Most of the world's great wines are wines of place, made with grapes of a particular vintage and from a particular vineyard. Climate, location, soil, and grape varieties all affect the quality of wines, as do the various vine-growing and winemaking methods. The length of time wine matures in the barrel and bottle also influences how the finished wine will taste.

ORIGINS OF WINE

The first wine may have come about when a Stone Age gatherer left a cluster of wild grapes in a clay or wooden bowl and forgot about them. Over a period of days, the natural yeast present on the grape skins would have caused the grape juice to ferment and turn into wine—not very good wine, but wine nonetheless.

There is evidence that wine was drunk in the Middle East as long ago as 4000 B.C. Even then, it was regarded as a special beverage. In early dynastic Egypt, for example, one of the many titles given to the god Osiris was Lord of Wine.

Wine was an important part of Greek and Roman life, too, with philosophers and poets debating the best vintages and vineyards. It was also a major element of trade around the Mediterranean, and it continued to be widely drunk and appreciated during the Middle Ages.

The Spanish brought *Vitis vinifera*, the European winemaking vine, with them to America in the early sixteenth century, and wine was made in Mexico within a few years of the conquest. From there, Spanish missionaries took winemaking first into South America and then north into California, Texas, and New Mexico during the late eighteenth century. From the 1780s, immigrants from many different countries began planting vines in Australia, and commercial winemaking was well established there by the 1830s, as it was in the United States.

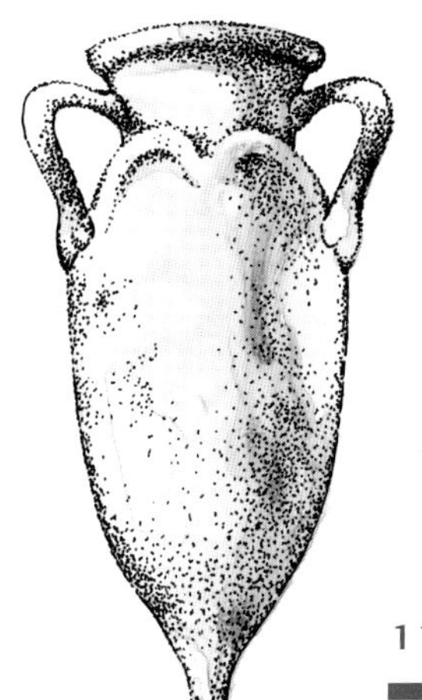

WINE VESSEL
In Greek and Roman times, wine was transported to underground cellars in large earthenware amphorae.

WORLD WINE REGIONS

The major classic wine producers are France, Germany, Italy, Portugal, and Spain. New World wine producers include the United States, Australia, New Zealand, Chile, Argentina, and South Africa.

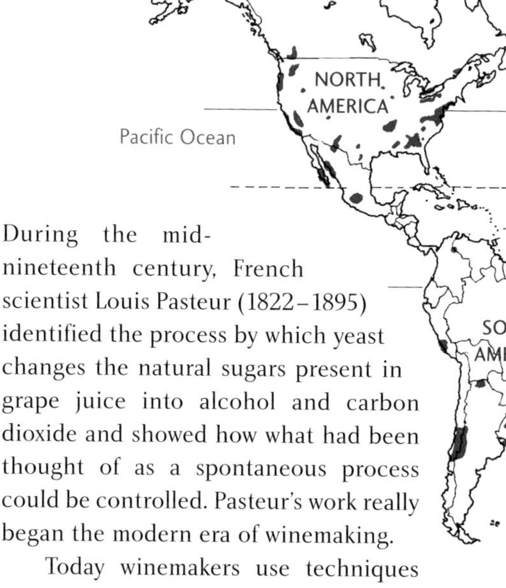

During the mid-nineteenth century, French scientist Louis Pasteur (1822–1895) identified the process by which yeast changes the natural sugars present in grape juice into alcohol and carbon dioxide and showed how what had been thought of as a spontaneous process could be controlled. Pasteur's work really began the modern era of winemaking.

Today winemakers use techniques such as controlling fermentation temperatures, and storing the fermenting wine in stainless steel, to create wines that are of a consistent standard.

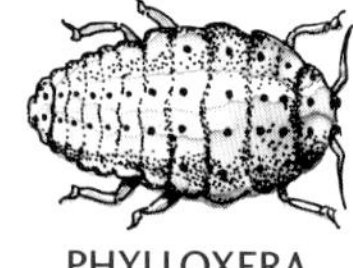

PHYLLOXERA

This root louse, which kills vines by eating their roots, originated in North America. It is still a serious problem in California.

Grape growers, too, have vastly improved the quality of grapes available; by endeavoring, for example, to keep vine diseases and pests under control. During the nineteenth century, European vines were affected by two diseases—powdery mildew and downy mildew. Later in the same century, the root-eating louse *phylloxera* (see left) destroyed many of the world's vineyards before it was stopped by the development of resistant rootstock from native American vines.

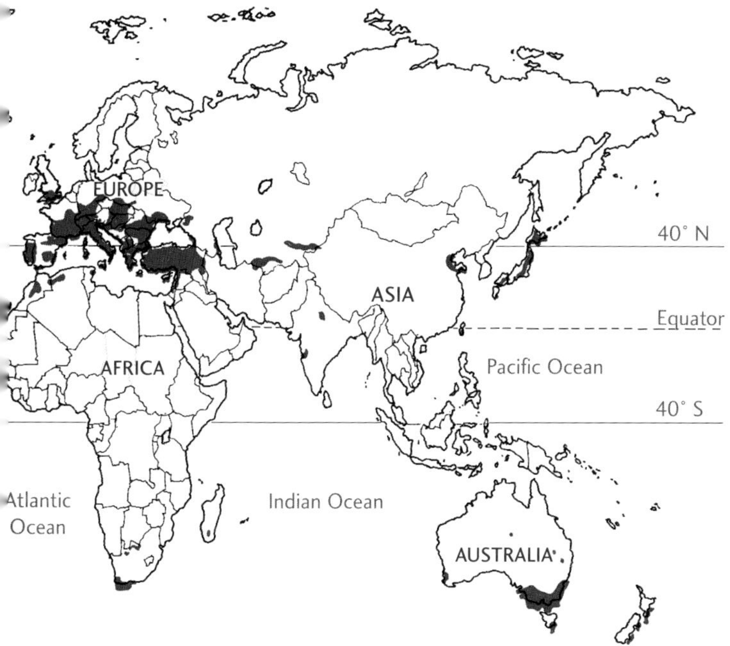

Wine is now made on every continent except Antarctica. The chief growing areas in the Northern hemisphere lie between 32° latitude and 51° latitude, and in the Southern hemisphere between 28° latitude and 42° latitude. There are exceptions, of course, and wine of a sort can be made much closer to the equator than the limits stated above.

The traditional, or classic, growing regions are centered in Europe, with France especially known for fine wines. In the last 20 to 30 years, wines from the newer regions of North and South America, Australia, New Zealand, and South Africa (often referred to as New World wines) have frequently matched in quality many of the wines from the classic areas.

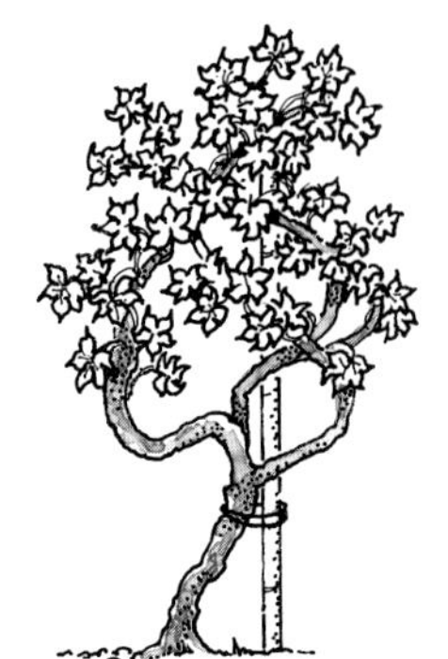

How Wine Is Made

Without good grapes there can be no good wine. Recognizing this simple fact, many vintners have taken to calling themselves "winegrowers," because they see how quality in the vineyards affects wine. There is constant experimentation to improve vine quality, from finding the right soils to deciding what kind of trellis system to use. One of the most important considerations in winemaking is determining when to pick the grapes. Once the grapes have been picked, they are taken to the winery where they are crushed—this is the first stage in the winemaking process.

STILL WINES

All grapes used in winemaking have clear juice—it is the skins of red grapes that provide the color for red wines, and for all good quality rosés, too. The first stage of winemaking involves crushing the grapes. White grapes are pressed to separate the juice from the skins before fermentation, whereas reds are fermented with the skins before pressing. Maturation in oak or steel follows fermentation, and the wine is then usually clarified before bottling.

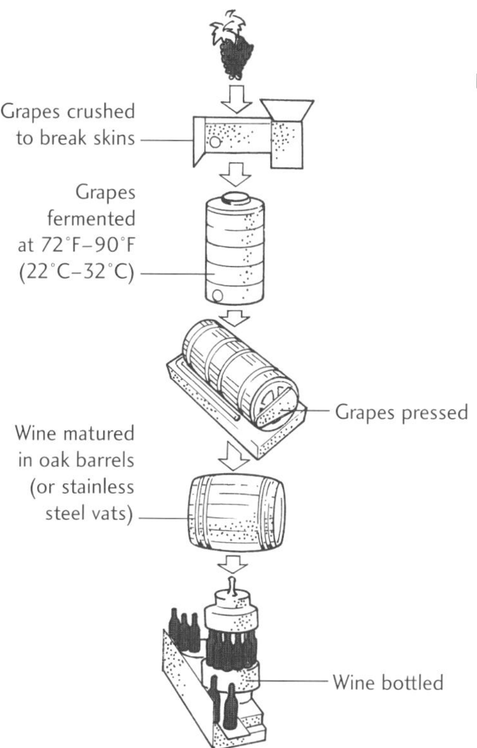

MAKING RED WINE

Red wine is fermented at much higher temperatures than white wine, which contributes to good color and tannin extraction.

RED WINE The crushed grapes are fermented with their skins, which adds color, tannin (an astringent element that enables wine to age), and flavor to the wine. The grapes are then pressed to separate the juice from the skins, and the young wine is matured in wood or stainless steel, depending on the style desired.

WHITE WINE The grapes are pressed just after crushing. Most white wines are fermented in

Racking

Racking off the lees, or sediment, involves moving red or white wine from barrel to barrel during the aging process. This helps to remove the lees and add trace amounts of oxygen, which softens the wine's harsher tannins.

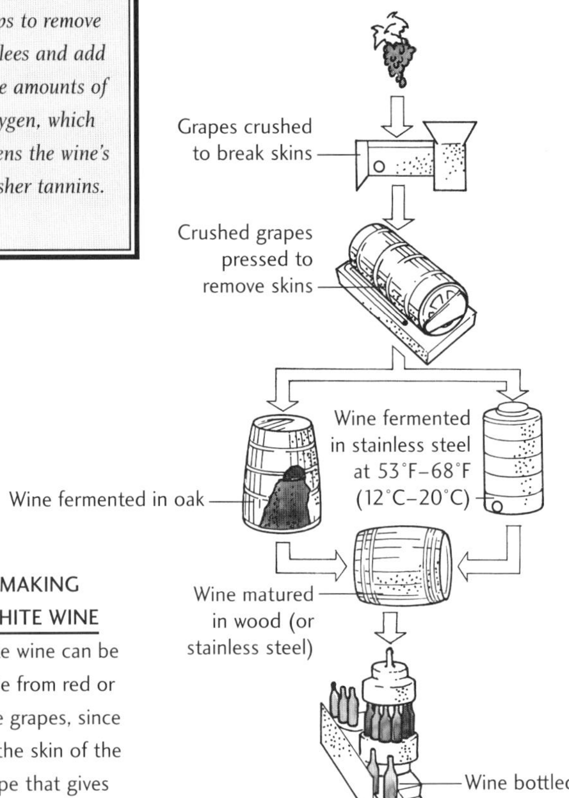

MAKING WHITE WINE

White wine can be made from red or white grapes, since it is the skin of the grape that gives wine its color.

stainless steel at low temperatures, which enhances the fruitiness of the wine. These wines can be transferred to oak barrels at a later stage. Other white wines, such as some Chardonnays, may be fermented in oak.

ROSÉ WINE True rosé wines differ from red wines in that the fermenting juice is kept in contact with the skins for a much shorter time, often only a few hours. This allows some color to be extracted, but very little tannin. Many inexpensive rosés are made by blending a little red wine or fermenting juice with white wine.

DESSERT WINE For the great dessert wines, the grapes are left on the vine until the regular harvest has ended. This concentrates sugar in the grapes. In certain fine wine regions, and in the best years, they may be affected by *Botrytis cinerea,* or noble rot. This causes the skins to break, so much of the liquid in the grapes evaporates, concentrating the sugars further.

Maturing in Barrel

The type of barrel used to mature wine is critical. New oak barrels impart wood tannins to wine, while older oak barrels add softness and complexity. The barrel also exposes the wine to small amounts of oxygen (the wood is permeable by air), which speeds up the maturation process. Barrel size is key, too, as it affects the ratio of wine to wood and oxygen. Generally, the smaller the barrel, the more rapid the maturation process. The most common barrel size is 59 gallons (223 liters).

Fortified Dessert Wines

Fortified wines include some of the world's great dessert wines. As well as the classic after-dinner ports, there are some wonderful dessert sherries, Madeira, with its great aging potential, lush vins doux naturels *from France, and sweet fortified Muscats from Australia.*

FORTIFIED WINES

Fortified wines are wines that have had brandy or some other grape spirit added to increase the alcoholic content during or after fermentation.

PORT Making port involves adding grape spirit to stop fermentation and maintain high sugar and alcohol levels. Vintage ports, made only in years when grape quality is excellent, are aged in wood for two years. Ruby and tawny (nonvintage) ports receive varying time in wood, depending on the style desired.

SHERRY This Spanish wine consists of two basic styles: dark, rich, dry Oloroso and pale, light, dry Fino sherry. Sweet sherry is made by sweetening either style before bottling. After fermentation, the wine is poured into wooden casks, called butts, for aging. The surface of the wine in some butts will develop a bloom of wild yeast called flor. Wines with flor are destined to become Fino sherries, and are lightly fortified with brandy. Wines without flor will become Olorosos, and are fortified more strongly than Finos. All sherries are aged and blended in a solera, a system in which younger wines are added to older wines over a number of years. As the new wine moves through the solera, it takes on the character of the older wines.

MADEIRA This fortified wine is made in a range of dry to sweet styles. In the eighteenth century, Madeira wine was often sent on long tropical sea voyages while still in barrel, which resulted in a mellowing of the wine in the ships' warm holds. Today, heat is applied to age the wine artificially. Cheaper wines are heated in tanks at 104°F–122°F (40°C–50°C) for at least three months. More expensive wines are kept in warm rooms at lower temperatures for up to a year.

CHAMPAGNE AND SPARKLING WINES

For wine to be called Champagne, it must be made from any or all of three different grape varieties (Chardonnay, Pinot Noir, and Pinot Meunier) grown in the Champagne region of France, and produced using the Champagne method—a lengthy, labor-intensive, and expensive process. Fine sparkling wines in other parts of the world are also made by the Champagne method (also called Traditional Method). Cheaper methods are used to make less expensive sparkling wines.

CHAMPAGNE METHOD In early spring, following harvest, still wines are tasted and assembled into the final blend, or cuvée.

The final blend is then bottled with a small portion of wine, sugar, and yeast, called the *liqueur de tirage,* and sealed, usually with a metal cap. The yeast begins a secondary fermentation in the bottle, producing carbon dioxide, which dissolves in the wine. This stage takes from ten days to three months. The wine is then left for several further months, or even years, to age in contact with the yeast.

At the next stage, *remuage,* the bottles are stacked, with their necks pointing downward, at

Wine Bubbles

What about those bubbles? During the production process, pressure inside the sealed bottle has kept the trapped carbon dioxide dissolved in the wine. But when the bottle is opened, the carbon dioxide bubbles up out of the wine and escapes into the air.

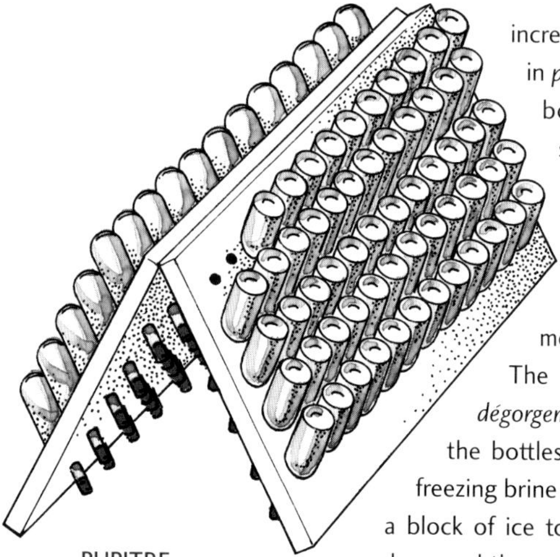

increasingly steep angles in *pupitres*, or racks. The bottles are turned slightly at regular intervals to shift the sediment into the bottle necks. Today, the process is mostly mechanized.

The next stage is called *dégorgement*. The necks of the bottles are plunged into a freezing brine solution that causes a block of ice to form in the bottle neck around the sediment. The bottle is then flipped upright, the metal cap is popped, and the ice and sediment shoot out. Next, the bottle is topped up with a mixture of reserve wine and sugar, called the *dosage*. The amount of sugar added determines the sweetness of the wine. The cork is then placed in the bottle and it receives further aging before it is finally released. The whole process from bottling to release takes at least a year.

PUPITRE

Champagne bottles are turned to lie at increasingly steep angles in racks called *pupitres*.

OTHER METHODS The most basic method for making sparkling wine involves pumping carbon dioxide into still wines. However, the better sparkling wines are made by conducting a second fermentation to create the bubbles. In the Charmat process, this fermentation may take place in large, sealed tanks. In the transfer method, the wine is fermented in one bottle and transferred to a fresh bottle after filtration. Bottle-fermented sparkling wine is generally of better quality than wine fermented in tank.

Studying the Bottle

You can learn a great deal from the wine bottle and label before you remove the cork. The bottle's shape can tell you something about the wine inside, including where it is from. Various shapes and colors have developed over the centuries. In recent years, some producers have abandoned the traditional shapes in favor of eye-catching bottles with wide, flanged mouths and other unusual features, some harking back to the handblown bottles of preindustrial Europe. The bottle label provides key information about the wine inside, and must also satisfy certain minimum legal requirements.

CLASSIC BOTTLE SHAPES

Some of the characteristic bottle shapes shown below are associated with particular wine regions.

RED BORDEAUX OR CLARET This green-cast bottle has been virtually universally adopted for the wines of Bordeaux in France, and for Cabernet Sauvignon, Merlot, Cabernet Franc, Malbec, and Petit Verdot almost everywhere.

BURGUNDY A bottle shape associated with the French wine region, this has been adopted almost everywhere for Pinot Noir in a dark green bottle, and for Chardonnay in a yellow-green bottle known as "dead leaf."

CHAMPAGNE The classic bottle for sparkling wine is similar in shape to a Burgundy bottle, usually deep green in color, and much heavier. Most Champagne bottles have a deep punt.

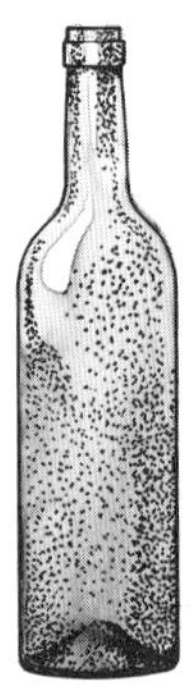

BORDEAUX OR CLARET

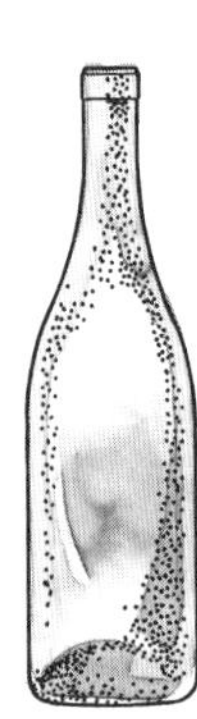

BURGUNDY

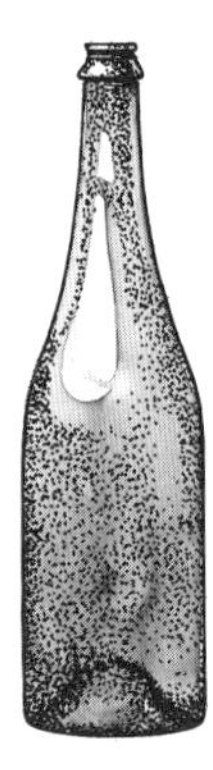

CHAMPAGNE

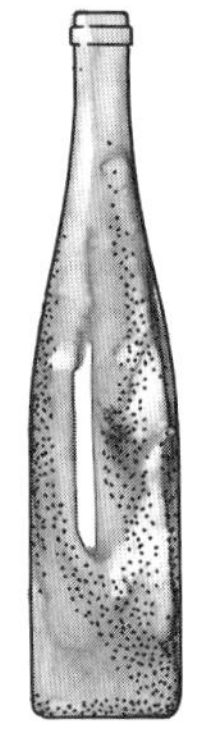

ALSACE OR RIESLING

ALSACE OR RIESLING Ranging in color from pale green to brown, this graceful, slender bottle is used for Riesling, and also for Gewürztraminer and other aromatic white wines in most parts of the world.

WHITE BORDEAUX A clear glass bottle originally used for sweet and dry white Bordeaux wines, it is used today for numerous other white wine styles throughout the world.

SHERRY This dark brown bottle has a roughly Bordeaux shape, but more rounded shoulders and a longer neck.

PORT Very dark green or almost black in color, this distinctive squat bottle is easily recognized by its slightly bulbous neck.

BOCKSBEUTEL The traditional bottle used in Germany's Franken region is green and round.

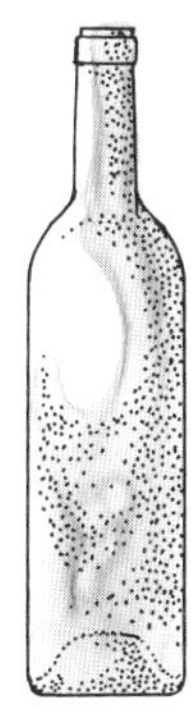

WHITE BORDEAUX

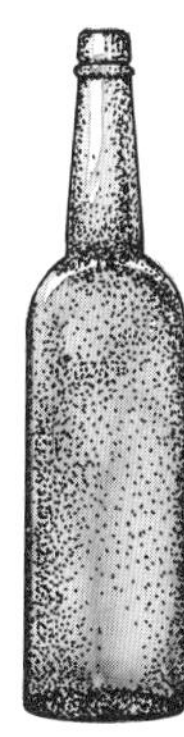

SHERRY

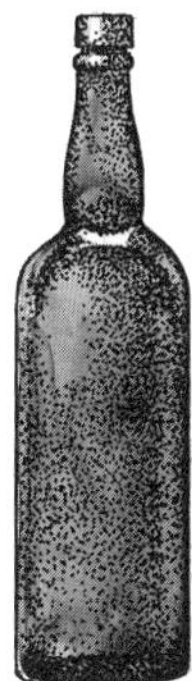

PORT

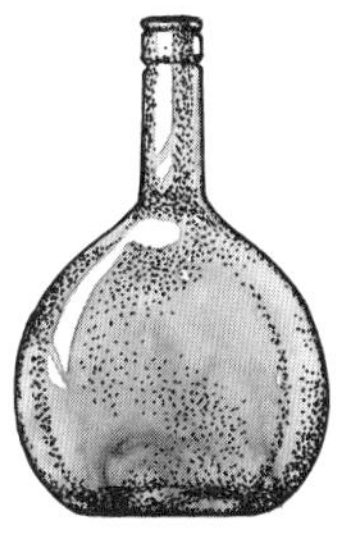

BOCKSBEUTEL

THE LABEL

There are four key pieces of information to look for on the front label:

- Where the wine was made, that is, the country and/or appellation (designated wine region) of origin
- What variety of grapes was used—especially important in newer winegrowing areas, but rarely shown on French wine labels
- The name of the producer
- The year the grapes were harvested

There are also certain legal requirements, which vary from country to country, including the volume of wine in the bottle, the alcohol content, and mandatory health warnings in some countries, including the United States.

Wine producers often use a back label to give more detailed information about the wine in the bottle, such as the blend of grape varieties used, or even a colorful story about the producer.

Misleading Labels

From time to time, phrases or words may appear on wine labels that have no legal definition, such as "Proprietor's Reserve," "Barrel Select," or "Cellar Selection." These are phrases that may attempt to give ordinary wines a quality aura.

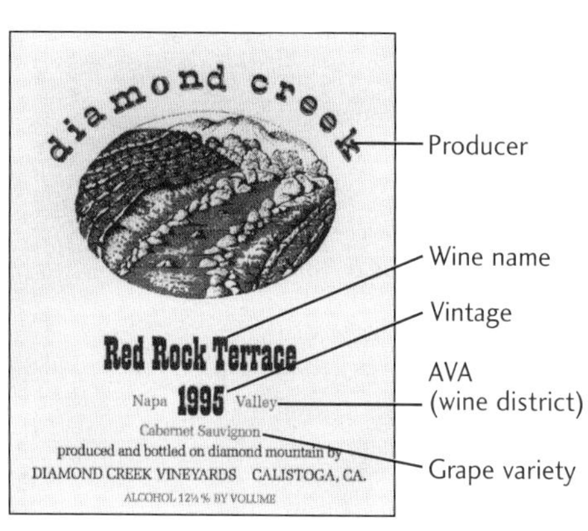

AMERICAN LABEL

The American wine label shows the grape variety, but gives no indication of wine quality (unlike French and German labels), which is why it's a good idea to get to know the producers.

FRENCH LABEL

The information on a French wine label tends to concentrate on where the wine comes from and not what it is made of.

QUALITY CLASSIFICATIONS

All the major winegrowing areas of the world have undertaken some quality classification of wines as a guarantee to the consumer that what they buy is what is written on the label. Most classifications are based on the French system of Appellation Contrôlée (AC), which specifies the

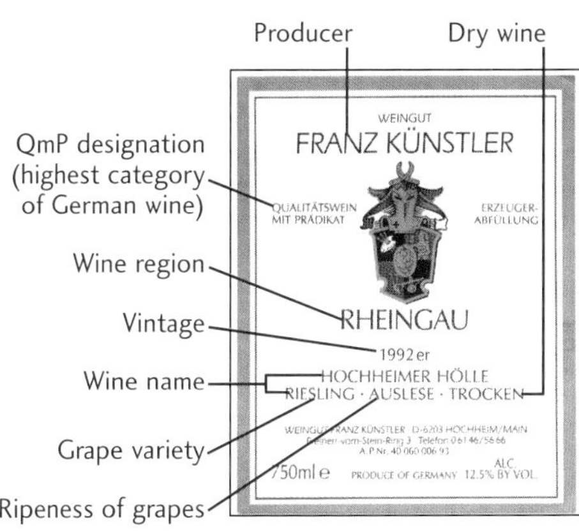

Ordinary or Special?

Some wine brands present the image of high quality wine with ordinary wine in the bottle. You can sometimes spot this by the lack of a specific place of origin—for example, a label may read California Merlot rather than Napa Valley Merlot.

GERMAN LABEL

This label provides detailed information about the grapes used to make the wine.

wine's exact origin. AC-approved wines must also meet certain requirements as to grape variety—for example, regulations for Champagne allow only three varieties (Chardonnay, Pinot Meunier, and Pinot Noir). Other regulations cover minimum alcohol levels, maximum production per hectare, and other aspects of grape growing and winemaking applicable to the particular region.

The French AC laws, established in 1935, have been the model for similar regulations in Italy, Spain, Portugal, and all major wine-producing countries of the European Union except Germany and Austria, where quite separate quality classification systems are used.

Australia, South Africa, the United States, and Chile have less strict quality assurance systems than France. The U.S. system differs fundamentally from the European systems. U.S. wine districts, called American Viticultural Areas (AVAs), simply define geographic areas, with some attention paid to soil types and climate.

U.S. producers have resisted attempts to regulate the grape varieties used, feeling that it is a decision for the individual wineries. However, variety names do appear on most U.S. labels, and for a wine to be called a Cabernet Sauvignon, for example, it must contain a minimum of 75 percent of that grape variety.

For details about wine regulations, see country-specific headings in A World of Wine (pages 64–135).

Estate Bottled

The term "estate bottled" is legally defined in the United States as wine made from grapes owned by the winery, or in a vineyard totally under the winery's control and in the same appellation. In France, mis en bouteille au château *indicates that the wine is made from grapes grown on the winery estate.*

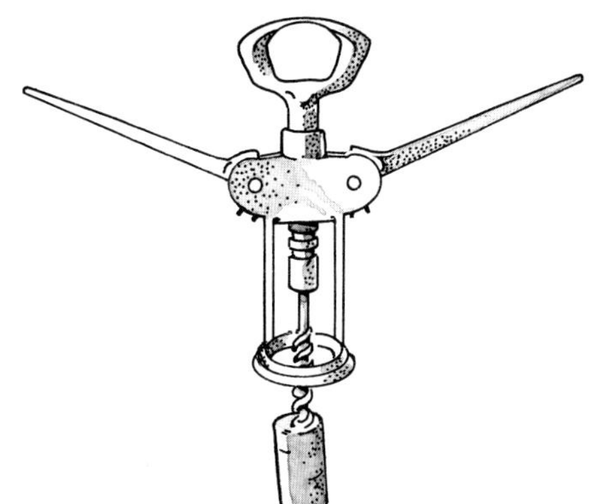

Opening the Bottle

Opening a bottle of wine can be tricky, but once it is achieved the rewards are self-evident. Many people enjoy the ritual of pulling the cork; in fact, even though a screw cap keeps wine just as well as a cork, there is some resistance by consumers to buying a quality wine without a cork. Even synthetic corks, which many wine producers have begun using for economic and quality reasons, have yet to be fully accepted. The following pages describe some of the many different tools and methods for extracting corks, along with useful tips for removing damaged corks and opening Champagne.

FOIL CUTTER

This device cuts the foil just below the lip of the bottle.

BASIC CORKSCREW

The basic pull-out consists of a worm and a handle.

SCREWPULL

The plastic frame of this self-puller acts as a fulcrum.

WINGED CORKSCREW

This corkscrew pulls the cork as the "wings" are pushed down.

HOW TO OPEN A BOTTLE OF WINE

The first step in getting to the wine is to remove the foil hood, or capsule, that covers the top of the bottle. Originally made of lead, foils are now usually made of plastic, tin, or even paper. In the days of underground cellars, the foil protected the cork from being nibbled by mice or rats, and also served as a secondary stopper should the cork fail. These days, foils are largely decorative, although they can be useful for identifying bottles of wine kept in a wine rack. Some producers have stopped using foils altogether, instead presenting the bottle with a patch of wax or plastic covering the top of the cork.

CUTTING THE FOIL

The foil may be cut with the small blade found on many corkscrews, or you may use a special cutting device which rotates, cutting the foil just below the lip of the bottle. This presents a neat, uncluttered look and prevents the wine from dribbling off the foil as it is poured.

TYPES OF CORKSCREWS

There is a wide, perhaps even confusing, selection of corkscrews available. The most basic style of corkscrew is simply a wire spiral, or worm, attached to a handle. The worm is twisted, or "screwed," into the cork, which is removed by pulling on the handle. The choice really depends on what style is easiest for you to use. The most important element of the corkscrew is the worm. It should be at least 2 inches (5 cm) long, so that it will penetrate deep enough into the cork to remove it without breaking or damaging it. Look for a round worm with a sharp point and an open spiral that will firmly grip the cork.

Many professionals prefer a simple corkscrew called the waiter's friend, which uses leverage to extract the cork. The ah-so, or butler's friend, has also become quite popular. The cork can be extracted without damage by inserting two thin blades between the cork and the bottle and twisting the cork out. However, this method does require dexterity.

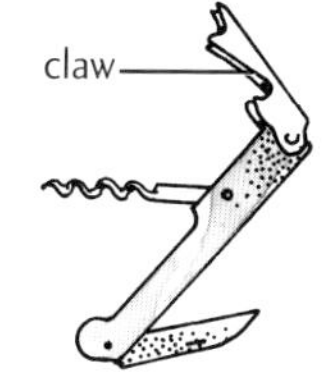

WAITER'S FRIEND

The claw provides leverage on the rim of the bottle.

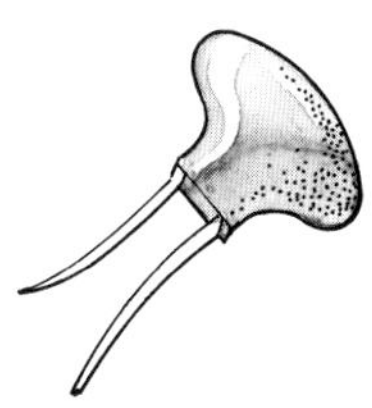

AH-SO

The two prongs are used to grip the cork and twist it out.

REMOVING THE CORK

The exact method of removing the cork from the bottle depends to a large extent on the corkscrew. Whatever style of corkscrew you use, the object is to pull the cork slowly so that the entire cork is removed from the bottle without leaving behind bits of it that look unsightly in the glass, although they do not actually affect the taste of the wine.

In the event a cork does break off in the bottle, it is possible to insert the corkscrew at an angle to remove the remainder of the cork, although this can be a tricky operation. Otherwise, you could use an ah-so, or failing that, push the cork carefully into the wine bottle. If you do not want pieces of cork floating in the wine, then you could decant it.

REMOVING A DAMAGED CORK

If care is taken, a broken cork may be removed from a bottle by inserting the corkscrew at an angle.

OPENING SPARKLING WINE

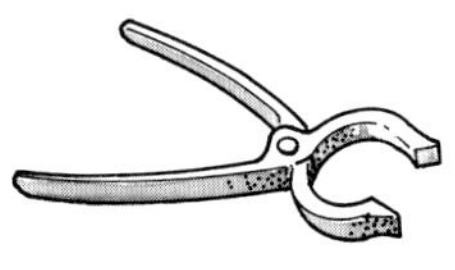

CHAMPAGNE PLIERS

You can use these special pliers to grip the Champagne cork as you carefully twist the bottle.

Never use a corkscrew to open Champagne or sparkling wine. Hold the bottle at a 45-degree angle to maximize the surface area of the wine, and keep a thumb over the cork. First remove the foil and wire cage, then slowly twist the bottle off the cork, either by hand or using a device called Champagne pliers. Bear in mind that Champagne corks are under enormous pressure. Don't be tempted to see how far you can propel the cork by suddenly popping it. Always point a bottle of Champagne away from you, and never point it in the direction of another person, even if you are only removing the foil. A faulty cork may explode out of the bottle when the foil is removed. Champagne corks have been known to cause serious injury and, in the United States, many producers have started putting a voluntary warning on the bottles.

Port Tongs

Opening vintage port that is more than 20 years old can be a problem, because the cork is often soft and crumbly. If you have port tongs, there is a simple solution. Heat the tongs red hot, then clamp them around the bottle neck for 20 to 30 seconds. Remove the tongs and wipe the same spot with a damp cloth. The neck should break off cleanly.

How to Taste Wine

How do I learn more about wine? That's a frequently asked question with an easy answer: taste it. The first step in tasting is to pour the wine into a suitable glass. The glass should be clear so that the color and clarity of the wine can be appreciated. It should also be large enough to swirl the wine without spilling it, releasing the aromas which are so important in tasting. There are some useful tasting terms to help you describe the wines you taste, and various scoring systems to assess them. It's useful to be aware of wine faults, too—their causes, and how to detect them.

THE TASTING PROCESS

Evaluating a wine involves four stages—looking, swirling, sniffing, and tasting.

LOOK
Examine the color of the wine against a white background, preferably using a natural light source.

LOOK

Tasting a wine begins with the eyes. What does it look like? Hold the glass against a white background to get a true idea of the clarity and color, which should be brilliant and clear in a red wine, and limpid and bright in a white wine. Hold the glass by its stem in order to keep the bowl free of smudges and handprints. Wines from hot climates generally have a deeper color than wines from cool climates. Older wines usually have a less intense color than young wines. Very old red wines may show slight browning at the rim, which you will see if you tilt the glass and look at the edge of the wine. Any cloudiness or discoloration may indicate wine defects.

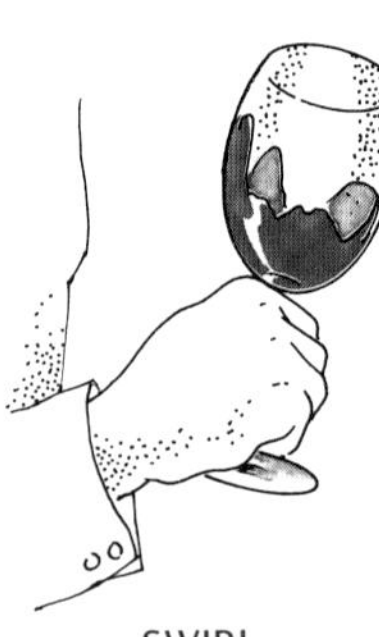

SWIRL
Holding the stem of the glass, swirl the wine carefully to release its aromas.

SWIRL

The next step is to swirl the wine in the glass. This introduces oxygen into the wine, which helps release the wine's essential aromas. A young wine should be swirled fairly vigorously, while an older wine should be treated more gently.

SMELL

Now put your nose over the rim of the glass and take a long, deep sniff. Really expand your nostrils to take in the smell. Try to think what memory you associate with the smell. You may want to repeat this process several times. The olfactory memory is one of the strongest memories we have, and the sense of smell plays a more important part in your perception of a wine than your sense of taste, which is fairly limited. What did the wine smell like? Professional wine critics have a special vocabulary for wine aromas, but most important is how it smells to you. Let your imagination run loose here and don't limit yourself to standard terms. Younger wines usually have stronger, more aggressive aromas, while older wines are generally more subdued and subtle.

SMELL

Put your nose over the rim of the glass, expand your nostrils, and inhale deeply.

TASTE

After satisfying the olfactory sense, move on to tasting the wine. Fill your mouth about half full and swish the wine around thoroughly. Two things are happening now: first, more aromas are being released into the nasal cavity, which is where the real tasting happens; and second, you are covering all parts of your mouth, tasting with the whole palate to gain a complete impression of the wine. Some people describe this process as "chewing."

TASTE

Take a generous mouthful of wine and swish it around your whole mouth.

SPIT OR SWALLOW

Now you may either swallow the wine or spit it out. Spitting is a must if you are tasting a number of wines in a formal tasting situation. When you swallow the wine,

Some Useful Tasting Terms

ACIDITY A natural element of grapes, acidity helps carry the lively, refreshing flavors in wine. There are several types of acidity in wine.

APPLEY Really the taste of malic acid from the grapes (the chief acid found in apples), this sensation is often found in young, unoaked Chardonnay and moderately priced sparkling wine.

BALANCE This refers to the relationship among different elements of the wine, such as acidity, fruitiness, tannins, and oak.

BERRYLIKE A wine that has ripe fruit flavors reminiscent of berry fruits, such as blackberries, may be described as berrylike.

BODY The weight of the wine in the mouth, this is a combination of factors such as tannin, fruit concentration, and alcohol.

BOUQUET The smell of a wine, particularly a mature or maturing wine that has spent some time in bottle, is called the bouquet.

COMPLEX A wine worth some consideration with deep, rich flavor elements of fruit, acidity, and oak, may be called complex.

EARTHY Reminiscent of the smell of fresh loam and leafy forest floor, this is usually considered a positive term.

FINISH This is the taste that lingers after you have swallowed wine.

FLOWERY OR FLORAL These terms are used to describe aromatic white wines such as Riesling or Gewürztraminer.

NOSE Used as a noun, "the nose" is the overall aroma of a wine; used as a verb, "to nose" a wine is to smell it.

OAKY If you can distinguish an excessive taste or smell of oak in a wine, it is "oaky" and out of balance.

TANNIN A substance found in the grape and also in new oak barrels; some tannin is necessary to give wine structure and balance, particularly red wines, but too much can be a defect.

pay attention to how it tastes as it slips down your throat. How long does the aftertaste linger? If the aftertaste is hot, the alcohol level is probably too high, or the wine is out of balance in some other way. A good wine is all about harmony. The wine should be full of flavor, with all the elements—fruit, tannin, and acid—in balance.

NOTEBOOK

It's a good idea to make notes to remind you later about the wines you have tasted.

TASTING NOTES

It is helpful to jot down a few notes while tasting a wine. Notes help fix the wine in your memory and are fun to come back to when you retaste a wine to see how consistent your palate is, or how the wine has changed in the interim. The notes need not be formal—a simple description of your impressions of the wine's aroma, taste, and finish should suffice.

Tasting terms are described more fully in the A to Z of Wine (pages 136–257); the chart (shown left) lists key terms.

SCORING SYSTEM

Scoring wines is popular among both professional and amateur wine tasters. There are many ways to score a wine. While the 100-point system is the most common, a simple 10-point system will work perfectly well. Some systems assign a numerical score to wine elements such as appearance and aroma in an attempt to make them seem more "scientific."

100-Point System

This scoring system rates the best wines at 90 and over, while 80–89 is average to well above average. Scores of 70–79 are acceptable, but wines rating below 69 should be avoided. This system is used by most consumer wine magazines.

TASTING GLASS

The large surface area of wine in this unusual wine-tasting glass allows the wine to breathe fully and release its aromas.

WINE FAULTS

Faulty wines, which are the result of errors in winemaking or storage, are not as common as they once were. The one exception is corkiness, a problem of which producers are increasingly aware. Modern winemaking technology has saved the consumer from many unpleasant wine-tasting experiences. However, there are still a few faults to look out for.

CORKED WINE

One of the most common faults is corky, or corked, wine. It is caused by a mold in cork bark that may contaminate the cork used in wine bottles, and thence the wine. This corkiness masks the flavors of the wine and, at its worst, leaves the wine smelling like wet cardboard, with an unpleasant flavor. On the other hand, the cork taint may be so light that even experts have trouble detecting it. In such wines, the flavors and aromas are dulled and cut short, leaving the typical consumer thinking it is simply poor wine. Cork producers and vintners are working to combat the problem, although cork mold can be hard to detect before the wine is bottled. It is estimated that three or four bottles out of 100 are corked.

OXIDIZED WINE

A wine that has been exposed too long to air, either during the production/bottling process or because of a faulty cork, is said to be oxidized. The wine takes on a dull brownish color and an unpleasant, sour apple taste. Oxidized wines are less common than corked wines.

VINEGARY WINE

A vinegary wine—sharply unpleasant to smell or taste—is a wine that has been infected by the same bacteria that produce vinegar and is virtually undrinkable.

OTHER WINE DEFECTS

Brettanomyces, or Brett, is a wild yeast that can give wine a metallic flavor if a high level is present—a low level of Brett does not spoil wine. Another wine spoilage compound, called mercaptan, is formed after the fermentation process. A foul odor (somewhat skunklike) may form and the wine is ruined. Cloudy wine, caused by instability during fermentation, or by the wine refermenting in the bottle, is generally the result of poor winemaking.

Sulfur in Wine

This is not strictly a fault, since sulfur dioxide is used in winemaking as a sterilizing agent and an antioxidant. A tiny amount is also produced naturally during fermentation. There are strict legal limits, however, because a small percentage of the population is allergic to the sulfites in wine. The amount added is falling as technology improves. If too much sulfur dioxide has been added, the wine may smell like burnt matches and give a burning sensation in the throat.

Serving Wine

How should wine be served? There are times when a tumbler, filled with rough red wine and served to friends with a bowl of pasta, is all that is necessary. Most of the time, if you have taken the trouble to select a fine wine, why not give it proper treatment? In addition to serving the wine in clean, clear glassware of the appropriate shape and capacity, it is useful to serve wine at the proper temperature, which varies with the type of wine. Some wines also benefit from decanting. And when the guests have gone, there are ways to preserve any leftover wine for enjoyment later on.

GLASSES

There are dozens of different shapes of wineglasses—specialists have developed glasses for most of the major wine varieties and regions—but you could start out with two basic types: the classic red-wine glass, which is fine for all sorts of table wine (even for port and sherry), and the sparkling wine flute. As your wine knowledge increases, you can build up your collection of glasses.

Avoid tinted or colored wineglasses, as they hide the appearance of the wine. Also to be avoided are glasses with wide mouths, especially for Champagne, since sparkling wine loses its bubbles too quickly and the aroma escapes before it can reach your nose.

It is important to look after your wineglasses carefully. Keep them in a closed cupboard, free of dust and distracting odors, and stand them upright to avoid trapping stale air in the bowl.

TYPICAL GLASSES

The classic red wine glass has a generous bowl to capture red wine's aromas. The sparkling wine flute's tall, narrow shape preserves the bubbles in sparkling wine.

Cleaning Wineglasses

Before use, glasses should be properly washed, rinsed, and dried with a clean cloth to remove any detergent residue, which can ruin a wine's flavor and will destroy the bubbles in sparkling wines. It is a good idea to wash wineglasses without detergent using a short cycle in the dishwasher—and as soon as the cycle ends, open the door so that the glasses don't collect odors from the dishwasher.

CLASSIC WINEGLASSES

The glasses below have different capacities and shapes to suit different types of wine. There are many other traditional glasses that can be used for serving other wines, such as Riesling and Chianti.

RED WINE This tulip-shaped glass has plenty of room in the bowl to swirl the wine and sample the bouquet, which is concentrated around the rim of the glass.

WHITE WINE This glass has a smaller bowl than the red-wine glass, as white wine's bouquet does not develop as dramatically as that of red.

SPARKLING WINE FLUTE The narrow shape of this glass preserves the bubbles and directs them vertically up the glass.

RED BURGUNDY/PINOT NOIR These wines release their aromas very quickly, so the wider bowl and tapering sides of this glass have been designed to maximize these aromas.

RED WINE

WHITE WINE

SPARKLING WINE FLUTE

RED BURGUNDY/ PINOT NOIR

RED BORDEAUX This large glass, with its gently tapering sides, provides maximum contact with the air, allowing the aroma and flavor of red Bordeaux and similar wines to develop.

PORT Port is traditionally served in small quantities, and this slim, tapering glass allows you to serve the correct quantity while allowing room in the bowl to swirl and appreciate vintage port's complex bouquet. This glass is suitable for serving most fortified wines, but is larger than the traditional sherry glass.

SHERRY The narrow and slightly tapering shape of this glass, which is called a copita, is perfect for capturing the remarkable bouquet of good Spanish sherry.

ISO TASTING GLASS This roomy glass funnels the wine's bouquet straight to the taster's nose. Developed by the International Standards Organization (ISO), it is a superb professional tasting glass, but because it is made of very thin glass it is not suitable for everyday use.

Filling Glasses

When filling a wineglass, about two-thirds full is just right for both red and white wine. Sparkling wine flutes can be slightly fuller. If you are using an oversize glass or conducting a wine tasting, fill the glass about one-third full.

RED BORDEAUX

PORT

SHERRY

ISO TASTING GLASS

SILVER DECANTER FUNNEL

DECANTING

Some people decant any wine served, while others never decant at all. The best approach is somewhere between these two extremes. When serving a fine vintage port, or an older red wine that might have thrown a sediment, you should decant for clarity, leaving the sediment in the bottle. At the other end of the scale, some very young wines should be vigorously decanted. This aerates the wine and helps soften the youthful tannins.

When decanting an older wine, set the bottle upright for several hours, or even a couple of days, prior to opening and decanting. Pull the cork carefully so as not to disturb the sediment, which should have settled to the bottom of the bottle. Pour the wine gently and steadily with a light beneath the neck of the bottle, so that you will be able to see the sediment when you reach it. A candle may look romantic, but a flashlight will get the job done just as well. When you can see the sediment, stop pouring.

If you don't want to bother with decanting a bottle of wine, pour off half a glass an hour or two before you wish to drink it. This will increase the surface area of wine exposed to the air and allow it to breathe. Simply pulling the cork

DECANTING

When decanting a bottle of wine, hold the neck of the bottle over a source of light so that you will be able to see the sediment. Stop pouring as soon as the sediment reaches the neck.

an hour ahead of drinking does not let the wine breathe to any appreciable extent.

The bouquet of older wines fades quickly, so they should be decanted immediately before drinking. Younger wines (and some big Italian wines, such as Barolo) benefit from being left in the decanter for several hours before drinking. When decanting a younger wine, just hold the bottle upright and let it glug and splash into the decanter.

The choice of decanter is mostly a matter of personal taste. As with wineglasses, decanters should be clear; they should be lightweight enough to pass around the table without great effort.

CHILLING WINE

There are a number of ways to chill white wine (or red wine, if it is too warm) to the correct temperature for serving. For real emergencies, when there is no ice available, put a bottle in the freezer for 10 to 15 minutes. Don't forget about it, or you will end up with a frozen bottle of uncorked wine on your hands—wine expands as it freezes and pushes the cork out of the bottle. As a general rule, freezers are best avoided.

For fast chilling, the refrigerator itself is a poor method. Most home refrigerators are set at between 39°F and 45°F (4°C and 7°C). At that temperature, it can take an hour or more to lower the temperature of a bottle of wine by 10°F (5.5°C).

DECANTERS

Decanter shapes have changed over the years, but most are still made of glass and stoppered.

The best method by far is to put the wine in an ice bucket or wine cooler with a mixture of ice and water—water conducts heat and will draw warmth from the bottle fairly swiftly. In fact, the temperature of a bottle of wine fully submerged in water and ice can drop 10°F (5.5°C) in 10 to 15 minutes. Ice cubes alone, surrounded by air, are not effective, since air is a poor conductor of heat and cannot therefore extract heat from the bottle.

Once the wine is chilled, you can keep it at the correct temperature at the table for a few hours by placing the bottle in an insulated container.

Ideal Serving Temperatures

The correct serving temperature for wine is important. Shown below is a guide to the best temperatures for major wine types.

Big red wines such as Bordeaux, California Cabernet, and Rhône reds	64°F–68°F (18°C–20°C)
Medium-weight reds such as Pinot Noir, Rioja, and Zinfandel	60°F–64°F (15.5°C–18°C)
Lighter reds such as Bardolino, Beaujolais, and northeast Italian reds	55°F–60°F (13°C–15.5°C)
Whites such as Chardonnay, Sauvignon Blanc, Alsatian whites, and most sweet wines	45°F–50°F (7°C–10°C)
Champagne, fine sparkling wines, and rosés	42°F–45°F (5.5°C–7°C)
Inexpensive whites and sparkling wines	40°F–42°F (4°C–5.5°C)

WINE COOLERS

The gel-filled cooler (shown far right) is useful for chilling wine quickly. Place the cooler in the freezer for a few hours, then wrap it around an unchilled bottle of wine—it will cool the wine in a few minutes, and will keep it cool for a few hours.

The insulated stainless steel cooler (right) keeps already-chilled wines cool.

WINE COOLERS

These practical coolers will keep chilled wine cool for the duration of a meal.

WARMING WINE

If you want to take the chill off red wine, one method is to decant the wine into a decanter warmed with hot water. Alternatively, pour out a few glasses in a warm room. You can also heat wine in a microwave oven (follow manufacturer's instructions), but take care not to overheat. Never apply direct heat to the bottle.

DECORATIVE STOPPERS

Wine bottle stoppers serve as useful closures for opened bottles of wine.

LEFTOVER WINE

An opened bottle of wine can be kept for a period of a few hours up to several days. The simplest method is to replace the cork and put the bottle in the refrigerator, where darkness is as important as the cool temperature. In this way, wine will stay fresh for one to three days. If it is a white wine, simply take it out when you want to drink it; for a red wine, remove it from the refrigerator a few hours before you plan to consume it. You can replace the cork with a wine bottle stopper if you wish. Stoppers are useful if you have leftover sparkling

CHAMPAGNE STOPPER

PUMPING DEVICE AND STOPPER

NECK LABEL

POURING DISC

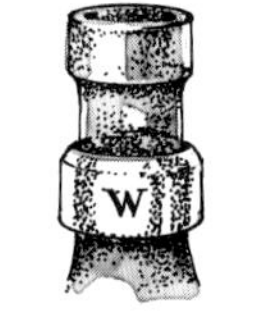

BOTTLE COLLAR

wine, because it isn't possible to put the cork back in a bottle of bubbly. To keep wine fresh longer, inert nitrogen gas (which is odorless and tasteless) with a little carbon dioxide can be sprayed into the opened bottle. The nitrogen mixture sinks to the level of the wine and the oxygen is held above it. This will keep wine for several weeks. The gas comes in handy canisters and is available from most wine shops and some grocery stores. A miniature pumping device that sucks air from the bottle will preserve wine for a few days (the pump should be fitted over a rubber stopper inserted into the mouth of the bottle). None of these methods is recommended for older wines, however, which quickly lose flavor and bouquet no matter what you do.

WINE ACCESSORIES

There is a whole range of paraphernalia for serving wine available for the dedicated hobbyist. Decanting devices include wine thieves, decanting funnels, and mechanical decanting cradles, which are useful for decanting older ports. Among other accessories are neck labels for wine bottles or decanters, which are handy for identifying wine; pouring discs, which can be inserted in the bottle to avoid drips; decorative bottle collars; and coasters to protect table surfaces. If you are organizing a wine tasting at home, you might like to add a spittoon to your wine accessories.

Style Guide

This section aims to provide you with an approach to trying different kinds of wine, based on what you already know you like. The information is divided into five main sections, which deal with key red, white, rosé, sparkling, and fortified wine styles. In addition to describing the individual wine styles, the following pages tell you about the grapes and winemaking techniques used to achieve them. There are also suggestions for foods to pair with each wine style. More information about the grapes used to make the wine can be found in the Grape Varieties section (pages 55–63).

CLASSIC RED WINE

Red Bordeaux wine based on Cabernet Sauvignon is harder and more tannic than Merlot-based red Bordeaux.

RED WINES

The range here is from great tannic wines that need aging to fruity, young wines for immediate drinking.

BORDEAUX STYLES

The diversity of styles within this category is wide. At one end of the scale are lush, velvety wines based on Merlot, from California and from St-Émilion and Pomerol in the Bordeaux region of France, that are eager to please at first sip. At the other end of the scale are more tannic, Cabernet-based wines from the Médoc in Bordeaux and from Australia and California that tend to project a harder style with deeper flavors, and are not so immediately accessible. The Merlot style pairs well with many foods. Match it with dishes ranging from roast duck to grilled fish. The Cabernet-based wines are good with roast beef, leg of lamb, or steak.

RED BURGUNDY

The Pinot Noir grape, with its subtle flavors and fruity complexity, makes fine red Burgundy wine. There, in its native French region, the best wines take on a warm, silky texture, somewhat akin to that of Merlot but with more depth and focus. Oregon Pinot Noir is usually lighter. A long list of foods pair well with this companionable wine, ranging from *coq au vin* through rabbit with mustard to poached salmon. In California, where the style tends toward more forward fruit than in

France, Pinot Noir matches well with spicy Asian dishes, but also tastes good with grilled fish.

JUICY REDS

This style of wine is becoming increasingly popular worldwide. Lighter Cabernet Sauvignon and Merlot wines, whether from Australia, California, Washington State, Chile, or the south of France, display an eager versatility and accessibility when made in a style for everyday drinking, and are capable of bringing immediate pleasure. Other good examples of this style include young Tempranillos from Spain, Crus Beaujolais from France, and Bardolino and Dolcetto from Italy. Match these wines with foods from hamburgers to stews and grilled meats.

WARM, SPICY REDS

Built on big, hearty flavors, often with hints of spice and lively fruit, this engaging style is found in many regions from the Rhône Valley of France, through northern Italy with its Nebbiolo-based wines, to northern Spain, California, and Australia. Besides Nebbiolo, the style includes Sangiovese, Grenache, Syrah, and Zinfandel-based wines. Important stylistic nuances exist within the overall category. Sangiovese, for example, if blended with Cabernet Sauvignon, makes a rich, flavorful wine that complements grilled steak. This family of wine matches well with game and hearty stews.

Alcohol and Style

The alcohol content of a wine affects its style, as alcohol tends to add weight, texture, and warmth. Wines that are out of balance, with a high alcohol content, may even be described as hot. The lower-alcohol wines, such as many German wines and Portuguese Vinho Verde, feel lighter on the palate.

WHITE WINES

Styles here range from oaky Chardonnays, through dry or sweeter Rieslings, to lusciously sweet dessert wines.

CLASSIC CHARDONNAY

Based on integrated oak with an underlying focus on pure Chardonnay fruit, this style offers great complexity of flavors. Originally developed in Burgundy, in France, but since copied in California and elsewhere, the style is achieved by fermenting and then aging the wine for 12 months or more in small oak barrels. Good food matches include simple roast chicken, baked or broiled fish, or pasta in a cream-based sauce.

Terroir

Where a wine is grown is a major factor in establishing its style. This sense of place, called terroir, *is found in all of the world's great wines.* Terroir *includes the soil, microclimate, sun exposure, and all other environmental factors affecting the vineyard.*

FLINTY CHARDONNAY

This style of Chardonnay, originally from the Chablis district of Burgundy, has a flinty, steely flavor and pure expression of Chardonnay fruit. It is generally an unoaked wine with a refreshing flavor and is seldom made so successfully elsewhere, although there is some good unoaked Chardonnay produced in California, New York State, Michigan, Oregon, Australia, and New Zealand. This wine style pairs well with oysters, broiled white fish, and clam and mussel stews.

SPICY CHARDONNAY

Not as rich and complex as the classic style, this popular style of Chardonnay is forward and often oaky, with a buttery richness. Flavors tend toward tropical fruit and deep citrus with occasional touches of melon or ripe apple. A popular wine style in Australia and California, spicy Chardonnay makes an excellent aperitif and also tastes good with sauced pastas and light grilled meats.

DRY RIESLING

A good dry Riesling, whether from Alsace, in France, Australia, or California, New York, or Washington State, offers a distinctive floral aroma and engaging fruit, along with a backbone of acidity. It pairs well with many foods but is, perhaps, best consumed on its own in order to appreciate the vivid flavors.

DRY WHITE

Although a good food companion, a glass of chilled dry Riesling is very drinkable on its own.

SWEETER-STYLE RIESLING

An off-dry Riesling from Germany or one of the New World wine producers has the same distinctive flavors as dry Riesling, with the addition of a honeyed flavor and richer texture on the palate. These wines are superb served as an aperitif, but will also pair well with a strong blue cheese, Asian fare, or even some of the new chili-laced fusion dishes.

PERFUMY WHITES

Gewürztraminer is a classic example of the aromatic, spicy wine style, especially as grown in the Alsace region of France. Pinot Gris from Alsace or Oregon is another good representative of this style. Either wine may be dry, although they are probably at their best with a hint of sweetness on the finish. Viognier from France, and also from California and Virginia in the United States, offers apricot and pear flavors. Gewürztraminer's intense spice and tingly acidity make it a favorite with spicy Asian dishes. It also goes well with smoked meats and smoked fish. Oregon Pinot Gris lacks the full-blown flavor of the Alsatian-style Gewürztraminer but has enough spiciness to pair with the same foods, as does Viognier.

WINE WITH FISH
Sauvignon Blanc matches well with most fish dishes.

ZIPPY, TANGY WHITES

The classic Sauvignon Blanc from Bordeaux or the Loire Valley, in France, has lively, tangy acidity with herbaceous fruit. More extreme styles from New Zealand and, to a lesser extent, from Australia emphasize the intense varietal flavors. Other wines in this style include lighter Rieslings, especially the *trocken*, meaning "dry," wines from Germany, Albariño from Spain, light Vinho Verde from Portugal, and Soave from Italy. Sauvignon Blanc, in particular, can be served with almost any fish dish, and the high acidity of the wine matches well with tomato-based sauces.

FOOD-FRIENDLY DRY WHITES

These are wines with a neutral or unaccented fruit character and a clean, crisp finish. Often fairly high in acidity, they include Trebbiano (in all its manifestations), Pinot Grigio (Pinot Gris) from Italy,

Muscadet from the Loire Valley, some of the fresh, young Spanish white wines, unoaked Sauvignon Blanc from California, Sémillon from Australia, and many others. Wines in this style match particularly well with fish, simply cooked meats, and light pasta dishes.

LUSCIOUS SWEET WHITES

The lush, honeyed flavor of a good dessert wine is unmistakable. The aromas fill the nose and the flavors flood the mouth. Superb dessert wines made all over the world include Sauternes from France, Canadian Icewines, German Riesling, Tokay from Hungary, fortified Muscat from Australia, and late-harvest botrytized Sauvignon Blanc from California. In addition to complementing desserts, these are excellent wines to drink with an aged blue cheese or a creamy cheddar. They also taste good with nuts.

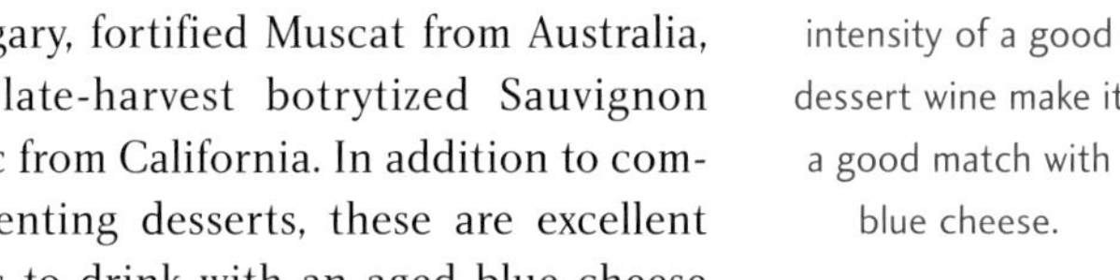

BLUE CHEESE

The sweetness and intensity of a good dessert wine make it a good match with blue cheese.

ROSÉ WINES

A good, dry rosé has lively fruit balanced by good acidity and a mineraly edge. The best dry rosés come from the south of France and northern Spain and are often based on the Grenache (called Garnacha in Spain) grape. Dry rosés are excellent food wines and are especially suited to popular Mediterranean dishes such as the Spanish classic, paella.

CHAMPAGNE

A top-of-the-range sparkler is an ideal accompaniment to caviar or oysters.

SPARKLING WINES

Dry or off-dry sparkling wine has firm acidity and a fine thread of fruit, often disguised by a rich creamy style. A top-of-the-line Champagne from France or a Champagne-method sparkling wine from California goes well with oysters or caviar.

FORTIFIED WINES

Port and sherry are the most important fortified wines, and range from richly flavored ports to dry and sweet sherries.

PORT

Ruby, tawny, and vintage port are sub-styles of Portugal's classic wine. All have a rich depth of flavor, a warmth in the mouth, and a lingering finish. A lighter ruby port has bright fruit that flirts with the palate, while tawny and vintage ports are powerful and bold. Outside Portugal, good-quality ports are made in Australia, California, and South Africa. Port is a classic with cheese and nuts.

SHERRY

This Spanish wine is made in a range of dry to sweet styles. Dry sherry has a mineraly, earthy character with a penetrating aroma. Sweet sherry has a nutty, sometimes raisiny flavor that fills the mouth and has a lasting finish. Dry sherry is a classic aperitif. It also pairs well with Spanish tapas. Sweet sherry matches with soft and cheddar-style cheeses.

Grape Varieties

How a wine tastes depends to a large extent on the grape variety or varieties used to make the wine, although terroir, *growing methods, and winemaking techniques also play a part. Virtually all of the world's wines are made from varieties of* Vitis vinifera, *a species of vine that originated somewhere near the Black Sea in prehistoric times. This section describes the major red and white wine grapes. For notes on minor varieties, see the A to Z of Wine (pages 136–257). In the listing for each grape you'll find information on where it is planted and the kinds of wine it makes.*

VITIS VINIFERA

Virtually all of the world's wines are made from the vine species known as *Vitis vinifera.* Although some local wines are made from other species of vine, vinifera is responsible for all of the world's great wines. There are well over 1,000 varieties of vinifera, but most wines are made from a few dozen varieties. These varieties differ in their adaptability to climate and soils.

RED GRAPES

This section describes the principal red grapes used to make red, rosé, and sparkling wines. Some of these grapes go by different names in different countries.

CABERNET SAUVIGNON This grape can make complex, rich wines with aromas and flavors ranging from black cherries to briery berries. At its best, Cabernet has good aging potential. It is one of the chief grapes used in France's red Bordeaux, and it certainly makes California's best red wines. It is a key grape in several of Italy's Super-Tuscan wines. Cabernet also makes superb wines in Australia and in Washington State, and delicious, if lighter, wines in Chile.

NAPA CABERNET SAUVIGNON

Between 1,000 and 2,000 bottles of this fine Cabernet Sauvignon wine are produced annually by the Bryant Family Vineyard, based in the Napa Valley, in California.

GAMAY Gamay has appealing, cherry-red berry fruit and good acidity. It is usually rather light on the palate. The grape is best known in the wines of the Beaujolais district of France, where it makes light, winning nouveau wines from the most recent harvest, as well as deeper, more complex Cru

Beaujolais wines. In California, the grape that many people thought was Gamay has now been identified as Valdiguié. In future, the name Gamay will not be used in California, unless, of course, true Gamay vines from France are planted there.

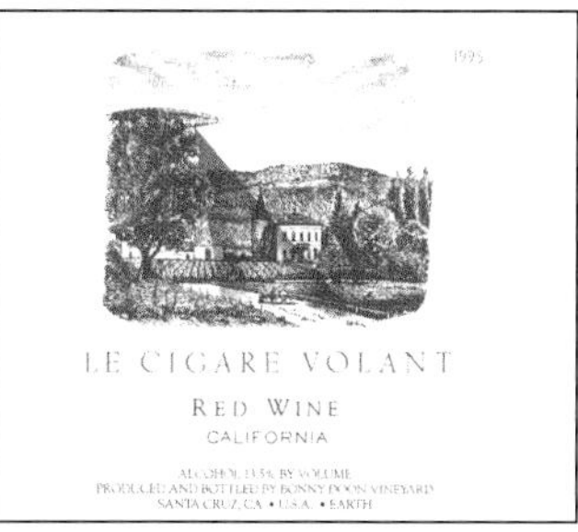

CALIFORNIA BLEND
This spicy red wine from California is a blend of Grenache and Syrah grapes.

GRENACHE At its best, Grenache makes a wine of substantial fruit with the possibility of some aging. A common variety in the south of France, it is a valuable blending grape for the wines of the Rhône Valley. Grenache is the principal grape in the *vins doux naturels* wines of Banyuls in southern France. In Spain, where the grape is called Garnacha, it is the main and often only grape in the wines of the Priorato, in Catalonia, which age beautifully for decades. In Rioja, it is blended with Tempranillo to give fruit and power to the wines. In the nineteenth century, Grenache was planted extensively in California and used in inexpensive table wines. There has been a recent revival of interest, especially in cooler, coastal vineyards.

BORDEAUX MERLOT
This is a Merlot-based wine from St-Émilion's top-quality AC in the Bordeaux region of France.

MERLOT The most planted wine grape in Bordeaux, Merlot was once thought of elsewhere only as a grape to blend with, and soften, Cabernet Sauvignon. It has now come into its own worldwide. At its best, notably in Pomerol and St-Émilion, in France's Bordeaux region, it makes a silky wine with lush fruit, tending toward ripe cherries and blackberries with traces of spice. Merlot is very sensitive to vineyard site, preferring poor soils with low yields. Excellent Merlot wine is made in many parts of the world, including California and Washington State, Chile, and South Africa.

NEBBIOLO One of the world's great red wine grapes, Nebbiolo grows best in cool areas with morning fog, such as the hills of Piedmont, in northern Italy. Nebbiolo wines, which include three of Italy's best—Barolo, Barbaresco, and Gattinara—have good tannic structure and high acid, an ideal combination for long aging. Nebbiolo is called Spanna in parts of Piedmont, and a number of everyday table wines are sold under that name. Some Nebbiolo is grown in California and in South America, but the quality has yet to reach the Italian standard.

PINOT NOIR This grape is responsible for the great red wine of Burgundy. Pinot Noir makes a velvety wine with lively fruit, tending toward red cherries in younger wines. The greatest Pinots deepen with age and take on a complexity, concentration, and finesse rarely matched by any other wine. Pinot Noir is the most planted red wine grape in Germany, where it is called Spätburgunder and makes a light but engaging red wine, as it does in the Alsace region of France. In the United States, very good Pinot Noirs are made in Oregon and California, where they are at their best in the cooler regions. The grape is also grown in France's Loire Valley, in Australia and New Zealand, and in Chile. In the Champagne region of France, Pinot Noir is one of the three varieties (the other two are Chardonnay and Pinot

OREGON PINOT NOIR

Produced in the Willamette Valley AVA, the powerful Laurène wine, made from estate-grown grapes, is among the finest Oregon Pinot Noirs.

Meunier) used to make the world's most esteemed sparkling wine.

SANGIOVESE This great Italian red wine grape of Tuscany is the chief grape in Chianti and in Vino Nobile di Montepulciano. It is also responsible for the great Brunello di Montalcino, where it is known as Brunello. Sangiovese produces fruity young wines, as well as powerful, richly concentrated older wines, such as Chianti and Brunello riservas. In many Super-Tuscan red wines, it is blended with Cabernet Sauvignon or Merlot. Sangiovese has achieved some success in California, where it is sometimes blended with Cabernet Sauvignon.

SYRAH/SHIRAZ Both names refer to the same grape. The Australians call it Shiraz, and this name has been adopted by some producers in California, who distinguish between a jammy, fruity style of wine, which they think of as Shiraz, and a more Rhône-like interpretation of the grape which they call Syrah. Syrah or Shiraz makes outstanding red wines wherever it is grown. It has sweet black-cherry fruit which is well balanced by acidity and tannin. Syrah is the chief grape in the Rhône Valley's finest wines. In Australia, Shiraz is arguably the country's best red wine grape, consistently outperforming Cabernet Sauvignon. In California, Syrah is rivaling Cabernet.

TEMPRANILLO Grown throughout Spain, Tempranillo can be found under various names in Rioja, the Penedés region, Ribera del Duero, and Castilla-La Mancha. Rather light and fruity

ITALIAN SANGIOVESE

Altesino was one of the first producers in the Italian region of Montalcino to make a more modern style of Brunello (the local name for Sangiovese).

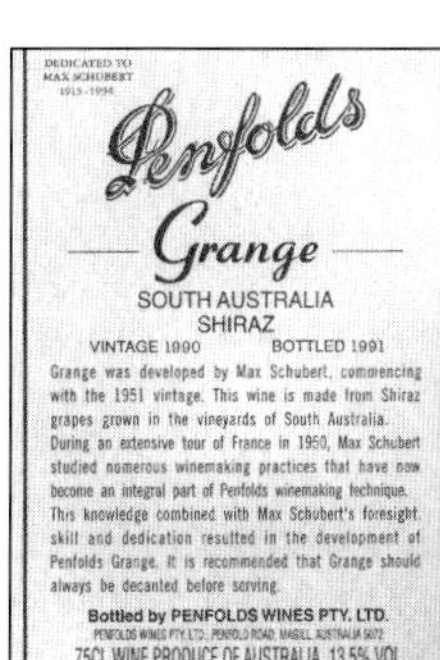

AUSTRALIAN SHIRAZ

Made from Shiraz grapes grown in South Australia, Grange is one of the country's finest red wines.

CALIFORNIA ZINFANDEL

This is one of the Martinelli family's top two wines from the Russian River Valley in California.

on its own, Tempranillo has strawberry and raspberry traces in the flavor and a somewhat leathery finish. In Rioja, Tempranillo is blended with Garnacha (Grenache) to produce the long-lived red wines of that area. In Ribera del Duero, where it is called Tinto Fino or Tinto País, Garnacha makes wine of great intensity used alone, and may be blended with Cabernet Sauvignon or Merlot. It is also grown in Portugal, and small plantings of Tempranillo have been made in California.

ZINFANDEL Widely planted in California, this grape is used to make several styles of wine. Lighter Zinfandel wines have aromas and flavors of raspberries and red cherries with a peppery, spicy finish. In a more robust style, Zinfandel has deeper, more concentrated fruit with black cherry and blackberry flavors. It grows well in areas of high daytime temperatures and cool nights, such as the Sierra Foothills and Sonoma County's Dry Creek Valley.

White Zinfandel

Called a blush wine, white Zinfandel is made by leaving the crushed and fermenting juice of red Zinfandel grapes in contact with the skins for a few hours until the juice picks up a reddish hue.

WHITE GRAPES

This section describes the major white grapes used to make still and sparkling white wine. Some of these grapes go by different names in different countries.

CHARDONNAY Generally regarded as the finest of white grape varieties, Chardonnay is planted all over the world, although the classic growing region is Burgundy in France. The mature grape is golden in color, and aromas and flavors range from green apples, melons, and ripe pears to tropical fruits such as mangoes, bananas, and papaya. Some styles achieve a buttery and/or creamy flavor. Although distinct regional styles for Chardonnay exist, it can be difficult to establish them, since Chardonnay is easily manipulated by the winemaker, and the use (or nonuse) of oak has a profound effect on the wine. Chardonnay is one of the three grapes used to make sparkling wine in Champagne.

ALSACE GEWÜRZTRAMINER

This delicious Grand Cru wine is made from late-harvest Gewürztraminer grapes grown in one of the best vineyards in Alsace, France.

GEWÜRZTRAMINER Surely one of the most distinctive of all the wine grapes, Gewürztraminer is noted for its intensely spicy aroma and flavors, and it may be compared to roses in full bloom with a touch of cloves and cinnamon. The top off-dry German styles can be delicious. At its best, in France's Alsace region, Gewürztraminer makes a dry wine with a rich mouthfeel unusual in a white wine. It is also grown in California, where it seems to lack the full-bodied richness of grapes from Alsace.

MUSCAT A family with many varieties, Muscat is one of the oldest and most widely planted of the wine grapes. Widely grown around the Mediterranean, it produces both dry and naturally sweet, lightly fortified wines, including Muscat de Beaumes-de-Venise and Muscat de Frontignan from France. Muscat à Petits Grains (or Moscato Bianco in Italy) is generally considered the best of the Muscats. Moscato Bianco is used in Asti (formerly Asti Spumante), the popular Italian sparkling wine. The same grape is known as Brown Muscat in Australia, where it is used to make Liqueur Muscat, a fortified sweet wine; and as Muscat Canelli in California, where it is sometimes made in a refreshing, lower-alcohol, slightly sweet style.

PINOT GRIS The color of this grape, as the name indicates, is grayish, shading to a light red. Wines made from Pinot Gris, especially those from Alsace, have a spicy aroma and flavor and a fairly full mouthfeel. In Italy, where the grape is known as Pinot Grigio, the practice is to pick just short of full maturity, which produces a crisp, easy-drinking wine style with good acidity and appley flavors. In Oregon, Pinot Gris makes very successful wines in the Alsatian style.

RIESLING This grape rivals Chardonnay as the world's greatest white wine grape. In its homeland in the Rhine and Mosel Valleys of Germany, Riesling makes wines of great delicacy with a light, perfumed aroma and a relatively low alcohol content. In more powerful versions, the wine takes on a honeyed mouthfeel and aroma. Riesling is made in a range of styles, from dry table wines to the late-harvest dessert wines of Germany. It is also made in Alsace, where it is mostly dry, and in Australia and California, where both dry and slightly sweet styles are made.

MOSEL RIESLING

The Sonnenuhr vineyard in Wehlen, in the Mosel region, produces some of Germany's most classic Rieslings.

SAUVIGNON BLANC Wine made from Sauvignon Blanc has a slightly spicy quality and very intense flavors for a white wine.

In France, it figures prominently in the dry whites of Bordeaux and is blended with Sémillon in the great sweet wines of Sauternes. Grown in the Loire Valley for the wines of Sancerre and Pouilly-Fumé, Sauvignon Blanc has also been successful in California, especially in the cooler regions. In recent years, excellent varietally intense Sauvignon Blanc has been made in New Zealand. A similar style is being made in cooler areas of Chile and Australia.

LOIRE VALLEY SAUVIGNON BLANC

La Grande Côte, an outstanding Sancerre wine, is made in the Loire Valley, in France, from the Sauvignon Blanc grape.

SÉMILLON Bronze-gold in color, this grape is often blended with Sauvignon Blanc, as it lacks acidity on its own. With rich fig and melon flavors, it makes a deeper wine than Sauvignon Blanc. In Australia's Hunter River Valley, unblended, it makes superb dry, unoaked wine with good aging potential. Sémillon's thin skin is prone to noble rot, and the grape is a major component in the sweet wines of Sauternes and Barsac, in France's Bordeaux region.

VIOGNIER A mere 20 years ago, Viognier was grown on fewer than 100 acres in France's Rhône Valley. Today it has made an astonishing conquest of the wine world. It became a cult favorite in the United States in the mid-1980s and early 1990s, with small plantings in Virginia and California. World demand led to more plantings in the Rhône and the south of France. It is also being planted in Tuscany, in Italy, and in Australia. Viognier makes a distinctive wine with delicate aromas and flavors of ripe apricot and pear, with a honeyed finish, even when dry.

CHAPTER 2

A World of Wine

A survey of wines made all over the world, from the classic European regions to vineyards and wineries in New World countries and beyond.

World Wine Regions

Wine is made on every continent except Antarctica. Because there are so many countries and regions that produce wine, this section deals in detail with only the most important areas and wines. What makes wine so fascinating is its seemingly infinite variety of styles and characteristics, which relate to the grape varieties used, local growing conditions, and winemaking techniques. Despite the ubiquity of some modern wine styles, the finest wines are always identifiably those from a particular area, reflecting specific soils, weather patterns, and vinification techniques.

FRANCE

Wine grapes were probably brought to France by the Greeks around 600 B.C., and vineyards were expanded under Roman rule to virtually every part of the country where grapes can ripen. These thousands of years of wine production have enabled French winemakers to hone their techniques to create some of the finest wines in the world, which other countries strive to emulate.

France currently produces roughly 20 percent of the world's fine wines—more than any other country. Because there are so many vineyard areas that have the top, AC (Appellation d'Origine Contrôlée) classification, the following sections on the main wine regions mention only the most important ACs.

French Classification System

France has the world's most complex system for classifying wines, with individual regions having their own rating systems within the overall scheme. The wines are divided into four main categories, described below in descending order of quality.

APPELLATION CONTRÔLÉE (AC) includes 45 percent of all wine made in any given harvest. These are the best wines of France including the great Bordeaux, Burgundies, and Rhônes. For further information, see Quality Classifications (pages 25–26).

VIN DÉLIMITÉ DE QUALITÉ SUPÉRIEURE (VDQS) is a tiny category of about 1 to 2 percent of total production. VDQS wines are considered virtually on a par with AC wines and are waiting to be promoted to that level by the Institut National des Appellations d'Origine (INAO).

VIN DE PAYS accounts for roughly 25 percent of all wines. These wines follow AC guidelines, but allow more grape varieties, lower minimum alcohol levels, and higher crop levels. Many of the exciting new wines from the south of France are Vins de Pays.

VIN DE TABLE includes 28 percent of production. Vin de Table is considered the most basic wine, and its production is in decline.

BORDEAUX

The region of Bordeaux is in the French *département* of the Gironde. It is home to approximately 250,000 acres (100,000 ha) of vines and over 13,000 producers. Roughly 75 percent of the wine is red, of which around 5 percent ranks among the best wine anywhere. The late-harvest dessert wines from Sauternes and Barsac are world famous, and certain dry whites from Graves are also world class.

The most widely planted red grape is Merlot, followed by Cabernet Sauvignon and Cabernet Franc, with tiny amounts of Petit Verdot and Malbec. Some of the great Bordeaux estates are dominated by a single variety—Château Pétrus, for example, is about 95 percent Merlot; but most red Bordeaux is a blend of two or three grape varieties. The Cabernet Sauvignon and Merlot blends have been copied around the world, with Cabernet Franc playing a significant role in certain Bordeaux châteaux.

Bordeaux districts are often referred to as "left bank," meaning to the west of the Garonne River, which runs into the Gironde estuary, and "right bank," meaning east and north of the Dordogne River. The large Entre-Deux-Mers (literally

translating as "between two seas") district is situated between the Garonne and Dordogne Rivers.

LEFT BANK This area is famed for the classic red Bordeaux wine style, which is dominated by Cabernet Sauvignon.

MÉDOC West of the Gironde estuary, the long narrow strip of land known as the Médoc is one of the world's great red winegrowing regions. It begins in the northern outskirts of the city of Bordeaux, extends for about 50 miles (80 km) along the estuary, and is never more than 8 miles (13 km) wide.

The great red wines of the Médoc, based on Cabernet Sauvignon, Cabernet Franc, and Merlot, are traditionally somewhat hard when young, but as they take on bottle age they mature into wines of great depth and elegance, capable in good years of extended aging.

The northern AC is simply Médoc AC. To the south, in generally better exposed vineyards, is Haut-Médoc AC, which includes six villages, each with its own AC: St-Estèphe, Pauillac, St-Julien, Margaux, Listrac, and Moulis. The first four of these villages produce some of the best known wines in the world. Made in the great stone châteaux that dominate the flat landscape, these wines include the First Growths: Lafite-Rothschild, Latour, Mouton-Rothschild, and Margaux; and the Second Growths: Pichon-Longueville-Lalande, Léoville-Las-Cases, and Cos d'Estournel. The communes of Listrac and Moulis, set back from the Gironde estuary on

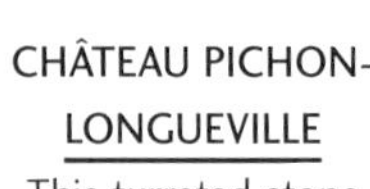

CHÂTEAU PICHON-LONGUEVILLE

This turreted stone château is situated in Pauillac, in the Médoc.

1855 Bordeaux Classification

This classification of Bordeaux red wines (all from the Médoc except Haut-Brion), devised by Bordeaux wine brokers for a World Exhibition in Paris in 1855, remains virtually unchanged. The brokers selected 61 wines, which they divided into five categories based on price, with the most expensive Premiers Crus first. In the list below, the châteaux are followed by the commune name.

PREMIERS CRUS (FIRST GROWTHS)
Lafite-Rothschild (Pauillac); Margaux (Margaux); Latour (Pauillac); Haut-Brion (Pessac/Graves); Mouton-Rothschild (Pauillac, since 1973).

DEUXIÈMES CRUS (SECOND GROWTHS)
Rauzan-Ségla (Margaux); Rauzan-Gassies (Margaux); Léoville-Las-Cases (St-Julien); Léoville-Poyferré (St-Julien); Léoville-Barton (St-Julien); Durfort-Vivens (Margaux); Gruaud-Larose (St-Julien); Lascombes (Margaux); Brane-Cantenac (Cantenac); Pichon-Longueville/Baron (Pauillac); Pichon-Longueville-Comtesse-de-Lalande (Pauillac); Ducru-Beaucaillou (St-Julien); Cos d'Estournel (St-Estèphe); Montrose (St-Estèphe).

TROISIÈMES CRUS (THIRD GROWTHS)
Kirwan (Cantenac); d'Issan (Cantenac); Lagrange (St-Julien); Langoa-Barton (St-Julien); Giscours (Labarde); Malescot-St-Exupéry (Margaux); Boyd-Cantenac (Cantenac); Cantenac-Brown (Cantenac); Palmer (Cantenac); La Lagune (Ludon); Desmirail (Margaux); Calon-Ségur (St-Estèphe); Ferrière (Margaux); Marquis d'Alesme-Becker (Margaux).

QUATRIÈMES CRUS (FOURTH GROWTHS)
St-Pierre (St-Julien); Talbot (St-Julien); Branaire-Ducru (St-Julien); Duhart-Milon-Rothschild (Pauillac); Pouget (Cantenac); La Tour-Carnet (St-Laurent); Lafon-Rochet (St-Estèphe); Beychevelle (St-Julien); Prieuré-Lichine (Cantenac); Marquis-de-Terme (Margaux).

CINQUIÈMES CRUS (FIFTH GROWTHS)
Pontet-Canet (Pauillac); Batailley (Pauillac); Haut-Batailley (Pauillac); Grand-Puy-Lacoste (Pauillac); Grand-Puy-Ducasse (Pauillac); Lynch-Bages (Pauillac); Lynch-Moussas (Pauillac); Dauzac (Labarde); Mouton-Baronne-Philippe (Pauillac); du Tertre (Arsac); Haut-Bages-Libéral (Pauillac); Pédesclaux (Pauillac); Belgrave (St-Laurent); de Camensac (St-Laurent); Cos-Labory (St-Estèphe); Clerc-Milon (Pauillac); Croizet-Bages (Pauillac); Cantemerle (Macau).

higher ground, produce wines with good style and structure, which are also good value.

GRAVES Starting at the edge of the city of Bordeaux, the Graves AC extends south for some 30 miles (48 km) along the Garonne's west bank. Red wines, dominated by Cabernet Sauvignon—with Cabernet Franc and Merlot also present—have a lean, mineraly quality with somewhat brighter fruit than Médoc wines. The dry white wines of Graves, made from Sémillon and Sauvignon, are considered the best in Bordeaux. In 1987, the Pessac-Léognan AC was carved out of Graves just south of Bordeaux city. Top châteaux formerly in the Graves AC, but now part of Pessac-Léognan, include Haut-Brion and Domaine de Chevalier.

SAUTERNES The Sauternes and Barsac districts, about 35 miles (56 km) southeast of the city of Bordeaux, produce the great dessert wines of d'Yquem, Suduiraut, and others made from late-harvest Sémillon, Sauvignon Blanc, and Muscadelle grapes. These wines vary greatly from vintage to vintage because the grapes are so subject to the whims of nature. In a good year, the proximity of the Ciron River raises the humidity of the vineyards sufficiently to produce, in the autumn, the noble rot that yields the best dessert wines.

CHATEAU D'YQUEM

Made mainly from Sémillon late-harvest grapes, the deliciously sweet wine is from the Sauternes AC of Bordeaux.

RIGHT BANK Wines made here tend to be softer than left bank wines.

ST-ÉMILION AND SATELLITES The St-Émilion AC, centered on the village of the same name, is charming and scenic compared to most of the Bordeaux region. The village overlooks the Dordogne Valley about 30 miles (48 km) east of the city of Bordeaux. The vineyards are planted largely to Cabernet Franc and Merlot, with some Malbec giving the wines a more supple style of red than is found in Médoc wines. However, the best wines of St-Émilion have a concentration and balance that promise good aging. Wines from some of the world's best châteaux, including Ausone, Cheval Blanc, Canon, Figeac, and Pavie, are produced in the St-Émilion AC. Certain surrounding areas, known as satellites, are allowed to add their name to St-Émilion; these satellites, such as Lussac-St-Émilion, produce similar, though lighter and shorter lived, styles of wine.

POMEROL On the north side of the Dordogne River, the small Pomerol AC produces some of Bordeaux's most attractive red wines. Pomerol vineyards are heavily planted to Merlot, which gives the wines a soft, rounded style. The better ones will improve for at least a decade or longer in the bottle.

The best known of all Pomerol wines, Château Pétrus is one of the most expensive red wines in the world. Only about 4,000 cases are made annually. Recent bottlings of another outstanding Pomerol wine, Le Pin, have sold at a higher price than Château Pétrus. Both are difficult to find. Other good Pomerol wines at a more reasonable price include Beauregard, Certan-de-May, and Clos René.

CHÂTEAU ST-PIERRE

This château is situated in the Pomerol AC, where the Merlot grape flourishes in the deep clay soil.

To the north of Pomerol, Lalande-de-Pomerol AC produces red wines that echo at a distance the great reds of Pomerol.

FRONSAC AND CANON-FRONSAC These two small ACs on the east bank of the Dordogne, west of Pomerol, are known for red wines of similar style. Canon-Fronsac is considered a superior AC to Fronsac.

CHÂTEAU BONNET

Bonnet is one of the best producers in the Entre-Deux-Mers AC.

CÔTES DE CASTILLON AND CÔTES DE FRANCS East of St-Émilion, Côtes de Castillon produces often quite attractive red wines, based chiefly on Cabernet Franc and Merlot. The old region of Côtes de Francs is undergoing a revival, and its red wines, based on Merlot, are showing very well.

ENTRE-DEUX-MERS This area between the Garonne and Dordogne Rivers is the most pleasing country in Bordeaux. Most of the wine from the Entre-Deux-Mers AC is dry white table wine and can be a very good value. An increasing number of red wines are made in the region, but regulations do not allow them to use the Entre-Deux-Mers AC. Instead, they must be labeled Bordeaux or Bordeaux Supérieur (see next page).

OTHER BORDEAUX WINES A number of simpler, less famous wines also hail from Bordeaux. This section describes a few of them.

CÔTES DE BOURG On the north bank of the Gironde, opposite the Haut-Médoc, the red wines of Bourg were famous before the Médoc wines. The average quality of the red wines, mostly made from Cabernet Sauvignon and Merlot, has recently improved.

BLAYE This large area northwest of Bourg is dominated by cooperative wineries and a few small châteaux striving to upgrade quality. There is a great deal of mid-quality red and dry white wine, which may be labeled Blaye AC or, for whites only, Côtes de Blaye AC. The best quality reds and whites, which may use only classic Bordeaux grape varieties, are labeled Premières Côtes de Blaye AC.

CHÂTEAU DE MALLE

The grand château in the small Bordeaux wine region of Sauternes is a major tourist attraction.

SWEET WINE APPELLATIONS East of the Garonne River are several appellations that form an enclave within Entre-Deux-Mers. Situated opposite Sauternes and Barsac, they benefit from a similar climate and are home to lesser-known dessert wines. The best of these ACs are Cadillac, Loupiac, and Ste-Croix-du-Mont. Sweet wines are also made in the larger Premières Côtes de Bordeaux AC.

BORDEAUX AND BORDEAUX SUPÉRIEUR About 40 percent of all Bordeaux red wine comes from the simple Bordeaux and Bordeaux Supérieur ACs, which cover the whole of the Bordeaux region. It is typically wine made outside recognized smaller ACs, although much of it comes from Entre-Deux-Mers, recognized only as a white wine AC. The word "Supérieur" signifies that the wine has a one-half percent higher alcohol content than other Bordeaux, but does not imply that the wines are superior in any other way.

BURGUNDY

This rambling winegrowing region runs from the isolated Chablis district, 90 miles (145 km) southeast of Paris, continues to Dijon and south through Beaune and Mâcon, and ends up in the Beaujolais district, which lies just north of Lyon. Total wine production varies between 25 and 30 million cases annually—just 10 percent of total production for all French AC wines.

The major difference between grape growing in Burgundy and Bordeaux is the size of the estates. Burgundy's vineyards are much smaller than those of Bordeaux.

The vineyards are at the heart of the Burgundy classification system, which can be imagined as a pyramid—the smallest vineyards at the apex are classified the highest and should offer the best quality. The best vineyards are named and classified as Grands Crus and the, slightly lesser, Premiers Crus (*cru* means "growth"). At the next level are named villages, or communes, each with its own AC (such as Chablis, Meursault, or Mâcon), and at the bottom of the pyramid are the larger subregional and regional ACs. This last category includes Bourgogne Rouge and Bourgogne Blanc, both of which can be made anywhere in the whole of Burgundy.

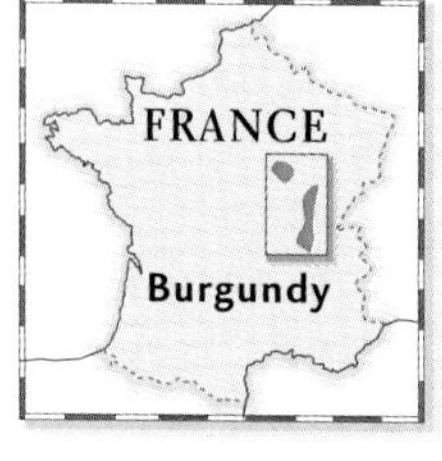

In Burgundy, perhaps more than in any other wine region, the vineyard is considered the most important element in winemaking. The concept of *terroir*, which includes the soil of the vineyard, the sun exposure, and the microclimate, is the key to understanding wine character. Wines from vineyards situated only a few yards apart from one another can differ a great deal if there is a difference in soil or sun exposure, for example. Throughout the region, winemaking methods are roughly the same. However, individual winemakers may use different techniques to achieve a particular style.

The great wines of Burgundy are made almost entirely from two grape varieties—Chardonnay for the whites and Pinot Noir for the reds. The major exception is the red wine of Beaujolais, which is made from the Gamay grape. Beaujolais can be a very attractive wine, but it is not, in general, the equal of the red Pinot Noir-based wines from the rest of the Burgundy region.

In some parts of the world, including the United States, the term Burgundy used to be regarded as the generic name for red wine. It is seldom used now. In a similar way, the name of the Burgundian district of Chablis has been applied in a general sense to inexpensive white wines.

Burgundy is divided into five main districts from north to south: Chablis; Côte d'Or, which is itself divided into the Côte de Nuits and Côte de Beaune; Côte Chalonnaise; Mâconnais; and Beaujolais.

OAK BARRELS
Classic Chardonnay, a style of wine originally developed in Burgundy, is traditionally fermented and aged in small oak barrels.

CHABLIS There are about 7,500 acres (3,035 ha) of vines in the AC of Chablis, centered on the small town of the same name. The exclusively white wine is bone-dry and has a flinty-mineraly flavor. Traditionally, Chablis has been fermented and aged in older neutral oak barrels, more recently in stainless steel vats; it was never exposed to new oak, a technique that distinguished the wines from the rest of Burgundy. Recently, a few producers have been using some new oak barrels in fermentation and maturation, believing that it adds complexity to the wine, in the style of the Côte d'Or.

The Chablis AC has its own system for rating wines. At the top of the hierarchy are seven designated Grand Cru vineyards. All on a single slope, these are named Blanchots, Bougros, Grenouilles, Les Clos, Les Preuses, Valmur, and Vaudésir. Below these in rank are about 40 Premier Cru vineyards, producing wines of varying quality. All other wines from the area are designated simply Chablis AC; Petit Chablis AC denotes outlying areas of the region.

WALLED VINEYARDS

Old stone walls with grand gateways surround many vineyards in the Côte d'Or.

CÔTE D'OR This gentle hillside extends for about 35 miles (56 km) just south of Dijon. Some of the world's greatest wines come from vineyards on the south and southeast-facing slopes of the Côte d'Or district. Both red and white wines are outstanding, offering an elegant richness found in few other places. The fruit is intense and deep, with flavors ranging in the reds from dark cherries through plums and ripe strawberries. The white wines offer flavors of ripe apples and buttery fruit in complex layers that make white Burgundy virtually unchallenged as the finest example anywhere of the Chardonnay grape, although California Chardonnay can sometimes get close.

The best wines are believed to come from halfway up the slopes, with the flatlands at the bottom reserved for Bourgogne Rouge and Bourgogne Blanc. Two vineyard areas sited higher up the slopes, categorized as subregional ACs Bourgogne Hautes-Côtes de Nuits and Bourgogne Hautes-Côtes de Beaune, are capable of producing good-value wines.

CÔTE DE NUITS The northern part of the Côte d'Or takes its name from the village of Nuits-St-Georges. About 12 miles (19 km) long and less than a mile (1.6 km) wide, this narrow strip produces mostly red wine. The most important villages are Chambolle-Musigny, Gevrey-Chambertin, Morey-St-Denis, and Vosne-Romanée. Some of the great Grand Cru vineyards are Bonnes-Mares, Clos de Vougeot, Chambertin, Clos de la Roche, Grands-Échézeaux, Romanée-Conti, La Tâche, and Richebourg.

CÔTE DE NUITS CHURCH

A familiar landmark in the Côte de Nuits, this twelfth-century church is surrounded by Premier Cru vineyards. The church itself has been converted into a wine cellar.

CÔTE DE BEAUNE Centered on the busy town of Beaune, Côte de Beaune AC is the southern part of the Côte d'Or. It is the home of the great white Burgundies from vineyards such as Le Montrachet and Corton-Charlemagne and those clustered around the villages of Chassagne-Montrachet, Meursault, and Puligny-Montrachet. Some outstanding red wines are also made there, particularly those from the ACs of Aloxe-Corton, Beaune, Pommard, and Volnay.

CÔTE CHALONNAISE This AC just south of the Côte d'Or takes its name from the city of Chalon-sur-Saône. It is less important than the Côte d'Or, but some good-value red and white wines are made there, especially in the ACs of Mercurey, Givry, and Rully.

MÂCONNAIS DISTRICT

Mâconnais vineyards of Pouilly-Fuissé nestle below the limestone rock of Vergisson, visible in the background.

MÂCONNAIS The Mâconnais is a large district near the town of Mâcon, south of Châlon-sur-Saône. It is known mostly for white wines made from the Chardonnay grape, including the popular Pouilly-Fuissé and Mâcon-Villages.

BEAUJOLAIS South of Mâcon is the district of Beaujolais. It is technically part of the overall Burgundy AC, but the wines, usually red, are totally different from those made in other parts of Burgundy. There are two major reasons for this difference. First, the soil in Beaujolais is clay and granite instead of the limestone found farther north. Second, Beaujolais wine is made from Gamay, not Pinot Noir. Very little white wine is made in the Beaujolais AC.

Recognizing that the great strength of Gamay is its forward fruit, winemakers make the wine in a lighter style for early drinking to emphasize that fruit. However, a good Cru Beaujolais, the highest classification for the Beaujolais AC, will age for several years. There are ten Crus Beaujolais: Brouilly, Chénas, Chiroubles, Côte de Brouilly, Fleurie, Juliénas, Morgon, Moulin-à-Vent, Régnié, and St-Amour.

RHÔNE

This area has been attracting increasing interest from wine connoisseurs looking for alternatives to more expensive wines from the Burgundy and Bordeaux regions.

Located south of Burgundy, the important wine-producing region of the Rhône stretches about 140 miles (225 km) from Lyon to Avignon along both banks of the Rhône River. It divides naturally into the northern Rhône, with its dramatic riverscape and granite soils, and the southern Rhône, with its milder Mediterranean climate as it fades into Provence. The wine styles are quite different, too.

The Côtes du Rhône AC covers the entire Rhône wine region, though in practice most wines bearing the name come from the south. The vast majority of Côtes du Rhône wines are sound, basic-quality reds, but whites and rosés may also be made.

NORTHERN RHÔNE The only red wine grape allowed in this region is Syrah, which produces wines with an earthy quality, good dark fruit, and firm tannins. The white wine grapes used are Viognier, which produces light, apricotty wines, and Marsanne and Roussanne, which produce weightier wines. The leading ACs in the northern Rhône for red wines are Côte-Rôtie, Hermitage, and Cornas, with St-Joseph and Crozes-Hermitage following close behind. At their best, these wines rival the world's best red wines and are capable of (indeed, need) extended aging for 10 to 15 years, and more in the best years. Very small quantities of top-level white wines are made in Condrieu AC from Viognier, and in Hermitage AC from Roussanne and Marsanne.

SOUTHERN RHÔNE In this area, the red wine is blended from a number of grapes. Up to 13 varieties are permitted in some places, the most important being Grenache, which is usually blended with Carignan, Cinsaut, and Mourvèdre. There are many new plantings of Syrah, too. The most famous AC in the region is Châteauneuf-du-Pape, with its intensely fruity red wines and mineraly whites. Gigondas and Vacqueyras are also important reds. Côtes du Rhône-Villages provides a regional AC for wines from the top villages in the area, with red wines dominating once again. However, the southern Rhône produces some outstanding rosés from Grenache-based blends, notably in Tavel and Lirac. There is also the elegant, naturally sweet, fortified Muscat de Beaumes-de-Venise.

LOIRE

The Loire River is the longest in France, about 600 miles (966 km) from its source west of Lyon, on the edge of Burgundy, to the Atlantic near Nantes. During the course of its run to the sea, the river passes through a series of viticultural areas where white, red, rosé, and a fair amount of sparkling wine are produced.

The Loire wines are not as well known outside France as they should be. The white wines, based chiefly on Sauvignon Blanc and Chenin Blanc, have a crisp acidity and vivid fruit. The red wines, which are mostly made from Cabernet Franc and Gamay, have a delicate balance and perfume.

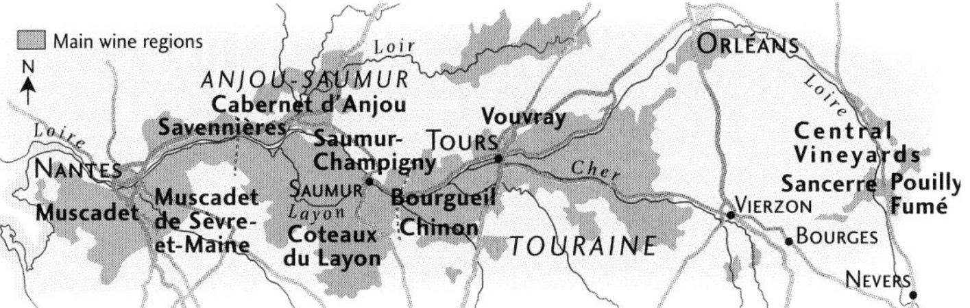

There are also superb sweet wines from Anjou, made chiefly from Chenin Blanc grapes. These wines can be affected by noble rot and, at their best, can rival the world's great dessert wines. Other sweet wines are made in a lighter, less concentrated style.

Loire wines worth knowing about, beginning at Nantes at the mouth of the river, include Muscadet, which is made from the grape of the same name, with the best considered to be Muscadet de Sèvre-et-Maine (look for *sur lie* on the bottle label, which indicates that the wine was aged in the vat on its lees).

The Anjou-Saumur district is the largest wine production center in the Loire Valley, producing wines of every color and style. As well as the wonderfully honeyed, sweet Coteaux du Layon AC, look out for the unusual, mineraly dry white Savennières AC. There are also rosés of inconsistent quality from Cabernet d'Anjou AC. Basic Anjou and Saumur reds

CHÂTEAU DE SAUMUR

Saumur is a center for sparkling white wines. The castle overlooks the Loire River.

are light, but Saumur-Champigny offers a fuller, finer wine. The sparkling Saumur, based on Chenin Blanc blends and made using the Champagne method, may be tart but the best offer excellent value.

Touraine has juicy red wines from Gamay and crisp, dry whites from Sauvignon Blanc. Chinon, the Loire Valley's best red wine, and Bourgueil and St-Nicolas-de-Bourgueil are made largely from Cabernet Franc. Vouvray makes superb whites from Chenin Blanc, with off-dry styles the most prevalent.

Farther up the river in the area known as the Central Vineyards (they are in the center of France), the villages Sancerre and Pouilly-sur-Loire have lent their names to the world's traditional benchmark styles for the steely, smoky Sauvignon Blancs, labeled Sancerre and Pouilly-Fumé. Light-style Pinot Noir rosés and reds from Sancerre are also good.

CHAMPAGNE LABEL

Champagne is the only AC that is not required to have Appellation Contrôlée written on the label.

CHAMPAGNE

Ninety miles (145 km) northeast of Paris is the Champagne region, where what many people consider to be the world's finest sparkling wine is made (see How Wine Is Made, pages 19–20). In the Champagne district, the only three grapes allowed for Champagne-method production are Chardonnay (which makes up about 25 percent of total acreage), Pinot Meunier (about 40 percent), and Pinot Noir (about 35 percent). The famous chalky soils in Champagne are rich in minerals, which growers believe add to wine character. On average, more than 20 million cases of Champagne are produced each year, in the following styles:

- Vintage Champagne. Made with grapes from a single vintage, only in the best years.
- Nonvintage (NV) Champagne. Made by blending wines from several years, which helps producers preserve their house styles.

The following Champagne styles may be vintage or nonvintage:

- Blanc de Blancs. Made only from Chardonnay, generally a lighter style of Champagne.
- Blanc de Noirs. Made only from Pinot Noir or Pinot Meunier, or a blend of these.
- Rosé. In the Champagne region, usually made by blending still red and white wines before making them sparkling.

Most Champagne is sold as Brut, a dry style with no more than 1.5 percent residual sugar. Extra Brut is a much drier style. Other styles, of increasing sweetness, are Extra Sec, Sec, Demi-Sec, and Doux, which has more than 5 percent sugar.

ALSACE

The vineyards of Alsace are about 20 miles (32 km) west of the Rhine, which forms the border with Germany and extends for some 80 miles (129 km) north to south along the lower slopes of the Vosges Mountains. Alsace was the first, and remains the only, major French region to use the varietal name on the

FORTIFIED CHURCH
This church at Hunawihr is a well-known landmark in the wine region of Alsace.

ALSACE RIESLING

Hugel is possibly the most famous producer in Alsace. This Vendange Tardive is one of Hugel's best wines.

label. Many Alsace grape varieties are also grown in Germany, but the Alsatian style is toward dry wines with spicy fruit.

The chief grapes are Riesling, Gewürztraminer, Pinot Gris, Muscat, Pinot Blanc, and Sylvaner for whites, and Pinot Noir for rosés and reds. Pinot Gris and Riesling are the most important for quality. Apart from Edelzwicker, which is ordinary blended wine, and the sparkling Crémant d'Alsace (see below), all Alsace wines are made from a single grape variety.

So far, 50 vineyards have been recognized as Grand Cru. These may grow only Riesling, Gewürztraminer, Pinot Gris, and Muscat, and must be well sited.

One of the main aims of Alsatian winemakers is to make wines of pure varietal character, so new wood is rarely used. Wines are aged in old oak, which does not impart oak flavors, or in stainless steel.

Besides the Alsatian table wines, there are three specialty wines:

- Vendange Tardive. Wine made from Gewürztraminer, Muscat, Pinot Gris, or Riesling, picked later than the normal harvest. It has a high concentration of flavor.
- Sélection de Grains Nobles. A very sweet wine made from grapes affected by noble rot, only in special years from select vineyards.
- Crémant d'Alsace. Champagne-method sparkling wine, usually made from Pinot Blanc and Pinot Noir.

LANGUEDOC-ROUSSILLON

There is a sense of excitement and change in this large area of southern France, traditionally a major supplier of red Vin de Pays and Vin de Table. The introduction of cool fermentation in the wineries, new plantings in the vineyards, and a revival of a sense of pride in the wines have led to an amazing leap in quality, both in the traditional wines and for wines made in the new international style.

The most important grape in terms of acreage is Carignan, although it is being partially replaced by Syrah, Grenache, Mourvèdre, and (in some areas) Cabernet Sauvignon, Chardonnay, and Merlot.

Vast amounts of red and white Vin de Pays wines are made in an international style from the latter and other classic varieties, mostly from new plantings near the Mediterranean coast. Traditional varieties are holding out in higher inland areas.

The largest AC in Languedoc is the Coteaux du Languedoc, where powerful, concentrated red wines are made from Syrah and Grenache. There is also a wide range of variable dry white wine made from local varieties. Some of the best wines in Languedoc include the fresh, lively reds from Corbières AC and the excellent Faugères AC reds.

Roussillon is on the border with the Catalonian region of Spain. This proximity has historically influenced the styles of its wines. Although Carignan has been the

CHURCH IN SOUTHERN FRANCE

A simple stone church marks the border between the old historical regions of Languedoc and Roussillon.

most important red grape, it is slowly being replaced by Grenache and Syrah. A little of the white grape Macabeo is often blended with the basic red wines of the area to add acidity. Macabeo is also vinified as a white wine on its own. There are excellent rosés and rustic-style reds from the Côtes du Roussillon and Côtes du Roussillon-Villages ACs. Sweet red wines from Grenache grapes, called *vins doux naturels,* are made in the Banyuls AC, on the Spanish border.

OTHER REGIONS

A significant number of good wines are made in parts of France that are off the traditional wine trails, most of which can be found in a great arc swinging from Provence on the Mediterranean almost as far as the Atlantic. During the past decade, many of these areas have dramatically improved the quality of their wines, and can offer good value as well as wines of nontraditional style and character.

VINES IN EARLY SPRING

Mont Ventoux marks the northern boundary of Provence, with the Côtes du Ventoux vineyards on the slopes below.

PROVENCE The Bandol AC, in Provence, produces superb rosé and red wines, based chiefly on Mourvèdre. The reds can age for up to ten years. The best wines from the touristy port of Cassis, on the French Riviera, are white, although rosés can be good. Wines are often overpriced there, as they are in another much-visited Provençal wine region, Bellet, in the hills near Nice. In general, Provence produces sturdy red wines and quantities of very drinkable rosé, both better than the whites.

SOUTHWEST FRANCE East of Bordeaux, the the Bergerac AC is planted to Merlot, Cabernet Sauvignon, and Cabernet Franc. The best reds are similar to St-Émilion wines, but have less body and concentration. The Monbazillac AC, in Bergerac, produces sweet white wines based on Sémillon, Sauvignon Blanc, and Muscadelle, which are similar in style to Sauternes.

Cahors, famed in the nineteenth century for its "black wines," so-called because of their extremely dark red color, still produces formidable red wines, chiefly from Malbec.

Irouléguy AC, in the Basque Pyrenees of southwest France, produces rustic red wines and the occasional rosé from Tannat, Cabernet Sauvignon, and Cabernet Franc.

The late-harvest sweet white wine of the Jurançon AC can be very good. Dry white wines are also improving.

The best wines in the Madiran AC, near the city of Pau, are sturdy reds, mostly made from the Tannat grape. Recent plantings of Cabernet Franc and Cabernet Sauvignon have improved the overall character of the wine.

EASTERN FRANCE Wines from the mountain districts of Jura and Savoie are rare outside the area but are worth trying. There are a number of white, rosé, red, and sparkling wines, many made from unusual grape varieties. The highly alcoholic *vin jaune*, or yellow wine, made from wine that grows a flor yeast, is from Jura. It is a dry, concentrated wine capable of great age.

VIN JAUNE

Made in the French district of Jura from the Savagnin grape, *vin jaune* is made in a similar way to Fino sherry, except that it is not fortified.

UNITED STATES & CANADA

Most of America's wine is from California. Canada's main wine production areas are in British Columbia and Ontario.

Wine has been made in what is now the United States since the 1560s, but it has been only in recent decades that the best wines from there have come to be seen as equal players in the world of wine. Wine is made in 45 of the 50 states, with

U.S. Classification System

The American Viticultural Area (AVA) system differs broadly from the European-controlled systems. AVAs define only geographic areas, which may or may not have common soils and climates. The AVA is not a guarantee of quality, simply of grape origin. Grape varieties, vinegrowing, and winemaking practices are not specified.

California producing about 90 percent of all U.S. wine. In quality, it is challenged by Washington, Oregon, and New York, with Michigan, Virginia, and a few other states making better wine with each vintage.

CALIFORNIA

More than half of California's wine is made from grapes grown in the hot, inland Central Valley, where irrigated vineyards produce crops of 10 to 15 tons per acre (25 to 37.5 tonnes per hectare), two to three times higher than coastal vineyards. Much of it is of poor quality and is used for blending into cheap jug and box wines. Most of the premium wines come from coastal regions or from inland hillside areas, such as the Sierra Foothills. The North Coast is the most established fine wine area, but several Central Coast areas are developing good reputations.

NORTH COAST North of San Francisco and including many of California's best wine regions, this area encompasses Napa, Sonoma, Mendocino, and Lake counties.

NAPA COUNTY Many people regard the Napa Valley as California's chief wine area. Grapes have been grown in the narrow valley just north of San Francisco Bay for about 150 years. Napa Valley is cooled by winds and fog off the bay.

The best red wine grapes are Cabernet Sauvignon, Merlot, Cabernet Franc, and Pinot Noir. There are also significant plantings of Zinfandel and Sangiovese. Good white wine grapes include Chardonnay and Sauvignon Blanc. However, because of the demand for high-quality red wine from Napa, few white wine vineyards are now being planted.

Napa red wines tend to have good tannic structure, with deep and concentrated fruit in the better wines. Flavors are usually bright and forward, so the wines are drinkable when fairly young, but those from good years repay extended cellar time. Many of the better red wines are blends of two or more of the five Bordeaux varieties, but there are also superb single-vineyard, single-variety wines.

Outstanding sparkling wines are made in Napa, though often grapes are taken from areas outside the region, such as Carneros (only partly in Napa) or other North Coast regions.

There are several American Viticultural Areas (AVAs) in Napa, ranging from those on the valley floor to steep, mountainside vineyards on both sides of the valley, where two separate arms of the Mayacamas coastal range extend almost to San Francisco Bay.

The catchall Napa Valley AVA includes almost all of Napa County and 15 to 20 different regions, of which several are sub-AVAs.

On the valley floor in the southern half of Napa Valley, the Oakville AVA is home to a number of famous wine producers, including Robert Mondavi. The Rutherford AVA cuts through the center

ROBERT MONDAVI WINERY

The well-known California wine producer is based in the Napa Valley.

of the valley from west to east, taking in foothill vineyards on both sides. It is renowned for excellent Cabernet Sauvignon.

On the east side of Napa Valley, the Stags Leap District AVA extends up into the hills. Cabernet Sauvignon is grown on distinctive red soil to produce the rich wines for which this AVA is known. Mount Veeder, Diamond Mountain, and Spring Mountain District are three hillside AVAs on the valley's western side, known for Cabernet Sauvignon, Chardonnay (Mount Veeder), and Zinfandel.

SONOMA COUNTY Like the Napa Valley, the Sonoma Valley can trace its wine history back to the days when California was a part of Mexico. It is a sprawling region with a number of distinct AVAs. Much of Sonoma is cooler than Napa, with several valleys open to fog and wind off the Pacific in the west, and to San Francisco Bay breezes and fog from the south. Pinot Noir and Chardonnay are key varieties. Cabernet Sauvignon rivals that of Napa in warmer areas, and the template for Zinfandel is in the Dry Creek Valley AVA.

STONESTREET
The Stonestreet winery in Sonoma County produces oaky, rich, dry Chardonnay.

Sonoma's warmest region, the Alexander Valley AVA, runs for some 12 miles (19 km) along both banks of the upper Russian River. Cabernet Sauvignon thrives there, producing ripe, juicy young wines that achieve elegance and roundness with age, the better ones lasting 20 to 25 years. Zinfandel and Merlot on the hillsides may be superb, and vineyards near the river produce good Chardonnay.

The Dry Creek Valley AVA runs from northeast to northwest along Dry Creek. The red iron oxide soils of the benchlands above Dry Creek produce rich Zinfandels with ripe berry fruit. Much of California's fast-disappearing acreage of old-vine Zinfandel grows there. Higher up the mountains are vineyards making lean, elegant Cabernet Sauvignon. Sauvignon Blanc thrives on deep soils near Dry Creek.

The Russian River Valley AVA is Sonoma's coolest region, with morning fog moving upriver from the Pacific, often lasting until midafternoon. Some of California's best Pinot Noir and Chardonnay are made there. Zinfandel and Merlot are grown in warmer vineyards above the river.

CHATEAU ST. JEAN

The tasting room for the Chateau St. Jean winery is situated in the Sonoma Valley AVA.

Only 10 miles (16 km) from the Pacific Ocean, Green Valley is a cool sub-AVA of the Russian River Valley AVA which has a growing reputation for Chardonnay and Pinot Noir, both for table wines and as a base for sparkling wines.

In the cool south of the Sonoma Valley AVA, Chardonnay has an intense appley flavor unusual in California Chardonnay. In the warmer north, a number of producers are making lean, tannic Cabernet with good aging potential, especially when grown on the valley's eastern side.

One of the first mountain AVAs to be defined, Sonoma Mountain is a sub-AVA of Sonoma Valley AVA. Situated above the fog line, it is slightly warmer than the valley floor, and so is ideal for growing Cabernet Sauvignon and Zinfandel.

CARNEROS The Carneros AVA hugs San Pablo Bay, a northern extension of San Francisco Bay, in both Napa and Sonoma counties. Much of the region was once under water, and the soils are poor. Wind sweeps off the bay, and during certain seasons, fog can obscure the sun for days. Until recently, there was little interest in planting wine grapes.

The best wines are made from Chardonnay and Pinot Noir, with an occasional excellent Merlot vineyard with southeastern exposure. The Pinot Noir typically has a light strawberry or raspberry flavor with floral aromas, but the best wines take on a velvety complexity. The Chardonnay has tropical fruit aromas and flavors. Most good California sparkling wine producers take grapes from Carneros.

DOMAINE CARNEROS WINERY

In the wine region of Carneros, this imposing building is a prominent landmark.

MENDOCINO COUNTY The northernmost area of the North Coast, this catchall county AVA contains several sub-AVAs, including Anderson Valley (see below) and Potter Valley. Much of the area is quite warm, since coastal mountains block cool Pacific winds, but there are some good Zinfandel vineyards at higher elevations, both near the coast in the Mendocino Ridge and Redwood Valley AVAs.

ANDERSON VALLEY This cool AVA in western Mendocino County, about 10 miles (16 km) from the Pacific Ocean, is gaining a reputation for Pinot Noir and sparkling wine. Zinfandel thrives in steep hillside vineyards above the fog.

CLEAR LAKE This AVA in Lake County has very hot days and, at higher elevations, cool nights. Sauvignon Blanc from Clear Lake has bright, lean fruit and a crisp, refreshing finish.

CENTRAL COAST Although the AVAs in this area are not as well-known as Napa and Sonoma, some of those listed below (north to south) are making wines that are just as good.

SANTA CRUZ MOUNTAINS Just south of San Francisco, this AVA is known for Cabernet Sauvignon from steep mountain vineyards.

ARROYO SECO Situated in a protected canyon in Monterey County, this AVA produces good Chardonnay, Riesling, and a limited amount of Cabernet Sauvignon.

EDNA VALLEY
VINEYARD
1995
Edna Valley
Chardonnay
PARAGON
Produced and bottled by
Edna Valley Vineyard
San Luis Obispo California USA
Alcohol 13.7% by volume

EDNA VALLEY CHARDONNAY

Edna Valley Vineyard produces one of the best Chardonnays in the cool Edna Valley AVA.

EDNA VALLEY This AVA in San Luis Obispo County, north of Santa Barbara, is cooled by winds off Morro Bay. Chardonnay here develops deep fruit and a ripe, complex mouthfeel.

PASO ROBLES This AVA in San Luis Obispo County has fine Cabernet Sauvignon and Zinfandel with a deeper, more pronounced blackberry fruit than North Coast Zinfandel.

SANTA MARIA VALLEY Situated in Santa Barbara County, this is one of California's best AVAs for Pinot Noir and Chardonnay. Rhône varieties also thrive in this cool region near the Pacific, showing great clarity and depth of fruit.

SANTA YNEZ VALLEY In this cool, coastal AVA in Santa Barbara County, Chardonnay and Pinot Noir are grown very successfully, along with recent plantings of Rhône varieties.

SIERRA FOOTHILLS The best wines from this catchall AVA on the western slopes of the Sierra Nevada mountains are Zinfandel, Syrah and other Rhône varieties, and Sauvignon Blanc. Fiddletown, one of a number of sub-AVAs within the Sierra Foothills AVA, produces rich, concentrated Zinfandel that rivals Dry Creek Valley as the best in California.

WASHINGTON STATE

Washington is an increasingly important wine region and the second-largest premium winegrowing state. Production of premium wine from *Vitis vinifera* began in the 1960s, so the industry is fairly new. Most of the major vineyards are planted on a high desert plateau east of the Cascade Mountains. Columbia Valley AVA, the main wine area, incorporates the Yakima Valley and Walla Walla Valley AVAs.

At a latitude of about 47°N, the growing season is cooler and shorter than in California. The influence of the Cascade Mountains means that there is little rainfall, so vineyards are irrigated year-round, which enables growers to manipulate crop levels and fruit intensity.

BOTTLING LINE
Fine wine production in Washington State is increasing annually.

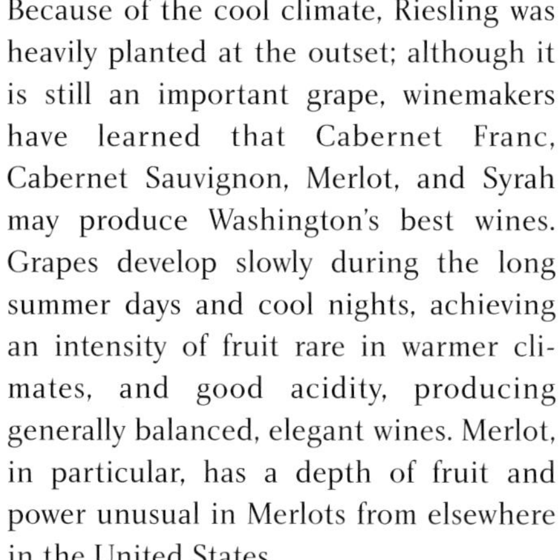

Because of the cool climate, Riesling was heavily planted at the outset; although it is still an important grape, winemakers have learned that Cabernet Franc, Cabernet Sauvignon, Merlot, and Syrah may produce Washington's best wines. Grapes develop slowly during the long summer days and cool nights, achieving an intensity of fruit rare in warmer climates, and good acidity, producing generally balanced, elegant wines. Merlot, in particular, has a depth of fruit and power unusual in Merlots from elsewhere in the United States.

Among white wines, although Riesling is successful (especially in a late-harvest dessert style), Chardonnay, Sauvignon Blanc, and Sémillon are all good, with the same depth of fruit as in the reds.

Unlike California, where inexpensive bulk wines make up much of the production, Washington devotes all of its wine production to premium varietal wines.

OREGON

The major winegrowing regions in Oregon—the Willamette, Umpqua, and Rogue Valleys—are all strongly influenced by damp, maritime air. Oregon is as cool as California's coolest regions and gets considerably more rain, always a threat at harvest time. The Willamette Valley is generally the coolest area and Rogue Valley the warmest. A little Cabernet Sauvignon is produced in the latter AVA, north of the California border.

Winemaking in Oregon is still very much a small family business, and total wine production is miniscule compared to California and Washington State. Oregon's leading wines are Pinot Noir, Chardonnay, and Pinot Gris. Oregonian winemakers pride themselves on following the Burgundian pattern for Pinot Noir. There is wide vintage variation; in a good year, Oregon Pinot has a ripe cherry complexity combined with medium body and good acidity. Even in poorer years, the aromas are usually there, though the wine may not deliver the desired fruit in the mouth. Of late, there has been a marked improvement in the consistency of Oregon Pinot Noir.

OREGON CHARDONNAY

The St. Innocent Winery in the Willamette Valley makes elegant, oaky Chardonnay from the Seven Springs Vineyard.

Oregon Chardonnay, at its best, combines a tart, almost mouthwatering acidity with a purity of fruit. Pinot Gris has proved a great success. Stylistically the wine falls between the lively fruit of an Italian Pinot Grigio and the complexity of an Alsatian Pinot Gris.

OTHER REGIONS

Outside the West Coast, New York, Michigan, and Virginia make some superb wines. Other states are producing a few acceptable, sometimes very good, wines. In New York State, European wine grapes (*Vitis vinifera*) were first planted on Manhattan Island (unsuccessfully) in the seventeenth century. Until the 1950s, New York wines were made only from native American varieties, such as *Vitis labrusca*, and from French-American hybrids, but following technological improvements in viticultural practices, growers and winemakers are now turning to the classic European varieties.

The two best winegrowing regions in New York State are the Finger Lakes AVA in north central New York, especially for Chardonnay, Riesling, Merlot, and Pinot Noir; and Long Island, which produces superb Merlot, Cabernet Sauvignon, and some good Chardonnay. Both regions offer varietal wines with good fruit and acidity. Long Island reds have fared well in blind tastings against California and French Bordeaux reds.

Michigan has won regional attention for its Chablis-style Chardonnays, dry and sweet Rieslings, Pinot Gris, and Cabernet Franc. The better vineyards are beside Lake Michigan, which moderates the harsh winter climate.

Virginia's climate is difficult for growing wine grapes, since the high humidity encourages outbreaks of rot and mildew. However, some Virginia producers have gained national recognition in recent years. The best grapes are Cabernet Sauvignon, Chardonnay, and Viognier.

Elsewhere in the United States, there are occasional good wines being made in Missouri, North Carolina, New Mexico, Ohio, Pennsylvania, and Texas.

Hybrid Grapes

A cross between varieties of two different species, usually a Vitis vinifera *and a native American vine, hybrid grapes were mainly developed to withstand harsh weather or vine diseases. They are important in the northeastern United States and Canada, where the red Chambourcin and the white Seyval Blanc and Vidal have made acceptable or better wines.*

CANADA

Canada's two chief winegrowing regions are about 2,000 miles (3,220 km) apart. The Niagara Peninsula in Ontario stretches for some 30 miles (48 km) along the southern edge of Lake Ontario. At the opposite end of the country, about 150 miles (240 km) inland from the coast of British Columbia, is the Okanagan Valley.

NIAGARA PENINSULA The best white wines from Niagara are Chardonnay, sweet and dry Riesling, and Vidal, a hybrid variety developed especially for cold climates, which makes superb dessert wines. Riesling and Vidal are used to make the world's largest quantities of luscious Icewines, made from frozen grapes. The best red wine is Pinot Noir, with Cabernet Franc and Merlot improving fast.

OKANAGAN VALLEY Noteworthy whites are Chardonnay (made in a steely Chablis-style), Pinot Blanc, Pinot Gris, and Riesling (both dry and sweet). The best reds are Pinot Noir, Merlot, and Cabernet Franc.

ICEWINE

Canada produces more Icewine than any other country. The wine is made from 100 percent British Columbia- or Ontario-grown grapes, harvested when naturally frozen on the vine. Grapes may not be frozen artificially.

Canadian Classification System

Ontario and British Columbia have their own appellation system, regulated by the Vintners Quality Alliance (VQA), which stresses the use of only Canadian-grown grapes. It does not define crop limits or grape varieties, but it does encourage high standards of wine production.

ITALY

Nowhere in the world, except perhaps Spain, have there been such dramatic improvements in the quality of wine as in Italy. Vines are planted almost everywhere in this Mediterranean country of contrasts, from the cool, alpine north to the hot south. The well-known wines of Tuscany and Piedmont are showing ever higher quality, and regions that once made unremarkable wine, such as the hot islands of Sicily and Sardinia in the far south, or the Veneto in the northeast, are also beginning to blossom.

102

A WORLD OF WINE

THE NORTHWEST

Piedmont is the most important wine-growing region in the northwest of Italy. It contains more than 40 classified zones of production, or Denominazioni di Origine Controllata (DOC), and almost half of all the wines made in the region now have DOC status.

The best red wines are based on the Nebbiolo grape. There are 12 DOCs based on Nebbiolo, including the famous DOCG (see Italian Classification System below) wines of Barolo, Barbaresco, and Gattinara. Wines made from Nebbiolo come in a range of styles, from light, fruity versions for early drinking (Nebbiolo d'Alba DOC, for example) to tannic, rich, concentrated wines from Barolo and Barbaresco. In the Piedmont region, Nebbiolo may also be called Spanna, which is an ancient name for the grape.

Italian Classification System

Vino da Tavola, or table wine, is wine produced with few restrictions, or in an area where no delimited zone exists. The recently introduced Indicazione Geographica Tipicia (IGT) is similar to the French Vin de Pays category and is increasingly used by the Super-Tuscans (see A to Z of Wine, page 243). Denominazione di Origine Controllata (DOC) guarantees that the wine has been produced in the named vineyard area according to specified production methods. DOCG (the G stands for Garantita) is meant to guarantee the quality of the wine.

BARREL-MAKING
The traditional craft of barrel-making is still practiced in Asti, in northwest Italy.

Both Barolo and Barbaresco need extended aging. They are traditionally held in large, neutral oak casks for many years before bottling, although modernist producers age them for a shorter time in new oak barrels. There is much dispute in the area over the changing style of the wines.

Barbera, another red variety, is widely planted, but (with rare exceptions) is used in the production of everyday table wines, although the Barbera d'Alba DOC can produce good-quality wine on occasion.

Dolcetto, which is also widely grown in Piedmont, makes a soft, fruity wine, often quite pleasant when young, although some require aging.

Italy's famed sparkling Asti DOCG, also produced in Piedmont, is made from the Moscato grape. The Gavi DOC produces a fruity, aromatic wine with a tangy, mineraly edge from the Cortese grape.

THE NORTHEAST

The most important growing regions in the northeast are Friuli-Venezia Giulia, Trentino-Alto Adige, and Veneto.

FRIULI-VENEZIA GIULIA Most Friuli wines are sold under the varietal name. The best DOC is Collio, home of some of Italy's best dry white wines. Leading white wines include Pinot Bianco, Pinot Grigio, Sauvignon Blanc, Gewürztraminer, Tocai Friulano, and Chardonnay. Red wines are also made in a fruity style. Merlot has been particularly successful in Friuli, and an approachable style of Cabernet

Sauvignon is also produced there; Refosco is a good local grape.

TRENTINO-ALTO ADIGE To the west of Friuli is Trentino-Alto Adige, where wines are made from the same varieties and in much the same style as in Friuli-Venezia Giulia, with most produced in stainless steel. In both regions, some producers have experimented with aging Chardonnay and Cabernet in small oak barrels, but few of the wines have the depth of fruit to stand up to the oak tannins. The local grape, Schiava, makes a light red wine for everyday drinking. Another red grape, Lagrein, makes a more intense wine.

VENETO A large wine region, the Veneto stretches from the shores of Lake Garda to Venice on the Adriatic Sea. Its best known DOC wines are Soave, Valpolicella, and Bardolino, which are all produced near Verona. Valpolicella and Bardolino are made from similar blends of native Italian varieties—mainly Corvina (the best), Rondinella, and Molinara. Bardolino tends to be a light, fruity wine, while Valpolicella, made in a DOC about 10 miles (16 km) away, has more body and, at its best, a silky mouthfeel. There are two special Valpolicellas—a sweet Recioto and a dry Amarone. These are traditionally made by drying the grapes on straw mats, resulting in a raisining of the grapes, which make wines of great power and intensity. The Amarone can be up to 16 percent alcohol. The white wines of Soave, made from Garganega and Trebbiano,

AMARONE

Amarone wines, from the Valpolicella DOC in Veneto, northeast Italy, are high in alcohol with distinctive bittersweetness.

can be light and fruity with rather low acid. When choosing either Valpolicellas or Soaves, look for the ones labeled "classico" or for wines from single vineyards.

There are other, sometimes excellent, wines made throughout the area from grapes such as Merlot, Cabernet Franc, Cabernet Sauvignon, and Pinot Nero (Pinot Noir). White wines include Pinot Bianco and Pinot Grigio. Native Prosecco white grapes are almost always made into a sparkling wine, popular in the cafés of Venice.

TUSCANY AND CENTRAL ITALY

Famous worldwide for Chianti, Tuscany has led the quality revolution in Italian red wines with the Super-Tuscans. Many of these are based on Sangiovese, alone or blended with Cabernet Sauvignon, Merlot, or Cabernet Franc. Made to escape too-rigid DOC rules, the Super-Tuscans helped establish more flexible regulations for Chianti production.

Sangiovese remains the most important grape in Tuscany. It is the principal grape of Chianti and of Vino Nobile di Montepulciano, and under the name Brunello is the only grape allowed in the famed Brunello di Montalcino.

In Umbria, Orvieto is an important and improving white wine, and Torgiano produces some interesting reds. Easy-to-drink wines from other areas include Frascati from Lazio, Verdicchio dei Castelli di Jesi from the Marches region, and Lambrusco from Emilia-Romagna.

CHIANTI SYMBOL

The Black Rooster is the symbol of the Chianti Classico Consorzio, a voluntary association of wine producers in the Chianti area.

CHIANTI Situated between Florence and Siena, Chianti Classico is at the heart of one of the world's best known wine regions. Chianti Classico DOCG is based on the historic Chianti boundaries; there are six other DOCG zones, the best known of which is Rufina. Quality varies from light, fresh, easy-drinking wines to intense, structured wines that are reminiscent of fine Bordeaux. Riserva wines must be aged for at least two years before release, and the finest can be aged for more than a decade.

BRUNELLO DI MONTALCINO South of Siena, this DOCG makes powerful wine that is 100 percent Sangiovese (known locally as Brunello) and must be aged for four years, including two in oak. The wine can usually be kept in bottle for years, but some producers are now making the wine for earlier drinking. Rosso di Montalcino is good value for younger drinking.

VINO NOBILE DI MONTEPULCIANO This DOCG is another Sangiovese-based wine which, at its best, combines the power of Brunello with the complexity of Chianti. Rosso di Montepulciano, bottled earlier, is a good, less expensive alternative.

CARMIGNANO West of Florence in the Montalbano hills, this DOCG makes a refined blend of Sangiovese and Cabernet.

BOLGHERI This up-and-coming DOC on the coast south of Siena is home to the prestigious red wine estates of Sassicaia and Ornellaia. The red wines are based on Cabernet Sauvignon,

Merlot, and Sangiovese, and are capable of aging for up to ten years.

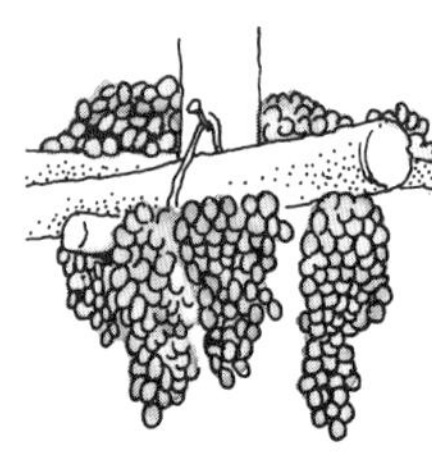

GRAPES DRYING

Trebbiano grapes are dried to make Vin Santo, Tuscany's famous dessert wine.

SAN GIMIGNANO AND OTHER WHITES Tuscany's best indigenous white wine is the Vernaccia di San Gimignano, which has recently achieved DOCG status. There are a number of pleasant, neutral white wines made in Tuscany, chiefly from the Trebbiano grape. An excellent dessert wine, Vin Santo, is made primarily from dried Trebbiano and Malvasia grapes.

UMBRIA The most famous Umbrian wine is Orvieto, a white wine made from Trebbiano in the area around the hilltop city of Orvieto. Traditionally it was slightly sweet, but the modern style is dry. The best Orvieto has complex flavors and a layered finish, which make it a versatile wine to match with food. Torgiano is a well-known red wine from Umbria.

LAZIO Frascati, made in the Alban hills south of Rome, is the traditional white house wine in Italy's capital. Rarely a great wine, chilled Frascati can be a pleasant and refreshing drink. It is made from Trebbiano and Malvasia.

MARCHES Verdicchio is a dry white wine which is made from the grape of the same name in the Marches region along the Adriatic coast. The best Verdicchio comes from the Castelli di Jesi DOC and makes a delicious accompaniment to the local seafood.

EMILIA-ROMAGNA This area to the southeast of Piedmont produces large quantities of fruity, fizzy, easy-to-drink Lambrusco wines, made from the red grape of the same name. The sweeter style is very popular in the United States, while the traditional dry version, consumed locally, matches the region's rich food.

MAKING PARMESAN

At home, Italy's famous Parmesan cheese is often eaten on its own with a glass of local Lambrusco.

SOUTH AND ISLANDS

During the past ten years, the quality of wine produced in the area south of Rome has greatly improved.

APULIA Situated on the Adriatic coast, Apulia is one of Italy's leading wine regions in terms of quantity. Most of the wine produced in the area is used for blending or export in bulk and is quite forgettable; however, recent advances in quality have resulted in some sturdy country red wines made from indigenous grape varieties, including Primitivo. Malvasia Nera and Negroamaro grapes can also produce above-average wines, such as the ripe red Salice Salentino and the smooth, elegant Copertino.

CAMPANIA The best wines of southern Italy come from the Taurasi DOCG near Naples, in the Campania region. Taurasi, recently granted DOCG status, is made from the Aglianico grape and is capable of extended aging. It is a powerful wine with layers of concentrated fruit.

BASILICATA Aglianico del Vulture, a DOC in Basilicata, is the home of concentrated red wines much in the style of Taurasi, and also made from Aglianico. Basilicata also produces some good dry white wines made from Pinot Bianco and Chardonnay grapes.

SARDINIA Wines from the island of Sardinia have improved noticeably in recent years. Traditionally the wines were powerful and highly alcoholic, but more recently the island has been producing lighter wines in a more modern, international style.

Sardinia's white wines are based on Vermentino, a grape of Spanish origin that also grows on the mainland. Good Vermentino is refreshing and can be delightfully aromatic. Other grapes used in white wines include native varieties such as Malvasia and Vernaccia.

There are two major red wines: Cannonau, which is believed to be a clone of Grenache (another grape of Spanish origin), offering medium weight and fairly deep fruit; and Carignano, which is related to Carignane.

SICILY The traditional wine of this extremely hot island was high-alcohol, fortified Marsala. However, modern viticulture has moved up into the cooler hillsides, where altogether better table wines are now being made. The best red wines are made from indigenous grapes Nero d'Avola and Perricone (also known as Pignatello); Grillo and Inzolia grapes produce the most successful white wines.

MARSALA
This dry Vergine fortified wine comes from the island of Sicily.

MARSALA Once believed to be one of the world's great sweet wines, Marsala was regarded for many years as a cooking wine and little else. However, great improvements have been made. Although most Marsala wines are now sweetened, the revival of a fine, complex unsweetened version, known as Vergine, is especially encouraging.

SPAIN

Spain has more acres planted to grape vines than any other country in the world. From the cool coast of Galicia in the northwest to the mountains of Andalucía in the hot south, the vine covers the land. As a winegrowing region, Spain is currently in a period of transition. There have always been good Spanish wines, but there have also been many wines of mediocre quality. The newer Spanish wines now catching the world's attention show consistently good quality, while remaining distinctively Spanish.

RIOJA AND NAVARRA

Rioja, Spain's first DOC, is traditionally the country's premier red wine. Today it is being challenged, but when Rioja is good it is still arguably one of the world's great red wines. Rioja is based on Tempranillo but may be a blend of Tempranillo, Garnacha, Graciano, Mazuelo, and Viura, a white wine grape. Better vintages can last for 20 to 25 years.

Rioja red wines are often tannic and somewhat leathery in character, with understated fruit. Some Rioja producers are making wines that put more emphasis on Tempranillo's graceful fruit, crafting wines for early drinking.

The structure and style of traditional Rioja owes much to the use of oak. A Gran Reserva, for example, must have a minimum of two years in oak (and three in bottle) before release. The traditional Rioja producers use very little new oak, so the time in barrel or large cask tends to lead to slight oxidation of the wine, especially the whites made in the traditional style. Modern producers are changing to new oak, or avoiding oak altogether, especially for white wines based on Viura.

Spanish Classification System

Denominacion de Origen (DO) forms the basis of Spain's appellation system and, like the French and Italian systems, regulates origin and some winemaking practices. Above this is a stricter, higher-quality DOC category (the C stands for Calificada). Wine regions aspiring to be granted the DO are categorized as Vino de la Tierra, closest to French Vin de Pays. A further category for larger regions is Vinho Comarcal. The lowest level is Vino de Mesa (table wine).

Excellent red wines based on Tempranillo are also produced in the neighboring region of Navarra, as are dry, fruity rosés from Garnacha. Navarra has welcomed new plantings of Cabernet Sauvignon, Merlot, and other international varieties, and good commercial wines have been made.

SEÑORÍA DE SARRÍA

This beautiful wine estate in Navarra produces fresh, fruity whites and rosés, and rich reds made from Tempranillo with some Cabernet Sauvignon.

CATALONIA

In Catalonia, near Barcelona, the Penedés region makes excellent red and white wines based on traditional Spanish varieties and a few plantings of Merlot, Cabernet Sauvignon, and Chardonnay. Most of the still wines are white. In the 1970s, cold-fermented white wines based on the local Parellada grape set a new fashion in Spain for fresh, floral white wines. Bold reds, made from Garnacha and, more recently, from Cabernet Sauvignon, have also been very successful.

The Penedés is best known in the United States for Cava, the sparkling wine made using the Champagne method, from three local white varieties—Parellada, Macabeo, and Xarel-lo—and, in certain wines, from Chardonnay. Good Cava is an excellent value bubbly.

In the mountains inland from the ancient Roman city of Tarragona, the winegrowing region of Priorato is making some interesting wines. Intense red wines made from Garnacha, grown on hillside terraces, are capable of extended bottle aging and can also be drunk young.

In the 1980s, the planting of French varieties, along with modernization of winemaking processes and the introduction of new oak, resulted in the production of new wines that have been extremely successful in Spain and elsewhere.

SOMONTANO

This cool, older region in the foothills of the Pyrenees in northern Aragon is currently undergoing a revival, with plantings of international varieties including Chardonnay and Merlot. Traditional varieties have also been improved.

RIBERA DEL DUERO AND RUEDA

Ribera del Duero, the winegrowing region north of Madrid, has long been known as the home of Vega Sicilia, the most famous and expensive wine in Spain. Many other fine red wines come from the area, based on Tinto Fino, or Tinto del País (local names for the Tempranillo grape). Small amounts of Cabernet Sauvignon, Merlot, and Malbec are also planted there. Most of the red wines are drinkable when young, but are capable of developing great elegance and style with aging. Where the Duero River crosses the border into Portugal, it becomes the Douro, traditionally associated with port.

One of Spain's best white wines, made in the nearby DO of Rueda, is from the Verdejo grape, a

VEGA SICILIA UNICO

Spain's top wine, Vega Sicilia Unico, is rich and slow to mature.

distinctive native Spanish variety that has been revived. It is made both as a fresh, fruity, unoaked wine and as a complex, barrel-fermented wine.

GALICIA

A hilly, green region in the far northwest corner of Spain, Galicia has a very rainy climate. There, in the Rías Baixas DO, the exciting aromatic white wine Albariño is made from the grape of the same name. It has soared in popularity in the last few years, and when Albariño is good, few Spanish whites can match it.

Other good DOs in Galicia include the mountainous Valdeorras and Ribeiro.

OTHER WINE REGIONS

Andalucía, in southern Spain, includes the sherry district of Jerez; and the DOs of Montilla-Moriles, which produces sherry-style wines, and Málaga, where wine production is decreasing. Castilla-La Mancha, in central Spain, is the largest delimited wine area in Europe. Valencia, to the east, produces sweet Moscatels.

JEREZ (SHERRY) Only wines produced in the Jerez y Manzanilla DO are allowed to be called sherry. Two major factors that contribute to the quality of wines produced in this region are the chalky *albariza* soil where the best vines grow, and the Palomino Fino grape.

There are a number of dry and sweet styles of sherry, all derived from two basic types, Fino and Oloroso, made primarily from Palomino

SHERRY

Since January 1996, within the European Union, the only country allowed to use the name sherry on a bottle label is Spain.

grapes. Chilled Fino sherry is the classic aperitif wine. Manzanilla, a near cousin of Fino, should also be served chilled. Amontillado is technically a type of Fino, often made sweet by adding sweet wine to it. Oloroso, the other basic type, is darker, with an intense nose and a nutty, rich flavor. It is made in both dry and sweet styles. Naturally sweet sherries, based on Pedro Ximénez and Moscatel grapes, are considered to be in the Oloroso category.

CASTILLA-LA MANCHA Spain's hot central plateau was known in the past for producing large quantities of poor to average-quality wine. However, recent advances in winemaking have led to significant improvements in the region's wines, especially the reds. Refreshing wines, made from Cencibel (the local name for Tempranillo), are turning up regularly, especially from the Valdepeñas DO. Cold fermentation techniques have also resulted in some fresh, fruity whites made from Viura, Chardonnay, and Airén, the world's most widely planted grape.

LA MANCHA

The landscape of La Mancha is dotted with squat windmills and vineyards as far as the eye can see.

VALENCIA Situated on the Mediterranean coast, Valencia produces plenty of fairly simple, drinkable red, white, and rosé wine. Much of it comes from cooperatives and is made from both international and native grapes, such as Monastrell for full-bodied reds and Bobal for light reds and rosés. It is also the home of sound but unspectacular sweet wines based on the Moscatel grape.

PORTUGAL

Portugal has resisted the rush toward the sometimes bland international wine style, preferring to use traditional grape varieties for ports and Madeiras, and now for new table wines.

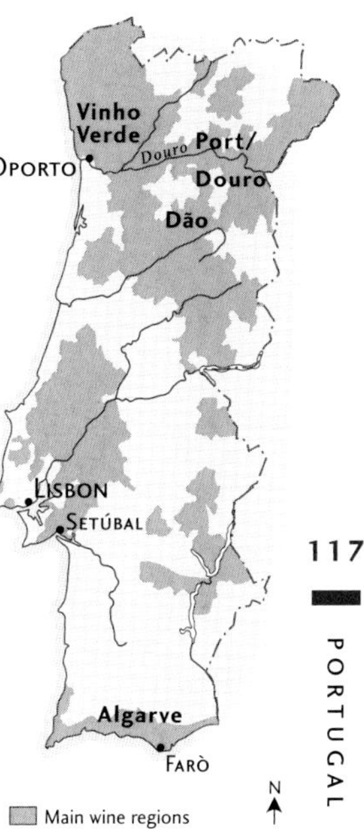

PORT

Made from a bewildering variety of red wine grapes grown in the Douro River valley, port comes in several styles, relating in part to the amount of time the wine spends in barrel.

- Simple ruby ports. Wines aged for about three years in wood.
- Tawny ports. A nutty style aged for longer in wood than ruby port. The best selections are labeled as 10, 20, or 30 years old.
- Vintage ports. Wines made from a single vintage, bottled after two years in small oak barrels; made for extended aging—up to 40 years—in bottle. Vintage ports are released only in exceptional years.
- Single Quinta (meaning farm in Portuguese). Vintage ports from a single estate.
- Late Bottled Vintage ports. Made from a single vintage, held from four to six years in wood before bottling, whereupon they are ready to drink.
- White port. A rather coarse, heavy style, which can be dry or medium dry.

BARCOS RABELOS

New port was traditionally carried down the Douro River on square-sailed boats called *barcos rabelos*.

TABLE WINE

The 1990s saw great developments in Portuguese table wines. The Dão DOC produces excellent red wines with deep fruit which will repay several years of aging. The Touriga Naçional, a grape important in port production, is also being used in table wine, both in the Douro and in the Dão.

DOURO VALLEY New table wines are being made in the Douro Valley, which may well turn out to be the best area for red wines.

VINHO VERDE A popular light wine from the northwest of Portugal, Vinho Verde is made in both red and white versions, but the best wines are white from the DOC of the same name. They are light and fruity with a slight sparkle and only 9 to 10 percent alcohol. Vinho Verde means "green wine," which in this case means a young wine released in the spring.

MADEIRA This subtropical island produces historically renowned fortified wines of varying sweetness. The best of them are excellent and can survive to a very great age.

Portuguese Classification System

As in France, Portugal has a four-tier system, starting with Vinho de Mesa, or table wine, at the bottom. The next tier, Vinho Regional, includes large areas equivalent to large French Vin de Pays areas. Above these, quality wines are divided into Indicação de Proveniencia Regulamentada (IPR), candidates for promotion like French VDQS, and Denominação de Origem Controlada (DOC), the highest quality.

GERMANY

Germany's wine reputation rests on Riesling. Grown in vineyards along the Rhine River and its tributaries, including the famous Mosel River, Riesling at its best has an elegant grace, astonishing fruit, and great depth. In reality, Riesling makes up only about 20 to 25 percent of German vineyards, but when we think of the best German wines, it is generally Riesling that comes to mind. Much of the simpler wine is made from Müller-Thurgau.

RHINE

The Rheingau, Rheinhessen, and Pfalz are the three chief wine regions along the Rhine River.

The Rheingau region includes many of the finest vineyards in Germany. They are planted mostly to Riesling and Spätburgunder (the German name for Pinot Noir). Rheingau wines are, at their best, ripe and full-bodied, with richly concentrated fruit. Well-known wine villages include Rüdesheim, which is also famous for its street of wine pubs, the Drosselgasse, Eltville, and Hochheim, where some of the most powerful Rieslings in the region are produced. Rheingau is also home to the famous Schloss Johannisberg vineyard, which makes elegant wines that are capable of aging for at least ten years.

German Classification System

German wine law ranks all wine primarily by the ripeness of the grapes, or grape sugar content, at harvest, rather than by vineyard location or grape variety. German growers striving for higher quality want the classification system amended to give more weight to vineyard location.

Quality levels, beginning with the lowest (least ripe grapes), are:

TAFELWEIN (table wine). Made from normally ripe or slightly underripe grapes and consumed primarily in Germany, this wine may be chaptalized, which involves adding sugar at fermentation.

LANDWEIN (country wine). This is similar to French Vin de Pays.

QUALITÄTSWEIN BETSTIMMTER ANBAUGEBIET (quality wine from a specific region). These wines must be made in one of 13 specific winegrowing regions from approved grape varieties. They may also be chaptalized.

QUALITÄTSWEIN MIT PRÄDIKAT (quality wine with distinction). These are quality wines from riper grapes and are given an extra classification as listed below in order of increasing ripeness at harvest, beginning with Kabinett and finishing with the rare Trockenbeerenauslese and Eiswein. No chaptalization is allowed.

KABINETT These are usually light wines made from fully ripe grapes, intended to be light quaffing wines or to go with light food. The sweetness level can range from dry to medium-dry, with relatively low alcohol levels.

SPÄTLESE (late-harvest). Believed to be of superior quality, these wines are made from grapes picked after the normal harvest. Due to the later harvest, the fruit intensity and flavors are increased. Ranging from *trocken* (dry) to medium-sweet, these wines make fine aperitifs.

AUSLESE (select picked). Wines with intense flavors, these are made from grapes harvested as very ripe, select bunches. Often regarded as dessert wines, Auslese wines can also be *trocken* (dry).

German Classification System (continued)

BEERENAUSLESE OR BA (selected berries). For these wines, grapes are individually harvested, specially selected for their overripe quality. BA wines are remarkably rich dessert wines; in fact, with a glass of BA, no other dessert is needed.

TROCKENBEERENAUSLESE OR TBA (dry berries, select picking). These are individually harvested berries, overripe and shriveled on the vine with *Botrytis cinerea*, or "noble rot," almost like raisins. TBA wines are thought by some connoisseurs to be the best dessert wines in the world, having great intensity and depth.

EISWEIN (Icewine). These are wines of BA intensity, made from grapes harvested and crushed while frozen. Because the juice is concentrated by freezing, the wine has remarkable depth and sweetness.

Rheinhessen is the largest of the German quality wine regions, of which there are currently 13. Only a small percentage of Riesling is planted there, in the district known as the Rheinterrasse, which overlooks the Rhine. Among well-known villages producing high-quality wines are Nierstein and Oppenheim, whose best wines have lush fruit and can be very appealing.

Shielded by the Haardt mountains to the west, the large Pfalz wine region has a warmer climate than Rheinhessen. Rieslings from the better vineyards have ripe aromas and are generally more full-bodied than Rheingau wines. Many other varieties are grown in Rheinhessen and Pfalz.

WINE HARVEST

Carved wooden shutters typical of the Rheingau region depict scenes from the wine harvest.

MOSEL RIESLING

This medium-sweet wine comes from the Leiwener Laurentiuslay vineyard on the eastern side of the Mosel River.

MOSEL

More than half of the vineyards in the wine district of Mosel-Saar-Ruwer are planted to Riesling. The best vineyards are on very steep terraces above the Mosel River and its tributaries. Mosel Riesling has an elegant fragrance and, at its best, is among the world's finest white wines. Whatever the degree of sweetness, there always seems to be the right matching acidity to produce wines of great balance and character. Top wine villages include Bernkastel, Wehlen, and Trittenheim.

BADEN AND FRANKEN

Baden, Germany's southernmost wine-growing district, is extremely large. Recent developments in the region have shown that the warmer climate is capable of producing fuller, softer red and white wines than in the rest of the country. A little Riesling is planted there, and many of the best non-Riesling German wines are made in Baden.

The Franken district is southeast of Frankfurt on the Main River. The most important vineyards, on the hillsides surrounding the city of Würzburg, are planted to Müller-Thurgau and Sylvaner. Unlike most other German wines, Franken wines are usually dry with bold flavors. They are sold in distinctive green flagon-shaped bottles called Bocksbeutels.

SWITZERLAND, AUSTRIA, & EASTERN EUROPE

The wines of Switzerland are generally for local consumption; Austria makes some good red and excellent sweet white wines. Much ordinary red and white wine comes out of Eastern Europe, but some countries, such as Hungary, are improving.

SWITZERLAND

There are 35,000 to 40,000 acres (14,164 to 16,187 hectares) of vines in Switzerland, most in the French-speaking regions of Valais, Vaud, and Geneva. Most make charming, if lightweight, white wines from the Chasselas grape, and light, red wines from Pinot Noir and Gamay.

AUSTRIA

Austria has a similar classification system to Germany. The best Austrian vineyards are planted along the Danube, where the Riesling is especially good. The climate is warmer and drier than in Germany, and most years there is no problem making red wines. The Burgenland district, south of Vienna, produces outstanding red wines from the Blaufränkisch grape (called Lemberger in Washington State), and some fine sweet whites from a variety of grapes, including Gewürztraminer.

About 70 percent of Austria's wine is white, much of it made from the Grüner Veltliner grape and best drunk young. Typically, the wines are drier than German wines, although there is plenty of off-dry wine too. The best dry white wines are Rieslings made in Wachau, and other good dry white regions include Kamptal and Donauland.

Austria is also renowned for dessert wines from the Neusiedler See area of Burgenland, where noble rot affects every vintage. Light, fruity reds are also made in Burgenland, from Blauburgunder (the local version of Pinot Noir).

EASTERN EUROPE

A vast quantity of wine is made in Eastern Europe. Most of it is very ordinary, although some of the red and white wines from Hungary have good potential.

Bulls' Blood of Eger, a famous Hungarian red wine, and Tokay (Tokaji), one of the world's great dessert wines, also from Hungary, are joined by a range of more commercial international dry white and red wines.

Bulgaria has long had a following in the west for large amounts of sound red and dry white wine, made using classic varieties and some local grapes.

The Czech Republic's cool-climate vineyards make mainly white wine, and Slovenia's northeastern vineyards produce Lutomer Laski Rizling.

Croatia makes bulk white wines, while the best vineyards produce reds. Romanian wines can be good but are erratic.

TOKAJI ASZÚ

Very sweet, concentrated wine comes from the region of Tokaj-Hegyalja, in northeast Hungary.

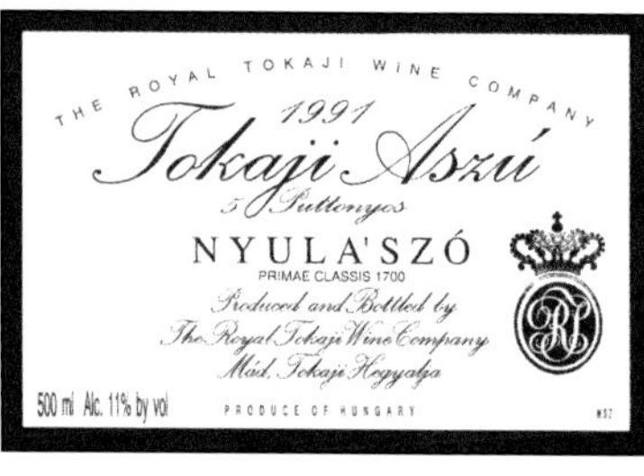

SOUTH & CENTRAL AMERICA

There is a long history of winemaking in South America, particularly in Argentina and Chile. After years of shipping inexpensive, ordinary wines to the world market, both countries have concentrated on improving quality during the late 1980s and 1990s and have been hugely successful.

CHILE

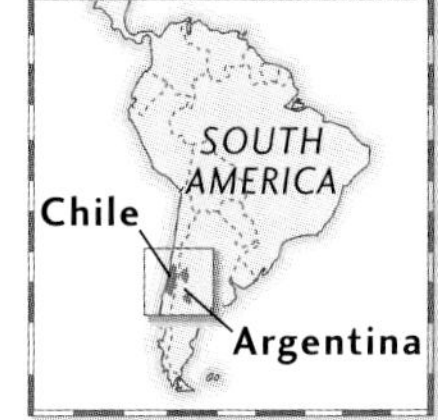

The French influence on winemaking in Chile has been and continues to be important. Chilean winegrowers looked to France in the nineteenth century when establishing their modern wine industry, and today Bordeaux and other foreign winemakers, particularly from the United States, are investing heavily in Chilean wine. The cooling influence of the Pacific Ocean in the west and the Andes Mountains in the east provides an ideal environment for the cultivation of vines. In addition, because the vineyards are so remote, they have been free of *phylloxera*.

Chile's Mediterranean-style climate and vast supply of irrigation water from the Andes Mountains enabled growers to produce abundant crops, which used not to promote quality in Chilean wine. However, many Chilean vineyards are no longer overcropped, resulting in greater intensity of flavor in the wines.

THE ANDES
The high Andes Mountains, a backdrop for the Guallatiri church in Aconcagua, moderate the climate in Chile's vineyards.

At this point, the best Chilean red wines are made from Cabernet Sauvignon, Merlot, and Carmenère, a red grape once widely planted in Bordeaux. Cuttings of Carmenère were brought to Chile in the nineteenth century and for years it was misidentified as Merlot. Newer plantings are true Merlot, however.

There are also some good whites. A great deal of Chardonnay is produced, and much of it has improved enormously in recent times. Sauvignon Blanc is also producing cleaner, more distinctive wines these days, especially in Casablanca.

Near the coast, Casablanca is Chile's top white wine region, while the Central Valley (including the regions of Maipo, Rapel, and Maule) is the heart of Chile's quality red wine production.

ARGENTINA

Argentina, which produces four times as much wine as Chile, was slow to recognize the need for premium wine production. It was only in the 1990s that Argentine winegrowers began to realize the importance of limiting crop size and matching the right vines to the right locations in order to produce quality grapes.

Argentina's largest production area is around the city of Mendoza, in the Andes foothills. As in Chile, Argentina's best wines are red. The Malbec grape makes wine of great distinction and character there, especially when grown in the foothills of the Andes Mountains, where it produces a robust, fruity wine which is capable of extended aging. Other red grapes cultivated include Cabernet Sauvignon, Merlot, Barbera, Nebbiolo, Syrah, and Tempranillo.

A distinctive white wine made from Torrontés, a Spanish grape variety, has a pronounced floral, Muscat-like aroma and flavor. Chenin Blanc is widely planted. Chardonnay develops more character in Argentina than it does in Chile.

ESCORIHUELA

The Escorihuela bodega, or winery, is in Mendoza, the largest wine-producing region in Argentina.

OTHER COUNTRIES

Elsewhere in South America, Brazil makes huge amounts of cheap, forgettable wine. However, a serious effort is underway in Uruguay, where the potential to produce fine wine is greater than in Brazil. Consultants from California have been working in Uruguay for several years, modernizing the vineyards and winemaking techniques. Wine is also made in Peru, where the hot climate means that two crops can be harvested each year, and in Ecuador and Colombia.

Mexico has a long tradition of winemaking and viticulture, with vineyards dating back to the sixteenth century, although the majority of the grapes go into brandy production. In the past few decades, however, the quality of wines from Baja California has improved dramatically. Baja producers are now forming joint ventures with California wineries, as has happened in Argentina and Chile.

AUSTRALIA & NEW ZEALAND

Australia is a cornucopia of fruity, affordable wines. New Zealand is the world's southernmost wine country. Both are producing some top-league wines.

AUSTRALIA

Australia offers the world superb varietal wine at reasonable prices. Many fine wines are produced there, too. Most of the country's vineyards are in the southeast, with some in the southwest corner.

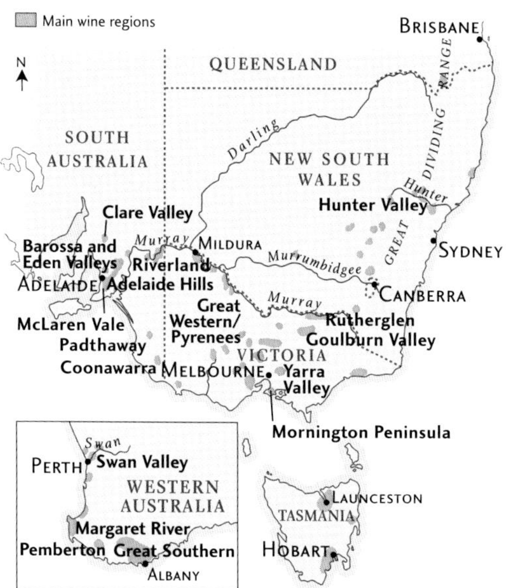

NEW SOUTH WALES The Hunter Valley, in New South Wales, some 100 miles (160 km) north of Sydney, was first planted in the 1820s and is Australia's oldest winegrowing region.

The region is well known for Sémillon with huge aging potential, both oaked and unoaked. Hunter Chardonnay and Cabernet Sauvignon are reliable wines, made in a variety of styles. Shiraz in a fruit-forward style is also good, with deep flavors that are long-lasting on the palate.

ROTHBURY ESTATE

Founded by Len Evans, this impressive winery is situated in the Hunter Valley, in New South Wales.

VICTORIA There are several important wine-growing areas in Victoria, ranging from the warm Rutherglen district, on the Murray River, famous for its fortified Muscats, to the cool Mornington Peninsula, known for its Pinot Noirs. Other top areas include the Goulburn Valley and the Yarra Valley, a source of good Pinot Noir for still and sparkling wines. World-class Cabernet Sauvignon is being made in Victoria—as is Shiraz, which is often made in a style reminiscent of the Rhône, rather than the jammy style seen elsewhere in Australia. There is even a sparkling wine made from Shiraz.

TASMANIA There has been a great deal of interest in the winemaking potential of the island of Tasmania, off the south coast. It is a generally cool area, and early plantings of Chardonnay, Riesling, and Pinot Noir showed promise. Some good sparkling wines have been produced.

CHATEAU TAHBILK

The family-run winery in Victoria's Goulburn Valley has been established since the nineteenth century.

SOUTH AUSTRALIA Roughly 60 percent of Australia's wine is produced in this state, ranging from bulk wines to some top-quality wines. Among the older districts are the Barossa, Eden, and Clare Valleys, and Coonawarra. Padthaway and Adelaide Hills are two newer areas.

Australian Classification System

Australia is working toward implementing an official system that will define geographic wine areas as zones, which will be further divided into regions. There are moves to single out specific vineyard sites that have demonstrated particular quality and reliability.

COMMEMORATIVE PLAQUE

This wooden plaque at the Yalumba winery, in the Barossa Valley, commemorates the planting of the first grapes there in 1849.

BAROSSA AND EDEN VALLEYS An hour's drive from Adelaide, the Barossa Valley rivals the Hunter Valley as Australia's most famous winemaking district. The glory of Barossa is Shiraz, much of it from old vines in vineyards with small yields, leading to concentrated wines with great intensity. On slightly higher, cooler land, the Eden Valley is well known for Riesling.

CLARE VALLEY North of Barossa, this hilly area with many small wineries produces superb dry Riesling, fine Sémillon and Chardonnay, and intense Shiraz and Cabernet Sauvignon with great depth of fruit.

MCLAREN VALE AND ADELAIDE HILLS South of Adelaide, the long-established McLaren Vale area is known for full-bodied red and white wines. East of Adelaide, vineyards have been planted more recently at higher, cooler altitudes in the Adelaide Hills. Chardonnay and Sauvignon Blanc grapes grow well there.

COONAWARRA AND PADTHAWAY These areas are in the far southeast of South

Australia. Coonawarra is famous for its rich, red soil with a limestone base and its relative proximity to the cool Southern Ocean. These factors have made it suitable for producing delicious Bordeaux-style wines from Cabernet Sauvignon and Merlot. Chardonnay and Sauvignon Blanc grow well in the Padthaway region to the north.

RIVERLAND Centered on the Murray River, this huge winegrowing district spreads through New South Wales, South Australia, and Victoria. Almost 30 percent of all Australian wine comes from Riverland grapes, much of it going into inexpensive bulk wines.

WESTERN AUSTRALIA The hot Swan Valley district near Perth has a reputation for Chenin Blanc, Chardonnay, and Verdelho. In Australia's southwest corner, there are three quality wine regions with cooler climates.

MARGARET RIVER Cabernet Sauvignon from this region can be rich, with concentrated fruit, and Chardonnay has great depth and structure.

PEMBERTON This new region in southwest Australia is showing great promise for Pinot Noir and other cool-climate varieties.

GREAT SOUTHERN The huge region includes the isolated vineyard areas Mount Barker and Frankland River. Chardonnay, Pinot Noir, and Riesling are among the wines that do well.

CAPE MENTELLE

An impressive Chardonnay is made in the Cape Mentelle winery in Margaret River, which is co-owned by the famous Champagne house Veuve Clicquot and founder David Hohnen.

NEW ZEALAND

Grapes grow on both North and South Islands, with the latter having the cooler climate. New Zealand wines are appearing more often in wine shops around the world as the industry develops and exports become more important.

Sauvignon Blanc is currently New Zealand's most important grape. It is made in an intensely fruity, aromatic style. Pinot Noir is another New Zealand specialty. Chardonnay and Cabernet Sauvignon grow well too.

GISBORNE In this region on the North Island, Chardonnay is made in a soft style, emphasizing ripe melon and pear flavors.

HAWKES BAY

An old Presbyterian church has been turned into a tasting room for wines made at the Akarangi winery in Hawkes Bay.

HAWKES BAY Also on the North Island, Hawkes Bay produces Chardonnay that has citrus fruit and is richer than in Gisborne. Cabernet Sauvignon, often blended with Merlot or Cabernet Franc, makes the best Hawkes Bay red wine.

MARTINBOROUGH Also known as Wairarapa, this region at the southern tip of the North Island is the home of small, quality-oriented wineries producing some excellent Pinot Noir.

MARLBOROUGH This area in the north of the South Island is New Zealand's largest wine region. It is well known for its piercing Sauvignon Blanc. Chardonnay and Pinot Noir can be equally good.

SOUTH AFRICA

Because of South Africa's political and economic isolation during apartheid, its winegrowers failed to keep up with the rest of the world. It was only in the 1990s that real progress began, starting with replanting in diseased vineyards. Almost one-third of South Africa's vineyards are planted to Chenin Blanc and less than 20 percent to the best international varieties.

South Africa's traditional premium wine regions are situated close to Cape Town and include the historic Constantia region, originally famous for its sweet wine and now producing outstanding Sauvignon Blanc, Chardonnay, and Cabernet Sauvignon.

The heart of the Cape winelands is Stellenbosch, a mountainous region known especially for its red wines made from Cabernet Sauvignon, Merlot, Shiraz, and the local Pinotage.

To the east, and part of the Paarl region, is Franschhoek, which is making a name for itself with white varieties and Cabernet Sauvignon. The rest of Paarl has a warmer climate. Formerly best known for its sherry-style wines, today it also makes good table wines.

One important newcomer, the warm, inland Robertson region, has the benefit of a limestone soil, particularly suited to Chardonnay. Besides producing good Chardonnay, Robertson makes Sauvignon

GROOT CONSTANTIA

Now a major tourist attraction, this historic wine estate was set up by Simon van der Stel about 300 years ago.

Blanc, Cabernet Sauvignon, and very satisfactory sparkling wines.

Newer wine areas showing promise include Walker Bay, South Africa's southernmost region, which has produced fine Pinot Noir and Chardonnay for several years; and the cool, high country of Elgin, not far from Franschhoek, which is producing good Sauvignon Blanc. New areas near the coastlands include Mossel Bay on the Indian Ocean, with plantings of Sauvignon Blanc and Pinot Noir.

Sauvignon Blanc, which is made in a fruit-forward style with pronounced citrus and melon flavors, is South Africa's leading white wine. The best red wines are powerful Bordeaux-style reds. A South African specialty is the red grape Pinotage, developed by crossing Pinot Noir with the southern French Cinsaut grape. It is used to make wines with some aging potential.

South African Classification System

In South Africa, Wine of Origin (WO) laws provide a guarantee of region, vintage, and grape variety. The country is divided into WO regions, which are subdivided into districts and wards. Estate wines in South Africa are strictly controlled. There are fewer than 100 designated estates, and grapes must come from defined estate-owned vineyards.

OTHER COUNTRIES

In North Africa, the best reds come from Morocco, where they are rich and sweet. Wine is also made in Algeria, with 75 percent of wine production in the western coastal province of Oran. Wine is also produced in Lebanon, where the two main producers have vineyards in the Bekaa Valley. Israel produces large amounts of sweet, red wine, as well as some fine dry whites, reds, and sparkling wine from the Golan Heights.

In Europe, Greece has recently established a wine classification system and has made improvements in both vineyard conditions and winemaking facilities. Some native Greek varieties are worth seeking out. Cyprus makes reds, whites, rosés, and some fortified wines. The main production area is centered around the Troodos mountains.

GREEK WINERY
This is the state-of-the-art interior of the Kourtakis winery in Greece.

England has planted a small amount of farmland in the south to vines. Although the soil is suitable, the climate is often too damp and there is not enough sun. The wines, mainly white, with some Champagne-method sparkling, are uneven, but some are proving good.

In Asia, vine planting in China is on the increase, mainly in the north where the climate is moderate. Japan makes some quality wine from grapes grown in the country, but relies mostly on imported grapes or wine. India produces some wine.

CHAPTER 3

A to Z of Wine

A comprehensive reference resource including entries on wine regions and grapes, definitions of technical terms, and profiles of people who have shaped wine history.

ABBOCCATO Italian for medium-sweet wine. In English, the term would be off-dry or medium-dry. The Spanish term is *abocado*.

ABFÜLLUNG German term meaning bottled by.

ABRUZZO Mountainous area in central Italy. The chief grapes grown are Trebbiano for white wine and Montepulciano for red and a little rosé. There have been recent improvements, but quality very much depends on the producer.

AC/AOC Abbreviations of Appellation d'Origine Contrôlée, the highest French wine classification. AC regulations cover yields, grape varieties, and geographic origin. In practice, the term guarantees style and origin, not necessarily quality.

ACETIC ACID The main flavor found in vinegar, this acid is produced when bacteria attack wine exposed to oxygen.

ACID Vital constituent of wine, necessary to help achieve balance and structure and responsible for the fresh, lively taste of wine, especially white wine. Sweet wine should have higher acidity to balance the sugar.

Used as a tasting term, acid can have a pejorative meaning indicating that the acidity is too high.

ACONCAGUA Region in Chile, north of Santiago. It includes the warm Aconcagua Valley, which has produced some of Chile's most intense Cabernet Sauvignon; and the cool Casablanca Valley not far from the Pacific Ocean, which specializes in whites.

ADEGA Portuguese for winery.

ADELAIDE HILLS Small region a short drive from Adelaide, South Australia, producing high-quality wine. Its moist, cool climate is ideal for making good sparkling wines and top table wines, especially Sauvignon Blanc, Chardonnay, and Pinot Noir.

AFTERTASTE Flavor remaining in the mouth after wine is swallowed,

including the length of time the flavor stays on the palate.

AGING The maturing and improving of wine in barrel and bottle after it is made. Most wines are best drunk young, but there are wines that improve in barrel and bottle. Best wines for aging include the classic red varieties such as Cabernet Sauvignon, Merlot, Pinot Noir, Syrah, and Nebbiolo. Whites that age well include top Chardonnay, Riesling, and Sémillon. SEE BARREL AGING AND BOTTLE AGING.

AGLIANICO DEL VULTURE DOC Appellation in the Basilicata region of Italy where red wines capable of extended aging are made from the Aglianico grape, grown on the slopes of Mount Vulture.

Aglianico vineyards

AHR Small German wine region south of Bonn, named after the Ahr River, a tributary of the Rhine. The best wines are dry reds made from Spätburgunder (Pinot Noir) and Blauer Portugieser. Much of the red wine is made in a slightly sweet style for the local market. A lot of the wine is made in cooperatives.

AIRÉN Most widely planted white wine grape in the world, with most of the acreage in central and southern Spain. A skilled winemaker with modern equipment can make a fresh, lively wine from Airén; otherwise, it holds little appeal.

AJACCIO AC Appellation on the French island of Corsica producing above-average Corsican red wines.

ALBANA DI ROMAGNA DOCG In the hills south of Bologna, this was Italy's first DOCG for white wines, a political decision roundly condemned by wine experts who did not consider the wine worthy of DOCG status. The wine, from the Albana grape, is made in dry, sweet, and sparkling styles.

ALBARIÑO White wine grape used to make what is quite likely Spain's best white wine, certainly the most popular and most expensive. It is grown in the cool and rainy northwest of Spain in the Rías Baixas DO of Galicia. The wine, with refreshing acidity, has lively peach and apricot fruit, reminiscent of Muscat and Viognier. The grape is also grown in northern Portugal, where it is called Alvarinho.

ALBARIZA Distinctive white limestone soil found in the Jerez y Manzanilla (sherry) region of Spain. Vineyards on *albariza* soil produce some of the best Fino and Manzanilla sherries.

ALCAMO DOC Good dry white wine made from the Cattarratto grape of western Sicily, Italy.

ALCOHOL In a wine context, alcohol usually refers to ethanol, the main alcoholic compound in wine.

ALCOHOLIC CONTENT On wine labels, usually expressed as a percentage of alcohol by volume, or ABV. Most table wines range from 10 percent to 14 percent ABV. In the United States, table wine must be between 7 and 14 percent, and dessert wines must be between 14 and 24 percent.

ALCOHOLIC FERMENTATION The primary fermentation in which certain yeast enzymes convert grape sugar into alcohol.

ALEATICO Traditional Italian red wine grape, which makes a remarkable sweet red wine from Apulia, southern Italy. It is also grown on the islands of Corsica and Elba. The grape was widely grown in California before Prohibition and has recently been making a comeback in the Sierra Foothills region.

ALELLA DO Small Spanish appellation near Barcelona, where off-dry white wines have traditionally been made from Pansa Blanca, the local name of Xarel-lo. Newer wines include dry whites from Chardonnay and Chenin Blanc and red and rosé wine from Merlot. Some Cavas are also made.

ALENQUER IPR Portuguese region in Oeste, north of Lisbon. Over 30 grape varieties are permitted in the region, with much of the production going into brandy distillation. Watch this region for rising quality.

ALENTEJO Red wines from the two Portuguese provinces of Alto and Baixo Alentejo, which make up most of southern Portugal, have improved dramatically. Many wine authorities believe that Portugal's finest red table wines will come from this region in the future.

ALEXANDER VALLEY AVA An American Viticultural Area that follows the Russian River in northern Sonoma County, California. It is a relatively warm area with little summer fog penetrating so far inland. Cabernet Sauvignon makes a distinctive, juicy wine, good for early drinking and, in some instances, capable of bottle aging. Zinfandel and Chardonnay are worth looking out for, as is Sauvignon Blanc, especially if grown on benchland above the river. Recent plantings of Syrah also show promise.

ALGARVE Despite a long history of winemaking, this southernmost province of Portugal makes mostly unremarkable wines.

ALGERIA Following World War II, France looked to Algeria for a large part of its everyday red wines. Although wine production continues in Algeria, the future looks somewhat uncertain.

ALICANTE BOUSCHET Crossing of Petit Bouschet and Grenache grapes, still widely planted in southern France and in Spain, where it is called Garnacha Tinta. A red grape, producing wine of a deep color, it is often used for blending. It was very popular in California

during Prohibition, when it was sold to home winemakers because its thick skin could withstand shipping. Today, it is made as a varietal wine by a few California producers, mostly as a curiosity.

ALICANTE DO Region in central Spain, on the Mediterranean coast, known for high-alcohol, rustic red wines. Today, most of the wines from the area are made by cooperatives and are exported in bulk. The huge Doble Pasa traditional reds are worth trying.

ALIGOTÉ White wine grape, mostly planted in Burgundy, France. Most is undistinguished, but from old vines in a good year, it can make a pleasing wine with a tart lemony flavor. It is the wine traditionally blended with cassis (the blackcurrant liqueur) to make the aperitif Kir.

ALOXE-CORTON AC Important French AC in the Côte de Beaune, Burgundy. Its solid reputation is based on two Grands Crus: Corton, which produces mostly red wine from Pinot Noir and a little white wine from Chardonnay; and Corton-Charlemagne, which makes white wine only from Chardonnay.

ALSACE AC White wines from this French appellation are among the most distinctive in the world. The most important grapes are Riesling, Gewürztraminer, Pinot Gris, and Muscat (all "noble" grapes), and Pinot Blanc and Sylvaner. There is a small amount of red wine made from Pinot Noir. Unusually for France, almost all Alsatian wines are labeled

Sign for Hugel, the famous Alsace wine producer

by grape variety. With a few exceptions, the wines are dry-finished and are not usually aged in new oak, allowing the characteristic fruit of the variety to show well.

ALSACE GRAND CRU AC About 50 vineyards in Alsace, France, may use the Alsace Grand Cru AC, but only for wines made from the "noble" grape varieties Riesling, Gewürztraminer, Pinot Gris, and Muscat.

ALSACE SÉLECTION DE GRAINS NOBLES SEE SÉLECTION DE GRAINS NOBLES.

ALSACE VENDANGE TARDIVE Late-harvest wine from Alsace, France, made from grapes picked when slightly overripe. They yield an intense, concentrated, mouth-filling wine. Vendange Tardive may be made only from Gewürztraminer, Muscat, Pinot Gris, or Riesling.

ALTO ADIGE Region in northern Italy producing a range of well-made red and white wines. Fruity, young red wines are made from indigenous varieties, as well as from Cabernet Sauvignon and Merlot. The white wines, known for their

forward fruit and crisp, bright style, are made largely from Chardonnay, Pinot Grigio, and Riesling grapes. The wines are almost always varietally labeled.

ALVARINHO Portuguese name for Albariño. SEE ALBARIÑO.

AMABILE Italian word for semi-sweet wine.

AMADOR COUNTY Wine region in the Sierra Foothills AVA, California. Vineyards were first planted in the 1850s during the Gold Rush. Some of California's oldest vineyards, mostly Zinfandel, are still productive. Zinfandel remains the leading grape by a long way, with a little Barbera and Sauvignon Blanc.

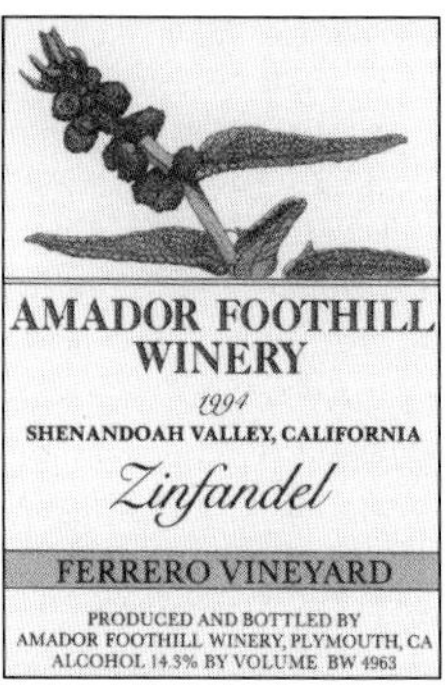

AMARONE DELLA VALPOLICELLA DOCG Dry red wine, made in Veneto, northeast Italy, from grapes dried on mats for months after the end of the harvest. Wines from the Classico region are the best.

AMONTILLADO Style of sherry in Spain. A true Amontillado is a Fino sherry, produced when the bloom, or flor, on the Fino dies naturally or is killed by fortification with alcohol to 16 percent. The more common Amontillados are sweetened to make a medium-dry style.

AMPURDÁN-COSTA BRAVA DO Area in Catalonia, northeast Spain, just across the border from the French region of Roussillon. Most of the wine is undistinguished, with much cheap rosé made from Garnacha and Cariñena, although efforts have been made recently to improve quality.

ANBAUGEBIET German term for growing region.

ANDALUCÍA Hot area of southern Spain, the home of Jerez y Manzanilla (of sherry fame), Condado de Huelva, Montilla-Moriles, and Málaga DOs. Sherry, a fortified wine, ranges in style from dry to sweet. Other wines from the area are generally sweet and fortified. Dry red and white table wine is also made in Andalucía.

ANDERSON VALLEY AVA Cool, isolated wine district close to the Pacific Ocean in western Mendocino County, California, best known for outstanding sparkling wines and, increasingly, for Pinot Noir.

ANJOU BLANC AC French Loire Valley appellation producing a wide range of dry to sweet white wines, based on Chenin Blanc with up to 20 percent Chardonnay or Sauvignon Blanc allowed. The best of these wines are dry.

ANJOU ROUGE AC French Loire Valley AC known for fruity Cabernet Sauvignon and Cabernet Franc blends, and for indifferent rosés.

ANJOU-SAUMUR French district in the Loire Valley producing a vast range of sparkling and still wines, including dry or sweet white wines from Chenin Blanc; and rosés and reds, the best of which are based on Cabernet Franc.

ANJOU VILLAGES AC French Loire Valley appellation created in 1986 for producers of top-quality red wines from Cabernet Sauvignon and Cabernet Franc grapes.

ANTINORI, PIERO Innovative Italian winemaker and head of the renowned Tuscan family firm with vast wine estates, Piero Antinori (1938–) created Tignanello, one of the first Super-Tuscan blends.

APPELLATION Used generally, it refers to a delimited and geographically defined winegrowing region.

APPROACHABLE Wines that are easy to drink, without particularly high acidity for whites, or high tannin levels for reds, are often termed approachable; this also implies that they do not need to be aged.

APULIA Region of southern Italy, called Puglia in Italian, where good progress is being made to improve wine quality. The best wines offer good value.

ARAGÓN Political and winegrowing region in Spain stretching from the Pyrenees mountains in the north to the central plateau. Traditionally, Aragón produces much of Spain's cheap red wine. Quality is improving, especially in the northerly region of Somontano, where Cabernet Sauvignon, Merlot, and Chardonnay have been planted.

ARBOIS AC Largest AC in Jura, France, well known for the sherry-like *vin jaune* and a sweet *vin de paille*. A sparkling wine made from Chardonnay is also good.

ARGENTINA Emerging wine producer. Recent foreign investments in its vineyards and wineries show faith in the potential quality of the wines, most of which come from the province of Mendoza, in the foothills of the Andes Mountains.

ARNEIS Italian white wine grape, which produces herbal, perfumed wines; at its best in Piedmont, northwest Italy.

AROMA Characteristic smell of a young wine, or of the grapes used to make the wine. As the wine matures, the aroma changes to bouquet.

AROMATIC Describes certain grape varieties, such as Muscat and Gewürztraminer, that give fragrant or spicy flavors in wine. Aromatic may also be used as a tasting term.

ARROYO GRANDE VALLEY AVA Established in San Luis Obispo County on California's Central Coast in 1990, vineyards in this appellation are planted chiefly to Chardonnay and Pinot Noir.

ARROYO SECO AVA Established in the early 1980s on benchland above the Salinas River in Monterey County, California. Chardonnay is the best grape in the AVA, although new plantings of Pinot Noir and Syrah are also looking good.

ARRUDA IPR Portuguese appellation, just north of Lisbon, making sound, inexpensive red wine from the local cooperative.

ASSEMBLAGE French word for the bringing together of separate lots of wine to make a final blend. It plays an important role in sparkling wine production, when dozens of base wines may be assembled for the final cuvée.

ASTI DOCG Light, sweet, sparkling wine once known as Asti Spumante is made in this DOCG in Piedmont, Italy. Sparklers made outside the DOCG are called simply Spumante

ASTRINGENCY Tasting term referring to a harshness in the wine caused by grape or oak tannins.

ASZÚ In Hungary's Tokay region, this is the name given to grapes affected by noble rot which are made into a sticky paste and used to sweeten a base wine.

ATLAS PEAK AVA California AVA in the eastern hills of Napa County, sparsely planted chiefly with Sangiovese and Cabernet Sauvignon.

AUCKLAND Fairly new winegrowing region on New Zealand's North Island, near the city of Auckland.

L'AUDE, VIN DE PAYS DE Large winegrowing region in Languedoc, France, best known for red wines.

AUSBRUCH Style of Austrian sweet wine, made from grapes affected by noble rot.

AUSLESE Classification category for German wine made from grapes picked after the regular harvest, which have a higher sugar level.

AUSTRALIA Producer of high-quality wines and a leader in technical innovations in wine production. Made from a number of grape varieties in New South Wales, Victoria, South Australia, Western Australia, and Tasmania, wines are characterized by intense fruit flavors. Shiraz has been the most successful red grape variety, helped by plantings of very old Shiraz vines that exist particularly in South Australia. Other good reds include Cabernet Sauvignon, Grenache, and Pinot Noir (in cooler areas). Oak-aged Chardonnay from Australia has proved extremely popular, though perhaps its Sémillon and Riesling whites show more class. Champagne-method sparkling wines are of increasingly high quality, and there is also a great tradition of fortified Muscat and ports.

AUSTRIA Producer of excellent dry Riesling, sweet wines, and light and fruity red wines made from Blauer Burgunder, the local name for Pinot Noir. Although Austrian wine laws are similar to German ones, Austria offers a much more varied selection of wines.

AUXEY-DURESSES AC Village AC in the hills above Meursault in the Côte de Beaune, Burgundy, France, making light red Pinot Noir wine, tending toward austere, and some Chardonnay. The wines are usually well priced for early drinking.

AVA Abbreviation of American Viticultural Area, the standard appellation classification in the United States. It denotes geographical areas, not quality levels.

AZIENDA AGRICOLA Italian term for estate or farm. The name may appear on a wine label only if the grapes used to make the wine were grown on the estate.

BACCHUS The name refers to the Roman god of wine, whom the Greeks called Dionysus, and to a German white wine grape.

Bacchus, the wine grape, is a crossing developed from a Sylvaner-Riesling cross and Müller-Thurgau. It is widely planted in Germany.

Bacchus

BADEN Large wine region in the south of Germany producing dry white and red wines. It has good potential for the future.

BAGA Grape widely planted in Portugal, especially in Bairrada, where it is sometimes called Tinta Bairrada. It produces a tannic red wine capable of some aging.

BAIRRADA High-quality wine region in northern Portugal, known for its dark, tannic red wines, mostly made from one grape, Baga.

BAJA CALIFORNIA Mexico's best wines come from this state, which occupies the peninsula extending south of California.

BALANCE A wine is in balance when all the elements, including acidity, tannins, alcohol, sweetness (if any), and oak (if any), come together in harmony.

BANDOL AC Good rosés and reds, based on the Mourvèdre grape, are made in this French AC on the Mediterranean coast in Provence.

BANYULS AC Small AC in Roussillon, southwest France, making fine *vins doux naturels,* mostly from Grenache. SEE VIN DOUX NATUREL.

BARBARESCO DOCG Important Italian DOCG in Piedmont, famous for powerful, long-lived red wines based on Nebbiolo. Barbaresco and Barolo are the classic examples of Nebbiolo wine. In most years, Barbaresco is softer than Barolo and matures earlier.

B

BARBERA When treated properly in the vineyard and pruned for smaller yields, this northern Italian grape can be quite good. Sadly, it is often overcropped, which leads to thin, acidic wines. Barbera is widely planted in California, where it is mostly used for blending in inexpensive table wines.

BARBERA D'ALBA DOC Most of Italy's best red wines made from Barbera grapes are from this DOC in Piedmont. It covers roughly the same area as the Barolo DOCG.

BARDOLINO DOC Italian wine region in Veneto making light red wines that are best drunk young.

BAROLO DOCG Famous red wine DOCG in the Italian region of Piedmont. The wine, which is made from Nebbiolo grapes, is initially austere and very tannic, and is capable of aging for decades.

BAROSSA VALLEY Top-quality wine region in South Australia that is home to some of Australia's largest wineries. Historically, Barossa was known for port-style wines, and for Shiraz and Riesling table wines, at which it still excels.

BARREL AGING Many red wines, especially Cabernet Sauvignon, and a few whites, notably Chardonnay, are aged in small barrels following fermentation for varied periods of time depending on the style of wine desired. Barrel aging tends to soften the wine and add to its richness. It also imparts some wood flavors and tannins.

Barrels for aging wine

BARREL FERMENTATION Some white wines, especially Chardonnay, are fermented in small barrels as winemakers believe that barrel fermentation creates a better balance between oak and wine and improves texture and mouthfeel.

BARRIQUE Traditional barrel used in Bordeaux, known as the *barrique bordelaise*, with a capacity of 225 liters (59 gallons). In the United States, most winemakers use this size of vessel.

BARSAC AC Appellation within the Sauternes AC in Bordeaux, France, producing good sweet wines similar in style to Sauternes.

BASILICATA Red wine capable of some aging is made in this area of southern Italy with only one DOC, Aglianico del Vulture.

BÂTARD-MONTRACHET AC Some of the world's greatest white wines, based on Chardonnay grapes, are made in this Grand Cru in France's Côte de Beaune, Burgundy. The wines have great intensity and, in good years, are capable of aging for at least a decade.

BATF Abbreviation for the Bureau of Alcohol, Tobacco, and Firearms, the U.S. agency that regulates the wine and spirit industries.

LES BAUX-DE-PROVENCE AC Small French AC in Provence, which regularly produces outstanding red and rosé wine. Much of the wine is made from grapes grown in organically farmed vineyards.

BÉARN AC Appellation in southwest France producing mostly red and rosé wines from a local cooperative. The wines are merely sound.

BEAUJOLAIS AC French red wine AC in southern Burgundy, famous worldwide for Beaujolais Nouveau, which has too often overshadowed the fine reds made in one of the ten Crus of the region. Made from Gamay, Beaujolais at its best offers forward fruit with fairly low tannins.

BEAUJOLAIS NOUVEAU Young red wine from Beaujolais, Burgundy, France, released on the third Thursday of November following the year's harvest. Traditionally, the wine was rushed to Paris's cafés and bistros in barrel. The subject of much hype in recent years, it is usually no more than a good quaff.

BEAUJOLAIS-VILLAGES AC Several designated villages in northern Beaujolais, France, can use this AC. The wines are very good for everyday drinking, with juicy fruit.

BEAULIEU Napa Valley winery in California where André Tchelistcheff created the wines that originally brought it distinction; its reputation, particularly for Cabernet Sauvignon, still flourishes.

BEAUNE The town of Beaune gives its name to the southern part of the Côte d'Or, Burgundy, France: the Côte de Beaune. It is home to the famous Hospices de Beaune, a charitable organization with large vineyard holdings in the Côte d'Or. The annual November auction of its wines in barrel provides a benchmark for Burgundy prices.

BEAUNE AC French AC in the south of the Côte d'Or, Burgundy, making first-class red wine.

BEERENAUSLESE German and Austrian wine category applied to wines from individually selected, overripe grapes, leading to rich, concentrated dessert wines.

BEKAA VALLEY Fertile valley in Lebanon, which has produced a few excellent red wines.

BELLET AC Small French AC near Nice, in Provence, producing distinctive red, rosé, and white wines.

BEREICH German term for a large wine district; the designation is often political in nature and not an indication of quality.

BERGERAC AC District in southwest France, east of Bordeaux, making wine from the same grapes used in Bordeaux. The red wines are good value and can be drunk young. SEE BORDEAUX VARIETIES.

BERINGER VINEYARDS Historic Napa property, founded in 1876 by Jacob and Frederick Beringer, making wines ranging from popular White Zinfandel to limited bottlings of acclaimed vineyard-select and winemaker reserve Cabernet Sauvignon and Chardonnay.

BERNKASTEL Pretty village in the heart of the Mosel Valley, with some of Germany's steepest and finest vineyards, planted with Riesling on slaty soil. The Doctor vineyard is widely considered the best, but Graben and Lay are also good.

BIANCO Italian word for white, often used as part of a wine name.

BIANCO DI CUSTOZA DOC District in Veneto, northeast Italy, producing dry white wine, similar in style to Soave.

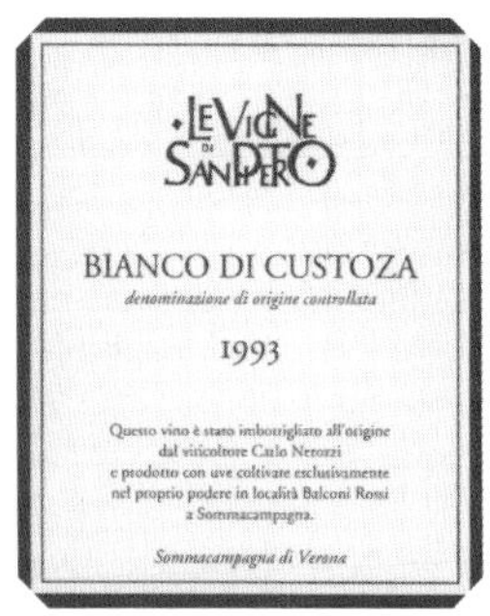

BIERZO DO Promising Spanish wine region between Galicia and Castilla-León. The red wines, based on Mencia grapes, have refreshing fruit, reminiscent of Galician wines.

BIODYNAMIC Form of alternative agriculture that bans the use of chemical fertilizers and sprays (except for sulfur). Soil fertility is emphasized in both biodynamic and organic farming, but biodynamics goes further: viticultural and enological practices are at least partly regulated by the positions of the planets and phases of the moon. Several top French producers are converting wholly or partly to biodynamic viticulture.

BIONDI-SANTI The most traditional and most expensive producer of Brunello di Montalcino in Tuscany, Italy, Biondi-Santi created the benchmark style for this wine and still produces one of the country's longest-lived wines.

BLAGNY AC French AC in the Côte de Beaune, Burgundy, producing good-value rustic red wines.

BLANC French word for white, as in *vin blanc*, or white wine.

BLANC DE BLANCS White wine, usually sparkling, made from only white grapes.

BLANC DE NOIRS White wine, most often sparkling, made from red-skinned grapes by pressing them gently, then quickly separating the juice from the skins before it picks up any color. In fact, the wine may sometimes have a slightly pink hue. Blanc de Noirs Champagne is made from Pinot Noir and/or Pinot Meunier grapes.

BLANCO Spanish word for white, as in *vino blanco*, or white wine.

BLANQUETTE DE LIMOUX AC French AC in Languedoc-Roussillon producing delicious, refreshing Champagne-method sparkling wine based chiefly on the Mauzac grape. It is known for its intense green apple flavors. Chardonnay, also planted there, can be sold under the Blanquette de Limoux AC.

BLAUBURGUNDER German name for Pinot Noir. SEE PINOT NOIR.

BLAUFRÄNKISCH Austrian name for the red wine grape known as Lemberger in the state of Washington. SEE LEMBERGER.

BLAYE AC Designation for lesser red and white wines of the Blaye region in Bordeaux, France.

BLENDING Art of assembling wines from different vineyards, regions, or even vintages, practiced to create a wine of better quality than any single wine in the blend. Sparkling wines and sherries are both classic blended wines.

BLUSH A name invented as a marketing ploy in California to avoid using the term rosé, which had become associated in the United States with cheap pink jug wines. Blush wines are usually light and sweet. The term blush was first used to describe the pink-hued White Zinfandel. SEE ZINFANDEL.

BOBAL Grape widely planted in central and southern Spain, where it makes densely colored red wines.

BOCKSBEUTEL Flagon-shaped wine bottle used in the Franken region of Germany.

BODEGA Spanish word for winery, wine store, or tavern.

BODY Tasting term for the impression on the palate of a wine's weight and texture.

BOLGHERI DOC Appellation on the Tuscany coast, now extended to cover some of the region's most prestigious reds made from Cabernet Sauvignon, Merlot, and Sangiovese. Watch out for interesting developments in this area. There is a separate DOC for Sassicaia, one of Italy's original Super-Tuscans.

BOLLINGER Highly regarded Champagne house, which has demonstrated top quality since the late Madame Lily Bollinger took over after World War II. The whole range of wines is dominated by flavors of Pinot Noir and long aging on the yeast. The RD (which stands for "recently disgorged," referring to the long aging on the yeast), kept for many years before release, and the Vieilles Vignes Françaises, made from old, ungrafted vines, are highly prized by Bollinger aficionados.

BONNES-MARES AC Outstanding Grand Cru for red Burgundy from France's Côte de Nuits, which has established itself as one of the most reliable and consistent of all.

BONNEZEAUX AC Loire Valley AC making one of France's great sweet wines. Based entirely on Chenin Blanc grapes, the wine is capable of extended aging in good years.

BORBA DOC Portuguese DOC in the up-and-coming region of Alentejo, especially known for red wines.

BORDEAUX Considered by many to be the home of fine wine, the Bordeaux wine region, named after the city in the Gironde *département* of western France, is home to some of the greatest names in France. Benefiting from a climate moderated by its proximity to the Atlantic Ocean and with soils ideally suited to wine production, the region is crossed by two important rivers, the Dordogne and the Garonne, which combine to form the Gironde estuary. These break up the important regions of Médoc, Graves, and Sauternes to the west, and St-Émilion and Pomerol inland to the northeast. The region was a pioneer in bottling at the property, in this case at the famous châteaux, thus controlling the process from grape to bottle. Long-lived reds, now imitated throughout the wine world, are based mainly on Cabernet Sauvignon, Merlot, and Cabernet Franc. The equally famous sweet whites are mainly from Sémillon, with some Sauvignon and Muscadelle. Dry whites rarely achieve the high quality levels of the best sweet whites and reds, with the exception of a small clutch of world-class dry whites from Pessac-Léognan, made from Sémillon and Sauvignon Blanc.

BORDEAUX AC Basic French AC for all Bordeaux wines not included in a site-specific AC. The wines are often good value.

BORDEAUX SUPÉRIEUR AC A French AC one step up from the basic Bordeaux AC. Yields are lower and regulations call for one-half percent higher alcohol content. In theory, this leads to wines with deeper, more concentrated flavors.

BORDEAUX VARIETIES The five red grape varieties of Bordeaux are Cabernet Sauvignon, Cabernet Franc, Merlot, Malbec, and Petit Verdot. These varieties, particularly Cabernet Sauvignon and Merlot, are planted in many of the world's winegrowing regions in the hope of producing Bordeaux-style reds. The white Bordeaux varieties are Sémillon, Sauvignon Blanc, and small quantities of Muscadelle.

BOTRYTIS CINEREA See Noble Rot.

BOTTLE AGING Process by which wines are held in bottle for a period of a few weeks up to several years. During bottle aging, elements in the wine such as acidity, tannins, phenolics, flavor compounds, and alcohol interact, creating new flavors and enriching existing flavor elements. Wine in larger bottles tends to age at a slower rate.

BOTTLE SIZES The standard bottle size is 750 ml (25.4 fl oz). Also common is the 1.5 liter (50.7 fl oz) bottle, called a magnum. Half bottles (375ml/12.7 fl oz) and quarter bottles (187ml/6.3 fl oz) are also made. There are a number of larger bottle sizes, the largest of which is the Nebuchadnezzar, containing 20 standard bottles.

Bottle sizes

BOTTLE VARIATION Wine experts agree that bottles of wine drawn from the same tank or barrel may differ to some degree, depending on storage and other conditions.

BOUCHES-DU-RHÔNE, VIN DE PAYS DES French Vin de Pays in Provence producing full-bodied red and rosé wines.

BOUQUET The complex smell of a wine that develops after it has been in the bottle for some time. It is different from aroma, which refers to the smell of a young wine.

BOURGOGNE AC French umbrella appellation including all the wines of Burgundy that do not have an AC of their own. Some Bourgogne AC wines, especially from top producers, may be good value, but quality varies greatly. The wines are almost always light in weight and texture and should be drunk young.

BOURGOGNE-CÔTE CHALONNAISE AC SEE CÔTE CHALONNAISE.

BOURGOGNE-HAUTES-CÔTES DE BEAUNE AC French appellation on the upper slopes of the Côte de Beaune, Burgundy, producing fruity, relatively inexpensive red and white wine.

BOURGOGNE-HAUTES-CÔTES DE NUITS AC In the hills behind Burgundy's Côte de Nuits; the best wines from this French appellation are the reds.

BOURGOGNE PASSE-TOUT GRAINS AC Red wine from Burgundy, France, which must contain a minimum of one-third Pinot Noir, the rest being Gamay.

BOURGUEIL AC Good red wines are made in this region of France's Loire Valley from Cabernet Franc, sometimes blended with a little Cabernet Sauvignon.

BOUVIER Austrian white wine grape used for dessert wines.

BOUZY Village in France's Champagne region known for its Pinot Noir, used for both Champagne and still red wine.

BOX WINES Inexpensive wine is sometimes sold in large containers consisting of a plastic bag inside a cardboard carton. As the wine is taken from the bag, usually by means of a spigot, the bag collapses, excluding oxygen from the wine. The package usually contains 4 to 13 quarts (4 to 12 liters) of wine and is especially popular in Australia, where it is called cask wine.

BRACHETTO Red grape variety from Piedmont, Italy, used to make a fizzy, usually sweet, wine. It is probably the same grape that the French call Braquet, which is grown in Provence and used in the wines of the Bellet AC.

BRANCO Portuguese for white, as in *vinho branco*, or white wine.

BRAZIL South America's third-largest wine producer after Argentina and Chile, Brazil makes a large amount of cheap table wine for the home market and exports little quality wine. The subtropical climate in the south of the country, where most of the vineyards are planted, has been a major problem. Wines of some quality started to emerge only in the 1970s, after foreign investment brought technological advancements, and more grape varieties were cultivated.

BREGANZE DOC Small Italian appellation in the hills near Verona. The best wines are reds made from Merlot and whites made from the distinctive Tocai Friulano.

BRETTANOMYCES Spoilage yeast, often called Brett, which can produce unpleasant off-flavors in the finished wine.

BRITISH COLUMBIA The wine industry in this Pacific province of Canada is centered in the Okanagan Valley a few miles north of the border with the United States. It is an exciting new area for Chardonnay, Gewürztraminer, Pinot Blanc, Pinot Noir, and Riesling.

BRIX U.S. measuring system which uses degrees to indicate the sugar level of wine grapes at harvest. When the brix measure is multiplied by 0.55, the approximate potential alcohol by volume of the finished wine can be determined. Most wine grapes for table wine are harvested at between 20°Brix and 25°Brix.

BROADBENT, MICHAEL One of the most respected modern wine writers and educators, Broadbent (1927–) revived the wine auction department at Christie's in London, England, making it internationally famous. His notebooks, which are the source of his *Great Vintage Wine Book*, record more than 60,000 wines tasted over the years. He has influenced the growth of the fine wine auction scene around the world and promoted a better understanding of fine wines.

BROUILLY AC Largest of the ten Beaujolais Crus, making big, fruity red wines in Burgundy, France.

BROWN MUSCAT SEE MUSCAT BLANC À PETITS GRAINS.

BRUNELLO Local name in Montalcino, Tuscany, Italy, for Sangiovese. SEE SANGIOVESE.

BRUNELLO DI MONTALCINO DOCG From vineyards below the Tuscan hilltop town of Montalcino, Italy, this is one of the most powerful and long-lived Italian red wines, made from Brunello (the local name for Sangiovese).

BRUT French term for dry sparkling wine with less than 1.5 grams per liter of sugar added before bottling.

BUCELAS DOC Historically important, though small, Portuguese appellation producing dry white wines capable of some aging.

BULGARIA Producer of some of Eastern Europe's best reds, especially drink-me-now, fruity versions of standard international red and white wines. There are also a number of good wines made from native grapes.

BULK PROCESS SEE CHARMAT.

BULLS' BLOOD OF EGER Once-legendary, rich red wine from Eger, northern Hungary.

BURGENLAND Austrian winegrowing region known for sweet white and dry red wines.

BURGUNDY Famed French wine region, which extends in a narrow strip from Auxerre, south of Paris, to Lyon. It is home to arguably the world's greatest white and red wines. The Chardonnay-based whites of Burgundy, at their best, have a richness and depth of flavor seldom found elsewhere. The reds, based on Pinot Noir, are rivaled only by the great red wines of Bordeaux and, perhaps, California. At one time, a fair amount of red wine from California was labeled Burgundy. There is still some "California Burgundy" around, now seldom seen except in jug wines.

Hospices de Beaune, Burgundy

BUTT Wooden cask that is used for aging sherry.

BUZET AC Appellation in Gascony, southwest France, making reasonable red wines from the same grape varieties and in the same style as Bordeaux. SEE BORDEAUX VARIETIES.

CABARDÉS VDQS French wine region near Carcassonne, in the Languedoc, known for full-bodied red wines made from standard Mediterranean varieties, as well as from new plantings of Cabernet Sauvignon and Merlot.

CABERNET D'ANJOU AC Rosé wine made from Cabernet Sauvignon and/or Cabernet Franc. Usually medium sweet, but with high acidity, it can be quite refreshing when drunk young.

CABERNET FRANC One of the five Bordeaux red varieties, used there chiefly for blending with Cabernet Sauvignon or Merlot. It is the best red grape variety in France's Loire Valley, where it is used to make several styles of wine, including rosé. It has long been used in northeast Italy and plantings are on the increase in California, where it is used in blends and as a varietal.

CABERNET SAUVIGNON Easily the most famous red wine grape, Cabernet Sauvignon spread from its base in Bordeaux, France, and is now grown virtually everywhere that wine is made. Many of the best Bordeaux wines are based on Cabernet, with some blending of wines from other varieties. Cabernet Sauvignon has helped establish California as a top wine region. It is a key part of Australian viticulture, and good Cabernets are turning up in Argentina, Bulgaria, Chile, and elsewhere. It is adaptable to a variety of soils and climates.

CADILLAC AC French AC in Bordeaux, on the other side of the Garonne River from the Sauternes AC, producing a similar style of sweet white wine, made mainly from Sémillon and Sauvignon Blanc.

CAHORS AC Wine region in southwest France producing tough, concentrated red wine from Malbec. The best wines are capable of extended bottle aging.

CALABRIA Both red and white wines from this region of southern Italy have improved. Most of the wine, based on native grapes, is consumed locally.

CALIFORNIA Wine has been made in California since the end of the eighteenth century, but only since the 1960s has the state achieved its reputation as a top wine producer. California was an early leader in technical innovations in both the vineyard and the winery. In general, California wines, both red and white, are made in a fruit-forward style, powerful and concentrated. The Cabernet-based wines can age very well. There is an ocean of California Chardonnay, including some very popular off-dry versions. The better Chardonnays from cool growing regions can rival the best white Burgundies.

CAMPANIA This southern Italian region has only recently been recognized as a producer of quality wine. A few producers, especially from the Taurasi DOCG, are making fine wines from the local Aglianico grape, and from Cabernet Sauvignon and Merlot.

CANADA Canadian wine has made a great leap forward in the 1990s, not because of any technological breakthrough, but because of the free trade agreement between the United States and Canada. With the loss of protective tariffs, Canadian winemakers have pushed the quality button. Now, outstanding wines are being made in both Ontario and British Columbia from Chardonnay, Pinot Noir, and Riesling in particular.

CANARY ISLANDS Spanish islands in the Atlantic Ocean, once well known for sweet wines made from Malvasia. Plenty of undistinguished red and white wine is made there. The best wines are made on the island of Lanzarote.

Vinegrowing in Lanzarote, Canary Islands

CANBERRA DISTRICT Cool growing region in Australia, at an elevation of more than 2,500 feet (762 m), making a reputation for good Riesling, Merlot, and Shiraz.

CANNONAU Grape variety used on the Italian island of Sardinia for rich, sometimes very tannic, red wines. The grape is the same variety as Grenache. SEE GRENACHE.

CANON-FRONSAC AC Underrated French AC on the right bank of the Dordogne River in Bordeaux. The red wines have attractive fruit and can age for ten years or more.

CANOPY The part of the vine growing above the ground, including the leaves and the grapes. How the canopy is trained and managed is one of the keys to modern viticulture. Canopy management can be used to help control crop size and the intensity of grape flavor.

CANTERBURY Winegrowing region on New Zealand's South Island. Its cool growing season is ideal for Sauvignon Blanc, Chardonnay, and Riesling, with a small amount of very good Pinot Noir.

CANTINA SOCIALE Italian term for cooperative winery.

CARBON DIOXIDE Natural gas used in winemaking to protect crushed grapes or wine from oxygen; also, an important by-product of the process of fermentation. In sparkling wines, dissolved carbon dioxide is trapped in the bottle and supplies the sparkle or bubble when the wine is uncorked.

CARBONIC MACERATION Process by which whole, uncrushed grapes are fermented in an atmosphere of carbon dioxide, which excludes oxygen. Fermentation takes place inside each grape, producing a low-tannin wine, which is suitable for early drinking. The most notable example is probably Beaujolais Nouveau, but the technique is increasingly applied elsewhere to make wines for early consumption.

CARCAVELOS DOC Portuguese appellation in the Estremadura region, west of Lisbon, known for its fortified wine, made in either a dry or sweet style.

CAREMA DOC Small Italian wine region in the foothills of the Alps in northern Piedmont, producing a perfumed, delicate red wine from Nebbiolo grapes.

CARIGNAN Grape responsible for large amounts of indifferent red wine from southern France. However, it can produce very drinkable table wine using partial carbonic maceration techniques. Old-vine Carignan can be made into a rich, concentrated wine. Carignan originates in Spain, where it is called Mazuelo or Cariñena. It is also widely planted in California, where it is called Carignane.

CARIGNANO DEL SULCIS DOC Appellation in Sardinia, Italy, showing great promise for rich, juicy red wines based on Carignan.

CARIÑENA DO The Carignan grape probably originated near the Spanish village of Cariñena, in Aragón, but growers there have switched to Garnacha, and even Tempranillo, in an effort to improve wine quality, which still lags.

CARMEL VALLEY AVA Small, fairly new AVA beside the Cachagua River in the coastal mountains just inland from Monterey County, California, showing great promise for Cabernet Sauvignon.

CARMENÈRE Grape variety once widely planted in the Médoc region of Bordeaux, France, but not replanted following the devastation of *phylloxera*. Cuttings were sent to Chile in the nineteenth century and were misidentified as Merlot. Carmenère is still grown in Chile, along with true Merlot.

CARMIGNANO DOCG Red wine blended from 85 percent Sangiovese and 15 percent Cabernet, is made in this region of Tuscany, west of Florence, Italy.

CARNEROS AVA Region at the northern edge of San Francisco Bay in California, including parts of both Napa and Sonoma counties. Cool and foggy, it provides perfect growing conditions for Chardonnay and Pinot Noir, used for table wines and as bases for sparkling wine. Merlot, if planted on a sunny hillside, also does well in Carneros.

CASA VINICOLA On an Italian wine label, the term means the producer bought the grapes or wine, like a French *négociant*.

CASABLANCA The cool climate of this valley in Chile, only a few miles from the Pacific between Santiago and the resort of Viña del Mar, is likely to make it one of Chile's most important quality winegrowing regions. Chardonnay, Merlot, Pinot Noir, and Sauvignon Blanc are all successful, and several new wineries have been built.

CASK Wooden container, larger than the standard Bordeaux barrel, for aging or holding wine.

CASSIS AC The city of Marseilles is slowly spreading across this French coastal wine region of Provence, which makes mostly white wine based on Ugni Blanc. Some red and rosé wine is made from Mourvèdre.

CASTEL DEL MONTE DOC Appellation in Apulia, Italy, making good red wines from the local Uva di Troia grape and Aglianico.

CASTILLA-LA MANCHA Spain's largest wine region is hot and dry. It produces mostly unremarkable red and white wines. Two DOs, La Mancha and Valdepeñas, have improved greatly in the last few years, using cool fermentation techniques to make fresh white wine from Airén and sound reds from Cencibel (the local name for Tempranillo).

CASTILLA LEÓN High plateau region of Spain, which has seen a dramatic improvement in wine quality since the late 1980s. Once known only for a single winery, Vega Sicilia, the DOs of Ribera del Duero (for red wines) and Rueda (for white wines) have done especially well, and the Cigales DO is showing great promise.

CATALONIA Large wine region in northeast Spain with several very good DOs, the best being Penedés, Costers del Segre, and Priorato. The Penedés region has been a leading DO in winemaking technology in Spain for several years. The region

has also led the way in the planting of international grape varieties. Oddly enough, the revival of the older, traditional Priorato DO has been the big story out of Catalonia in recent years.

CAVA DO Spanish DO for Champagne-method sparkling wine, traditionally based on three grapes: Macabeo, Parellada, and Xarel-lo. The Cava DO is not restricted to a delimited area, but 95 percent of Cava is made in Catalonia. Some producers are using Chardonnay in the cuvée.

CAVE COOPERATIVE French term for a cooperative of grape growers.

CELLAR Area where wine is stored, traditionally underground.

CENCIBEL Name given to the Tempranillo grape in much of central Spain. SEE TEMPRANILLO.

CENTRAL COAST AVA Huge AVA stretching from San Francisco Bay down the California coast to Santa Barbara. It includes a number of sub-AVAs, some quite site-specific and meaningful, such as Edna Valley, and some purely political, such

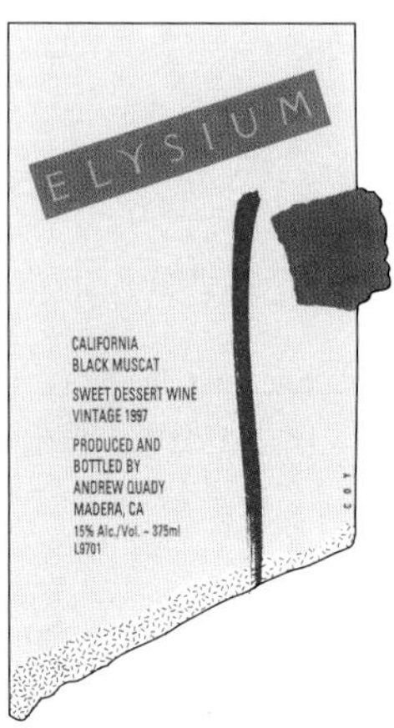

as San Francisco Bay. It is excellent Chardonnay country, and many cooler regions do a good job with Pinot Noir and Syrah.

CENTRAL OTAGO The world's southernmost wine region, on New Zealand's South Island, is showing promise for Pinot Noir, Gewürztraminer, and Chardonnay.

CENTRAL VALLEY (CHILE) Center of Chile's wine industry, including the Maipo, Rapel, Curicó, and Maule Valleys.

CENTRAL VALLEY (U.S.) More than half of California's grapes are grown in this vast inland region, stretching from Bakersfield in the south to Sacramento in the north. High-yielding, irrigated vineyards produce oceans of inexpensive red and white wine. In recent years, the Lodi-Woodbridge AVA, in the north of the Central Valley, has made a serious and successful effort to improve grape quality.

CENTRAL VINEYARDS Scattered vineyards in the center of France, in the Loire Valley, including the famous white wine areas, Sancerre and Pouilly Fumé. The vineyards are mainly planted with Sauvignon Blanc; some Pinot Noir is also grown for rosés and reds.

CÉPAGE French word for grape variety, often used in the United States to indicate the blend of the wine, as in a *cépage* of Cabernet Sauvignon and Merlot.

CÉRONS AC Appellation within the Graves AC in Bordeaux, France, where sweet white wine is made. Many producers also make dry white wines using the Graves label.

CHABLIS Region in northern Burgundy, France, making outstanding Chardonnay. The basic Chablis AC wines are best drunk young. Roughly 25 percent of the vineyards are ranked as Premier Cru, and these wines should have more depth and intensity than the basic Chablis AC wines. They are often the best-value wines in Chablis, too. The highest ranking for Chablis is Chablis Grand Cru. There are seven Grands Crus, typically giving wines of great intensity and depth and capable of extended aging. The best Chablis wines have a flinty, stony flavor and a lean purity of fruit.

CHACOLÍ DE GUETARIA DO Tiny DO in the Basque region of northern Spain making acidic white and red wines that pair very well with the local seafood. The whites, which comprise over 80 percent of production, are made from a local grape, Hondarribi Zuri. The red wines, made from Hondarribi Chalí, are starting to be available in the United States.

CHALK HILL AVA Sub-AVA within the Russian River Valley AVA in Sonoma County, California, best known for Chardonnay. The whitish soil is derived from volcanic ash.

CHAMBERTIN AC One of the great French Grands Crus of Burgundy's Côte de Nuits, it produces intense, long-lasting red wines based on Pinot Noir.

CHAMBOLLE-MUSIGNY AC This French AC in Burgundy's Côte de Nuits is capable of producing velvety red wine from Pinot Noir.

CHAMPAGNE In Europe, the term may be applied only to sparkling wine made in the Champagne region of France. The United States is one of the few nations in the world where Champagne is used as a generic term, and it is often applied to inferior sparkling wine.

CHAMPAGNE AC This region in northern France is the world's model for sparkling wine. The wine is made from only three grape varieties, the white grape Chardonnay and two red grapes, Pinot Noir and Pinot Meunier. For many years, the sparkling wines of Champagne were acknowledged to be the world's greatest sparklers; however, their dominance is now being challenged by sparkling wines from California and, to some extent, from Australia,

a challenge that has stirred some French producers to move toward improving quality.

CHAMPAGNE METHOD The world's serious producers of sparkling wine use this method, in which the wine undergoes a secondary fermentation in the bottle in which it is sold. On wine labels in Europe, the term is outlawed and has generally been replaced by Traditional Method.

CHAMPAGNE ROSÉ Style of rosé Champagne which is usually made by blending a little red wine with white wine.

CHAPTALIZATION Process of raising the alcohol content of wine by adding sugar to the grape must before or during fermentation. This heightens the texture and mouthfeel of the wine. It is common in many cooler northern regions, notably in France and Germany, where grapes usually fail to reach full ripeness. Chaptalization, as practiced in many northern European wine-producing areas, is not allowed in most premium wine-producing areas of the United States.

CHARBONO Rare red wine grape, which makes full-flavored wines in California. It may be related to the Italian grape, Dolcetto.

C

CHARDONNAY One of the world's great white wine grapes, it is responsible for the white Burgundies of France and is one of the three grapes used for Champagne. Chardonnay is now planted virtually everywhere that grapes are grown. Around the world, winemakers are producing extremely good wine from Chardonnay, especially in Australia and California.

CHARENTAIS, VIN DE PAYS DE Region in Cognac, France, producing young white wines based on Ugni Blanc (the chief grape used for Cognac) that can be quite drinkable. Some red wines are made from Bordeaux varieties. SEE BORDEAUX VARIETIES.

CHARMAT Also known as bulk process or *cuve close*, a bulk sparkling wine process in which a secondary fermentation takes place in a large, closed tank, rather than in the individual bottles.

CHARTA Organization of producers in Rheingau, Germany, dedicated to making high-quality dry Riesling.

CHASSAGNE-MONTRACHET AC Some of the world's great white wines made from Chardonnay come from this French appellation in Burgundy's Côte de Beaune.

CHASSELAS Grown in most areas as a table grape, Chasselas makes a drinkable white wine in Switzerland and in Baden, Germany.

CHÂTEAU French word for castle, also used to signify a wine estate.

Château in southwest France

CHÂTEAU AUSONE Situated on some of the best slopes of St-Émilion, Château Ausone maintains its reputation as one of the top red wines in Bordeaux, France.

CHÂTEAU BEAUREGARD Pomerol property in Bordeaux, France, making excellent red wine with, for the area, a high proportion of Cabernet Franc and Cabernet Sauvignon.

CHÂTEAU CANON Producer of concentrated, long-lived St-Émilion red wine in Bordeaux, France.

CHÂTEAU CERTAN-DE-MAY Small Pomerol property in the Bordeaux region of France, making superbly balanced red wine, which is capable of aging for a long time.

CHÂTEAU-CHALON AC The most prized and expensive *vin jaune*, from Jura, France.

CHÂTEAU CHEVAL BLANC Leading St-Émilion estate in Bordeaux, France, which uses an unusually high percentage of Cabernet Franc in its red wine. It may be kept for well over a decade.

CHÂTEAU CLOS RENÉ From the west of Pomerol in the Bordeaux region of France, this château makes red wine that is accessible and delicious when young. It also ages well.

CHÂTEAU COS D'ESTOURNEL Leading château in St-Estèphe, in the Haut-Médoc, and one of the most important in Bordeaux, France, making red wine with a high proportion of Merlot, relative to the Médoc region.

CHÂTEAU FIGEAC Top St-Émilion red wine from Bordeaux, France, and largest St-Émilion Premier Grand Cru. It should ideally be aged for at least ten years.

CHÂTEAU-GRILLET AC Home to the rare white wine made in the Rhône, France, from Viognier.

CHÂTEAU HAUT-BRION The only red-wine château outside the Médoc in Bordeaux, France, to be included in the famous 1855 classification. Situated in Pessac-Léognan, it usually lives up to its high ranking. A small amount of dry white wine is also made.

CHÂTEAU LAFITE-ROTHSCHILD Great French red wine from Pauillac, in the Haut-Médoc, Bordeaux. It has had a bad run, but seems to be back to First Growth standard. The wine can take up to 30 years in the bottle to achieve its potential.

CHÂTEAU LATOUR Powerful, classic French red wine from Pauillac, in the Haut-Médoc, Bordeaux. It lives up to its high reputation as a First Growth and makes good wine even in less good years.

CHÂTEAU LÉOVILLE-LAS-CASES Deep, concentrated red wine from St-Julien, in the Haut-Médoc, Bordeaux, France. It will age for up to 30 years.

CHÂTEAU MARGAUX Made at the most lavish of all the First Growth châteaux in Bordeaux, France, this wine from the Margaux AC in the Haut-Médoc usually lives up to its lofty reputation. The estate produces a fragrant, elegant wine with around 75 percent Cabernet Sauvignon, which gives it staying power.

CHÂTEAU MOUTON-ROTHSCHILD A great Médoc red from Pauillac, Bordeaux, France, promoted to First Growth status in 1973. It drinks well when young, but should be aged for at least 15 years. The labels, commissioned from artists each year, are collectors' items.

CHÂTEAU PAVIE Second-largest of the St-Émilion Premiers Grands Crus in Bordeaux, France. It produces immediately appealing red wines that do not lose their soft fruitiness even after a decade.

CHÂTEAU PÉTRUS Powerful, fabled red wine from Pomerol, Bordeaux, France, made almost entirely from Merlot. It is one of the world's most expensive wines.

CHÂTEAU PICHON-LONGUEVILLE-LALANDE French property in Pauillac, in the Haut-Médoc,

Bordeaux, making excellent red wines with a relatively high percentage of Merlot that are superb after 6 years, and magnificent after 20.

CHÂTEAU LE PIN Tiny French property in Pomerol, Bordeaux, making elegant and hugely expensive red wines from Merlot.

CHÂTEAU SUDUIRAUT Top sweet white Sauternes from Bordeaux, France, best after about ten years.

CHÂTEAU D'YQUEM One of the world's most expensive and best-loved sweet white wines from Sauternes, Bordeaux, France. The vineyard is large, but the yields are tiny—a reputed one glass per vine.

CHÂTEAUNEUF-DU-PAPE AC A vineyard area in the Rhône Valley, which has made great improvements in quality and now ranks as one of the best red wine areas in France, especially for wines from a single estate—look for the papal coat of arms embossed on the bottle. The best wines can age ten years or longer. There are 13 approved varietals. Only around 5 percent of the wine is white.

CHÉNAS AC One of the ten French Beaujolais Crus. The wines are surprisingly hard for Beaujolais when young and can age for five to eight years in a good vintage.

CHENIN BLANC This white wine grape merits more respect. It has great versatility and adapts well to different soils and climates. At its best in the Loire Valley of France, where it is often called Pineau de la Loire, it makes intensely flavored sweet wine and dry table wine. It is widely grown in South Africa, Australia, and New Zealand. In California, it has been used primarily for jug wine and, more recently, as a Chardonnay-stretcher.

CHEVERNY AC A number of wines in different styles, including red wines from Cabernet Franc, Gamay, and sometimes Pinot Noir, and often acidic white wines made from Sauvignon Blanc, Chenin Blanc, and Chardonnay are produced in this AC in France's Loire Valley.

CHEWY Tasting term often used to describe highly tannic wines.

CHIANTI DOCG Overall Chianti zone in Tuscany, Italy. Red wines of varying quality are made in seven zones—Classico, Colli Aretini, Colli Fiorentini, Colli Senesi, Colline Pisane, Montalbano, and Rufina. The chief grape is Sangiovese.

CHIANTI CLASSICO DOCG The heart of the Chianti zone in Tuscany,

Vineyards in Chianti, Italy

Italy, both historically and for modern winemaking. Classico wines may be made from only Sangiovese or may be blended with 10 to 15 percent Cabernet Sauvignon, Merlot, or Syrah. These wines, at their best, are richer, more intense, and have greater aging potential than other Chiantis. The Riservas can be especially good.

CHIANTI RUFINA DOCG Small Chianti zone in Tuscany, Italy, producing long-lasting red wines. The Riservas, in particular, can match the best Chianti Classico wines.

CHIARETTO Italian term for rosé.

CHILE This South American country made its reputation in the wine world by making large amounts of cheap, reliable red and white wine. This is still true, but Chile is now producing some high-quality red wines. Joint ventures with French and California wine partners have helped the drive for quality.

CHILES VALLEY AVA Although considered part of Napa Valley AVA, this sub-AVA in Napa's eastern hills, bordering Lake Berryessa, has different soils, a higher elevation, and a quite different microclimate.

CHINA With official government policy supporting wine production, China's vineyards are expanding rapidly, helped by investments from western wine interests. The Chinese market is still mainly skewed toward cheap everyday wines, but that could change as its economy improves. The chief grape varieties are Gamay, Cabernet Sauvignon, Chardonnay, and Riesling.

CHINON AC Probably the best red wines from France's Loire Valley are made in Chinon. Based mainly on Cabernet Franc, they are fruity when young but are also capable of extended aging in good years.

CHIROUBLES AC One of France's ten Beaujolais Crus. These light reds are delightful drunk young.

CHOREY-LÈS-BEAUNE AC Tiny village in the Côte de Beaune, Burgundy, France, producing good-value red wine based on Pinot Noir. Much of the wine is sold as Côte de Beaune-Villages.

CIENEGA AVA Hilly vineyard area tucked between Monterey and San Benito counties in California, important in the nineteenth century and now making a comeback.

CIGALES DO Spanish wine zone north of the city of Valladolid, with a growing reputation for dry rosé from Tinto País and Garnacha.

CINQUETERRE DOC Italian region in Liguria producing dry white wines of varied quality and a sweet white wine called Sciacchetrá, made by the *passito* method.

CINSAUT Red wine grape grown mostly in southern France, used mainly for blending. It is finding new popularity in California, where it was first planted in the nineteenth century. Cinsaut is also widely grown in South Africa.

CIRÒ DOC Appellation in Calabria, southern Italy, showing rapid improvement with plantings of Cabernet Sauvignon, which is blended with the local Gaglioppo.

CLAIRETTE DE DIE AC Ancient winegrowing region in the Rhône Valley of France, producing off-dry sparkling wine using a minimum of 75 percent Muscat. It can be quite charming when drunk young.

LA CLAPE Cru vineyard area within the Coteaux du Languedoc AC in southern France, producing interesting white, red, and rosé wines.

CLARE VALLEY Hilly region north of Adelaide, South Australia, making very good Riesling and Sémillon, and particularly rich Shiraz and Cabernet Sauvignon.

CLARET English term to describe Bordeaux red wines. The word originated several centuries ago from the French word *clairet*, used to denote lighter reds favored at one time by the English. Once widely used in California for red wine, the term has now virtually disappeared from wine labels in that state.

CLARKSBURG AVA Many believe the best Chenin Blanc in California comes from this winegrowing area on the Sacramento River delta, which is somewhat cooled by winds from San Francisco Bay.

CLASSED GROWTH Many of the best châteaux of the French Bordeaux region are grouped into various classification systems, including the famous 1855 classification (see page 71). Châteaux included in this classification are known as Classed Growths.

CLASSIC As a tasting term, it denotes a wine with a taste profile conforming to a good example of a particular varietal or region. On wine labels, it has no legal meaning.

CLASSICO Italian word signifying the historical center of a region, usually where the best wines of that region are produced.

CLEAR LAKE AVA Huge area centered on Clear Lake in Lake County, north of Napa, California. Daytime temperatures can easily reach 100°F (38°C), but the elevation moderates night temperatures. The best grapes are Sauvignon Blanc and Cabernet Sauvignon.

CLONE The term refers to vines that originated from a single plant propagated by taking cuttings. Clonal selection is a science of increasing importance for quality-minded wine producers. Clones of one variety vary greatly and can be selected for lower yields, better flavors, or greater disease resistance.

CLOS French word for a walled vineyard, especially in Burgundy. *Clos* is now often incorporated into a winery or brand name.

CLOS DE LA ROCHE AC Grand Cru in the Burgundy region of France, producing rich, red wines that can age very well.

CLOS ST-DENIS AC Small French Grand Cru in Burgundy, producing elegant red wines that can age for a minimum of ten years.

CLOS DE TART AC French Grand Cru producing good-quality red wines in Burgundy's Côte d'Or. It is entirely owned by Mommessin, wine merchants from Mâcon.

CLOS DE VOUGEOT AC Large Grand Cru vineyard in Burgundy, France, first enclosed by monks in the Middle Ages. Now it is owned by 80 growers, which helps explain the great variation in quality. At best, the wines are rich and deep with good aging potential.

CLOUDY BAY First New Zealand winery to achieve international acclaim, renowned for its dramatically varietal Sauvignon Blanc from Marlborough, which created a new international wine style virtually overnight upon its launch in 1985.

COASTAL REGION Large wine zone in South Africa which incorporates many of the best-known wine regions such as Stellenbosch, Paarl, and Constantia. Wines may be a blend from anywhere in the region.

COLARES DOC Portuguese DOC north of Lisbon, planted on sand dunes above the sea, producing tannic red wines from ungrafted Ramisco grapes and some white wine from Malvasia grapes.

COLD STABILIZATION Process involving lowering the temperature of the wine in tank to 32°F (0°C) or lower for a few days. It clarifies the wine, depositing naturally occurring tartrate crystals. SEE TARTRATES.

COLHEITA Portuguese for harvest or vintage, the term also refers to a tawny port from a single vintage.

COLLI BOLOGNESI DOC Italian winegrowing region in the hills near Bologna, where new wines are being made in an international style from Cabernet Sauvignon, Merlot, and Sauvignon Blanc.

COLLI EUGANEI DOC Hillside area in Veneto, Italy, producing a wide range of wines; the best are Cabernet Sauvignon and Merlot, or blends of these varieties.

COLLI ORIENTALI DEL FRIULI DOC Twenty different types of wine are made in this DOC in northeast Italy. Once known for sweet whites, the region is now becoming much better known for dry white and dry red wines, the latter made from Refosco, Schioppettino, Cabernet Sauvignon, and Merlot. The whites

Slopes of Colli Orientali del Friuli

are based on Tocai, Ribolla, Pinot Grigio, Pinot Bianco, and others.

COLLI PIACENTINI DOC The best wines from this area of Emilia-Romagna, Italy, are reds made from the Barbera grape.

COLLINES RHODANIENNES, VIN DE PAYS DE Good reds based on Gamay and Syrah may be found in this area of France's Rhône Valley.

COLLIO/COLLI/COLLINE Italian word for hill(s). When used as part of a wine name, these words indicate that the wine has been produced from hillside vineyards.

COLLIO DOC Some of Italy's best white wine comes from this DOC in Friuli-Venezia Giulia, ranging from the local Tocai Friulano and Malvasia grapes to international varieties including Chardonnay, Sauvignon Blanc, Pinot Blanc, and Pinot Gris. There are also some very good red wines, made mostly from Merlot, Refosco, and Cabernet Sauvignon.

COLLIOURE AC Most visitors to this pretty seaside village near the Spanish border in the Roussillon region of France pass through without realizing that there is a lovely local red wine. Intense and fruity when young, yet capable of some aging, it is based mostly on Grenache and Mourvèdre. This region also produces the Banyuls *vin doux naturel.*

COLOMBARD At its best, in France, this white grape variety produces fresh, dry white wine for early drinking. In California and elsewhere, it is more often used as a wine for blending. Traditionally, it was distilled in France for Armagnac and Cognac.

COLOMBIA In this tropical country in South America, vines set two crops a year, but must have the leaves pulled by hand to artificially create a short "dormant" period. A few California winemakers acting as consultants report that decent table wine can be made at higher-elevation vineyards.

COLUMBIA VALLEY AVA Huge viticultural area east of the Cascade Mountains in Washington including almost every vine in the state, and embracing the Yakima Valley and Walla Walla AVAs. A high desert area, it needs extensive irrigation. There are a number of microclimates within the area, and growers have been very successful with cool-weather Rieslings and Merlot, as well as with warm-weather Cabernet Sauvignon and Syrah.

COMMUNE A French wine village and the area surrounding it.

COMPLEX Tasting term for a very good, balanced wine with distinctive layers of aromas and flavors.

COMTÉ TOLOSAN, VIN DE PAYS DU Large appellation south and east of Bordeaux, France. The best wines are the reds and rosés.

COMTÉS RHODANIENS, VIN DE PAYS DES Sound red wines based on Syrah, Gamay, and Cinsaut, and an occasional worthy white wine from Viognier are best in this area of the Rhône Valley, France.

CONCA DE BARBERÁ DO Promising wine area in western Catalonia, Spain. Much of the production in the past has been sold to Cava producers, but there is increasing interest in Cabernet Sauvignon, Pinot Noir, and Chardonnay.

CONCENTRATE A concentrate of grape juice high in sugar can be made by reducing the water content of the grape. A large part of California's Central Valley grape production goes for concentrate. Used widely in California and elsewhere to enhance ordinary table wine, it is added before fermentation to boost the alcohol, or after fermentation to sweeten the wine.

CONCENTRATED Tasting term indicating that the fruit aromas and flavors of a wine are very powerful.

CONCORD American grape of the *Vitis labrusca* family, best for making juice and jellies but occasionally made into inferior wine in the eastern United States.

CONDRIEU AC French Rhône Valley AC producing expensive white wines made from Viognier, which are the model for the new Viognier producers in California.

CONSTANTIA WO Historically, South Africa's most important wine region. It has a cool climate and its wines, especially those made from Sauvignon Blanc, have attracted international attention.

COONAWARRA Once referred to as the Médoc of Australia, this southernmost winegrowing district in South Australia has earned its reputation from the high quality of its Cabernet Sauvignon and Shiraz, in particular. Only the original part of the region where the best wines are produced has the distinctive *tèrra rossa* (red soil) with its deep limestone subsoil, which is ideal for the production of fine wine.

COOPERAGE Production of wooden barrels for storing wine.

COOPERATIVE Winery that makes wine from grapes supplied by a union of growers.

COPERTINO DOC Italian winegrowing region in Apulia noted for hearty red wines.

COPITA Special glass for sherry.

CORBIÈRES AC Some of the best red wine of the Languedoc region of France comes from this AC. It is very good when young, but the best is capable of extended aging, for a decade or longer.

CORK The bark of the cork oak, *Quercus suber*, is used as a closure for wine bottles. In recent years, some producers have turned to artificial closures based on plastic or other material to eliminate the problem of cork taint, which affects an unacceptably high percentage of wine. Portugal is the main producer of cork. SEE CORKED.

CORKAGE Fee charged by restaurants to open and serve wine brought by the customer.

CORKED Wine fault caused by trichloranisole, or TCA, a mold in the cork, which gives the wine an off-flavor that has been compared to the smell of wet cardboard. An estimated three or four wine bottles out of 100 are corked. Cork producers and wineries are researching the problem, but no clear solution to corkiness has emerged.

CORNAS AC Northern Rhône French AC attracting attention for its Syrah-based red wines, which can age very well.

CORSICA French island in the Mediterranean, which has improved quality dramatically, as growers are replanting vineyards with Syrah, Cabernet Sauvignon, and other "noble" red varieties, as well as Chardonnay and Sauvignon Blanc.

CORTESE Italian white wine grape from Piedmont, capable of producing good everyday dry table wines.

CORTON AC French Grand Cru making both red and white Burgundy, although more red than white is produced. It is the only red Grand Cru in the Côte de Beaune. The best reds should take a decade to reach maturity.

CORTON CHARLEMAGNE AC Grand Cru for white wine only in the Côte de Beaune, Burgundy, France. The best wines are rich and buttery, with an aging potential of ten years or longer.

CORVINA Best and most widely planted of the trio of red grapes used in Italy's Valpolicella and Bardolino DOCs. It is dried on straw mats to make Recioto della Valpolicella and Amarone.

COSECHA Spanish word for harvest or vintage.

COSTERS DEL SEGRE DO Spanish winegrowing area dominated by the Raventos Cava family of Catalonia, owners of Codorniú, the world's biggest producers of Champagne-method sparkling wine. Located in a near-desert area north of the city of Lérida in western Catalonia, the most planted vines are international varieties.

COSTIÈRES DE NIMES AC Large area near Arles in the Languedoc area of France, making attractive red and rosé wines for early drinking. Only a little white wine is made.

CÔT Synonym for Malbec, widely used in Cahors, southwest France.

CÔTE French for hillside or slope, a favored position for vines.

CÔTE DE BEAUNE Southern part of the Côte d'Or in Burgundy, France, producing fine white and red wines.

CÔTE DE BEAUNE-VILLAGES AC French Burgundy appellation making red wine from Pinot Noir. Most producers use an individual village name, but the general AC is used if the wine is a blend of village wines.

CÔTE DE BROUILLY AC A hill in the Brouilly AC of Beaujolais, France, that is also a Beaujolais Cru. It produces concentrated wines capable of extended aging.

CÔTE CHALONNAISE The scattered vineyards near the town of Chalon-sur-Saône, south of the Côte d'Or in France's Burgundy region, form the Côte Chalonnaise district. Good wines are produced, from Pinot Noir and Chardonnay.

CÔTE DE NUITS The northern part of the Côte d'Or in Burgundy, France. It is home to some of the most famous wines in the world, producing mostly red wine from Pinot Noir.

Côte de Nuits vines

CÔTE DE NUITS-VILLAGES AC French AC in Burgundy producing both red and white wines from five villages in the Côte de Nuits.

CÔTE D'OR Center of France's Burgundy region. Some of the world's great vineyards stretch in a narrow belt for some 35 miles (56 km) south from the city of Dijon. Côte d'Or is usually translated as the "golden slope," but the name is actually an abbreviation of Côte d'Orient, or eastern slope, since the hillsides all face east.

CÔTE-RÔTIE AC Syrah ripens to perfection on the steep, "roasted" slopes of this northern Rhône AC, making arguably some of the best reds now in France. Some can age for ten years or more, but they are often attractive for drinking young.

COTEAU Similar to a *côte* (slope) but smaller. The plural is *coteaux*.

COTEAUX D'AIX-EN-PROVENCE AC First appellation in southern France to allow Cabernet Sauvignon to be blended with the traditional local grape varieties, such as Grenache and Syrah.

COTEAUX DE L'ARDÈCHE, VIN DE PAYS DE Area of France's Rhône Valley gaining some attention for varietal red wines from local Syrah and Gamay, as well as Cabernet Sauvignon and Merlot. The best white is from Viognier, though Chardonnay is also looking good.

COTEAUX DE L'AUBANCE AC Small AC in France's Loire Valley with a solid reputation for sweetish white wines from Chenin Blanc.

COTEAUX CHAMPENOIS AC French AC covering all still wine made in the Champagne region.

COTEAUX DU LANGUEDOC AC Large area in southern France between Montpellier and Narbonne. It is a center for hearty reds and good rosés. Quality is improving, especially in village Crus where the village name can be added.

COTEAUX DU LAYON AC French Loire Valley AC producing excellent sweet wines from Chenin Blanc. In good years, the grapes are affected by noble rot. The best wines are from village Crus, where the village name can be used on the label.

COTEAUX DU TRICASTIN AC Good everyday red and rosé wines are made in this southern Rhône region of France.

COTEAUX VAROIS AC Promising AC within the Côtes de Provence AC, southern France, where both red and white wines are produced from several varieties. The reds are showing the most potential.

CÔTES DE BERGERAC AC Hearty reds from Bordeaux varieties come from this area in southwest France. SEE BORDEAUX VARIETIES.

CÔTES DE BLAYE AC Once a center for sweet white wines in Bordeaux, France, the AC now makes mostly dry white wines, which can be good when young.

CÔTES DE BOURG AC Red wine made in a hearty style mostly for early drinking is the best bet from this Bordeaux area of France.

CÔTES DE CASTILLON AC Bordeaux AC in France turning out good-quality red wines which are also good value.

CÔTES DE DURAS AC Appellation next to Bergerac in southwest France making everyday red and white wines at reasonable prices.

CÔTES DE FRANCS AC Look for good red wines from this French AC east of St-Émilion in Bordeaux. The area has great potential.

CÔTES DU FRONTONNAIS AC Appellation north of Toulouse in southwest France making excellent red wines capable of aging, which are also good to drink right now.

CÔTES DE GASCOGNE, VIN DE PAYS DE Area in southwest France turning out a range of delicious white wines and small amounts of red and rosé.

CÔTES DU JURA AC Umbrella appellation for Jura, covering a large area. Wine quality is uneven. In general, whether red, white, or rosé, drink young.

CÔTES DU LUBÉRON AC Area near Avignon in France's Rhône Valley producing fresh red, white, and rosé wines for early drinking.

CÔTES DU MARMANDAIS AC Sound red wines based on the Bordeaux red varieties, with a little Syrah, are made in this AC in southwest France. SEE BORDEAUX VARIETIES.

CÔTES DE MONTRAVEL AC Area within Bergerac, southwest France, known for its sweet white wines.

CÔTES DE PROVENCE AC Large appellation in southern France, best for red and rosé wines, mostly for everyday drinking but improving steadily.

CÔTES DU RHÔNE AC About 85 to 90 percent of the wine from this umbrella appellation for the whole of the French Rhône Valley is red. The wines, which are generally good for everyday consumption, have improved noticeably in the last few years.

CÔTES DU RHÔNE VILLAGES AC Appellation in the Rhône Valley, France, for wines of better quality than the basic Côtes du Rhône AC. Sixteen villages in the southern Rhône are allowed to display this AC on their labels.

CÔTES DU ROUSSILLON AC Red wines are the best bet in this large appellation in the Languedoc-Roussillon region of France.

CÔTES DU ROUSSILLON-VILLAGES AC French appellation covering only red wine from villages in the north of the Côtes du Roussillon AC. The best wines are fresh and fruity, good for early drinking, and some have the potential to age for at least a few years.

CÔTES DE ST MONT VDQS Everyday red, white, and rosé wines from southwest France.

CÔTES DU TARN, VIN DE PAYS DES Area in southwest France making a number of agreeable red and white wines, best drunk young.

CÔTES DE THAU, VIN DE PAYS DES Some decent white wines are made in this part of the Languedoc region, southwest France.

CÔTES DE THONGUE, VIN DE PAYS DES With new plantings of international grape varieties, these Languedoc Vins de Pays are improving, especially the reds.

CÔTES DU VENTOUX AC Mostly red wine territory near Carpentras in the southern Rhône Valley, France. With skilled winemaking, this area is capable of making good wines for early drinking and occasionally for cellaring.

CÔTES DU VIVARAIS VDQS Traditionally, this southern Rhône region of France has made light- and medium-weight red wines, and the occasional white for early drinking. New plantings of Syrah and Cabernet Sauvignon are producing more promising wines.

COWRA Fairly new growing area in New South Wales, Australia, showing promise for Chardonnay and, perhaps, Shiraz.

CREAM SHERRY Sweet style of sherry. The best cream sherry is made by blending sweet wines from the Pedro Ximénez grape into an Oloroso sherry.

CRÉMANT French term for good-quality sparkling wine made by the Champagne method outside the Champagne district. Some of the best come from Alsace, Burgundy, Limoux, and the Loire.

CRÉMANT D'ALSACE AC Sparkling wine made in Alsace, France, using the Champagne method. It can be made from Auxerrois, Chardonnay, Pinot Blanc, Pinot Gris, Pinot Noir, or Riesling. Quality is good.

CRÉMANT DE BOURGOGNE AC The best sparkling wine from Burgundy, France, made chiefly from Chardonnay and a little Pinot Noir.

CRÉMANT DE DIE AC Rhône Valley sparkling wine made from the Clairette grape. This AC replaces Clairette de Die Brut AC.

CRÉMANT DE LIMOUX AC Appellation in southwest France covering sparkling wines made from Chardonnay, Chenin Blanc, and Mauzac. They are of good quality for early drinking.

CRÉMANT DE LOIRE AC French AC in the Loire Valley, which covers sparkling wine made in the Anjou and Touraine districts. The wines can have excellent fruit and are quite attractive when young.

CRIANZA Spanish term relating to the aging of wine. On a label, *crianza* refers to the youngest oak-aged category of wine. In much of Spain, such wine must not be sold until it is three years old and has spent six months in small oak barrels. In Rioja, the red must be aged 12 months in small barrels. *Sin crianza* denotes a young, fruity wine with little or no oak aging.

CRIOLLA Argentine name for the Mission grape of California, the País in Chile, and the Negra Corriente of Peru. The most widely planted wine grape in Argentina, it is thick-skinned and makes coarse white wine. It was probably the first grape cultivated in the Americas.

CROATIA The best wines in this former Yugoslav state are along the Dalmatian coast, where hearty red wines are made, including Cabernet Sauvignon. Indifferent white wine is made inland.

CROSS OR CROSSING New variety made by crossing two vine varieties from the same vine species.

CROZES-HERMITAGE AC Biggest AC in the northern Rhône, France, capable of producing full-bodied red wines with rich flavor and forward white wines for early drinking.

CRU French word for a particular piece of land or vineyard. Sometimes used, as in Champagne and Beaujolais, in reference to a larger area or a village.

CRU BEAUJOLAIS The ten best vineyard areas in northern Beaujolais, France, take the commune, or village, name as their appellation. They are known as the Crus of Beaujolais: Brouilly, Chénas, Chiroubles, Côte de Brouilly, Fleurie, Juliénas, Morgon, Moulin-à-Vent, Régnié, and St-Amour.

CRU BOURGEOIS French classification from the Médoc, Bordeaux, which ranks just below the 1855 classification. Wines vary a great deal in quality, but can be very good value.

CRU CLASSÉ Refers mainly to the 1855 Classed Growths of Bordeaux, but also to other wines from official classifications. SEE CLASSED GROWTH.

CRUSH American synonym for the entire harvest season.

CRUSHER Machine used to break the skins of grapes and crush them, to give yeast easier access to the sugars at the start of fermentation.

CRUSTED PORT An inexpensive alternative to vintage port, this style of port was created by port shippers. The young wine throws a "crust," or sediment, in the bottle and is therefore best decanted before drinking.

CUCAMONGA AVA Historically important winegrowing area east of Los Angeles, planted in the 1830s by Jean-Louis Vignes. He opened one of California's first commercial wineries in Los Angeles. Recently there has been an effort to revive winemaking in Cucamonga, based largely on the existence of a few old Zinfandel vineyards.

CUVE CLOSE SEE CHARMAT.

CUVÉE French word either for a particular blend which is marketed, or for a blend made partway through the winemaking process, as in Champagne where the cuvée is the blend of still wines made before undergoing a second fermentation.

CYPRUS Until recently, except for a few fortified dessert wines, little wine of note was made on this Mediterranean island. Today both the red and white table wines can be drinkable.

CZECH REPUBLIC Some adequate white wines, based chiefly on Pinot Blanc and Gewürztraminer, are made in the Czech Republic. With investment from the west, quality should improve over the near term.

DÃO DOC This region in north-central Portugal has long produced the best red wines in the country. The wines are mostly made from the traditional Portuguese varieties. Winemakers are now paying more attention to grape selection and to the technical side of winemaking.

DAVIS The University of California at Davis has been responsible for much of the research in enology and viticulture that has changed winemaking around the world in the past few decades.

DECANTING Process of pouring a wine from a bottle into a decanter. There are several reasons to decant a wine; the most common is to leave behind the sediment in an older wine. Young wines may also be decanted to release the fresh fruit in the wine.

DÉGORGEMENT Important step in the making of sparkling wine where sediment, which has been frozen, is removed from the bottle neck.

DEGREE-DAY SYSTEM SEE HEAT SUMMATION SYSTEM.

DEMI-SEC French term for medium-dry wine.

DÉPARTEMENT France is divided administratively into *départements*, like U.S. or English counties.

DEPTH Tasting term indicating that a wine has good weight on the palate and deep fruit flavors.

DESSERT WINE Sweet wine, sometimes fortified, served at the end of a meal with dessert.

DÉZALEY Swiss wine commune in Vaud producing first-rate white wines from the Chasselas grape.

DISGORGEMENT English term for *dégorgement*. SEE DÉGORGEMENT.

DO Abbreviation of *Denominación de Origen*, Spanish classified winegrowing area.

DOC Classification abbreviation of terms with the same general sense used in the classification systems of Italy, Portugal, and Spain. In Italy, a classified winegrowing area is designated *Denominazione di Origine Controllata*. In Portugal, the top regional classification is called *Denominação de Origem Controlada*. In Spain, DOC stands for *Denominación de Origen Calificada*, a classification above DO.

DOCG Abbreviation of *Denominazione di Origine Controllata e Garantita*, the highest level of the Italian wine classification system. Many DOCGs have been criticized as being political in nature.

DOLCE Italian word for sweet.

DOLCETTO Italian red wine grape grown chiefly in Piedmont, made into fruity wines best drunk young. The best examples from Dolcetto d'Alba DOC and Dolcetto d'Asti DOC have good structure to balance the black-cherry fruit character, and are ideal companions to Italian cuisine.

DÔLE A light red wine from the Valais district of Switzerland, it must contain a minimum of 51 percent Pinot Noir, the rest usually being Gamay.

DOMAINE French word for an estate. The term is now often used as part of a winery name in California, where it may well indicate foreign investment.

DOMAINE DE CHEVALIER Red wines from this great Pessac-Léognan estate in Bordeaux, France, are dry and tannic when young but achieve complexity and deep flavors when aged (15 to 20 years for the best vintages). This château also makes one of the region's finest dry whites; it is barrel-fermented and barrel-aged for 18 months.

DOMAINE DE LA ROMANÉE-CONTI This legendary domaine in France's Burgundy region owns a clutch of the most famous Grand Cru vineyards in the Côte de Nuits, making some of the world's most expensive red wines exclusively from Pinot Noir. DRC, as it is known, owns the Grand Cru vineyards of Romanée-Conti and La Tâche outright, in addition to large parts of Richebourg, Grands Échézeaux, and others. Standards have always been high, as they should be when considering the price this domaine can command for its wines.

DONAULAND Austrian wine region on the Danube.

DORDOGNE, VIN DE PAYS DE LA This wine region in southwest France is the source of good-value red and white wines and some rosés for early drinking.

DOSAGE A mixture of wine and sugar syrup, added to sparkling wine after *dégorgement*. This determines the degree of sweetness of Champagne or sparkling wine. Some very dry sparkling wines are made without *dosage*.

DOURO DOC Portuguese DOC along the Douro River, best known as the home of port. Increasing amounts of delicious red, white, and rosé table wines are now being made there from grapes also used for port production.

DOUX French term for sweetish wine. It equates to medium-sweet.

DOWNY MILDEW Fungal vine disease especially common in warm, humid climates; it can cause devastation in the vineyard.

DRIP IRRIGATION Form of irrigation whereby water is delivered in small amounts to the vine through a series of tubes; the water then drips directly onto the vine root system.

DRY Used to describe wines in which there is no discernible sweetness. It has a legal definition in Europe. Most people begin to perceive sweetness at about 0.5 percent residual sugar. However, high acidity may mask sweetness.

DRY CREEK VALLEY AVA Viticultural area in western Sonoma County, California, which follows the course of Dry Creek, west of Healdsburg. The best wines are Zinfandel, Sauvignon Blanc, and Cabernet Sauvignon. Recent plantings of Rhône varieties are also showing promise.

DRY-FARMED VINEYARDS Vineyards that are not irrigated.

DUBOEUF, GEORGES Duboeuf (1933–) has had a major impact on worldwide sales and acceptance of the French red wines of Beaujolais.

He controls almost one-third of the wines of Beaujolais and has established a reputation for high-quality, affordable wines. He also makes wine from the Rhône Valley and southern France.

DULCE Spanish for sweet.

DUMB Tasting term for wine that has little aroma or flavor. A similar term is "closed down." The term is often applied to wines that are expected to improve.

EARTHY Tasting term, often used positively to refer to the smell of rich loam or topsoil.

ÉCHÉZEAUX AC French Grand Cru vineyard on Burgundy's Côte de Nuits, well known for outstanding red wines capable in a good year of aging for 15 years or longer.

ECUADOR There has been a recent move to improve wine quality in this South American country by planting vineyards in the mountains where it is cool enough for the vine to lie dormant in winter. Plantings along the coast produce three crops a year.

EDELZWICKER Everyday blended white wine from Alsace, France, generally not of high quality.

EDEN VALLEY Relatively cool part of South Australia's Barossa Valley. It has excelled with Riesling, but all other classic grape varieties also do well, enjoying a longer, slower ripening period.

EDNA VALLEY AVA Cool winegrowing region in the south of San Luis Obispo County on California's Central Coast, best known for Chardonnay, which has a distinctive rich, butterscotch flavor. Pinot Noir also does well.

EINZELLAGE The smallest vineyard area that can be named on German wine labels, the Einzellage or vineyard name follows the village name as in Wehlener Sonnenuhr, which denotes wine from the vineyard, or Einzellage, of Sonnenuhr in the village of Wehlen.

EISWEIN German and Austrian term for wine made from grapes left on the vine to freeze, which concentrates the grape sugars since the liquid part of the grape has turned to ice. The finished wine is very sweet. Eiswein is rare, since the right conditions for making it do not occur every year. In North America, it is called Icewine. Good Icewines are made in Ontario, Canada, and the Finger Lakes AVA of New York State, and a small amount is made in Washington State. Randall Grahm, the innovative California winemaker, has made Icewine from harvested grapes frozen in commercial freezers, but this is not permitted in Europe or Canada.

EL DORADO AVA There has been a spurt of vineyard planting in this Sierra Foothills sub-AVA in El Dorado County, California. The AVA regulations limit plantings to between 1,200 feet and 3,500 feet (366 m and 1,067 m) in elevation. The best wine is Zinfandel, with Cabernet Sauvignon, Merlot, and Chardonnay only adequate.

ELEGANT Tasting term for a wine of great balance and smooth texture.

ÉLEVAGE French word with no real English equivalent. It refers to the entire process of maturing, or "bringing up" a wine in the cellar, between fermentation and bottling.

ELGIN Bordering the Franschhoek WO in South Africa, a relatively new wine area producing increasingly good white wines, especially from Sauvignon Blanc.

ELTVILLE Old German village on the banks of the Rhine River in the Rheingau area, planted almost exclusively to Riesling.

EMILIA-ROMAGNA Area in central Italy stretching from the Adriatic coast inland, where less than 20 percent of the wine produced is DOC-classified. The best-known wine, red Lambrusco, when dry, is a good quaff with the local foods.

EN PRIMEUR French term for wine sold on a futures basis before bottling. This system is widespread in Bordeaux, but not limited to that region. In the United States, the term used is "futures."

ENGLAND There was a time when English wine provoked a reaction of general amusement, but the wines, especially white and sparkling, are quickly gaining new friends. Despite the influence of the warm Gulf Stream, ripening wine grapes in England can be tricky. The most reliable grapes are German crosses, such as Bacchus, bred for cool climates. The hybrid Seyval Blanc also does well. At their best, the wines have a delicate, lean fruit that can be quite engaging.

ENOLOGIST Term increasingly used around the world for the person in charge of the technical side of winemaking, who may often be a visiting, consultant enologist. There are increasing numbers of enologists working in the wine industry today all over the world.

ENTRE-DEUX-MERS AC Much-improved Bordeaux AC responsible for some of the region's most drinkable white wines, indeed some of the best inexpensive whites in France. At its best, the wine is crisp and clean with forward fruit, suitable for early drinking.

ESTATE-BOTTLED In Europe, the term for wine bottled on the estate where it has been made. In the United States, the term has been expanded to include wine made from vineyards that the winery controls through a long-term agricultural lease, as well as from its own estate. The vineyards must be in the same AVA as the winery.

ESTREMADURA Region in central Portugal producing more wine than any other part of the country, but little of real quality.

ESTUFA Portuguese word for stove, now applied to the large tanks used to heat less expensive Madeira to speed its development.

ETHANOL Active alcohol in wine and other alcoholic drinks. It has no flavor or color, but does influence how the wine tastes. Wines with a high alcohol content can taste hot if other elements are not in balance.

ETNA DOC Wine region around Mount Etna, Italy, making pleasing reds from Nerello and good whites and rosés for drinking young.

EUTYPA Serious fungal disease of grape vines, sometimes called dead-arm or dying arm. The fungus causes the wood to rot and the vineyards may have to be replanted.

EVANS, LEN Journalist and media personality turned wine producer,

Len Evans (1930–) is the best known of a handful of people credited with transforming the Australian wine industry and putting Australian wine on the international quality map. His greatest achievement may have been creating the Rothbury Estate vineyard and winery in the Hunter Valley; but now that it has been sold, he is still making wine under the Evans Family Estate label.

EXTENDED MACERATION Process that allows newly fermented red wine to remain in contact with the skins and seeds for up to 25 to 30 days. The purpose is to rid the wine of harsh tannins and to increase color intensity and aroma.

EXTRA BRUT Champagnes and sparkling wines with either zero or minimal *dosage* (extra sugar) added. They taste very dry.

EXTRA DRY Sparkling wine labeled Extra Dry is not the driest made, since Brut and Extra Brut are drier. The residual sugar level may, surprisingly, be up to 6 percent for Extra Dry wines.

EXTREMADURA Vast Spanish region between Castilla-La Mancha and Portugal producing mostly wine for distillation or for bulk sales. However, improvements have been made in the past few years, especially in the Tierra de Barros region, a subzone of Ribera del Guadiana DO. Good everyday red wines are made from Tempranillo and Garnacha, some of which are capable of aging.

FALERNO DEL MASSICO DOC Falernian was one of the famous wines of classical Roman times. The region is currently undergoing a revival; early results show promise.

FATTORIA Italian word for a farm or wine estate.

FAUGÈRES AC Zone in the Languedoc region of southern France, making distinctive red wine with powerful fruit and lasting flavors. The chief grapes used are the traditional Mediterranean varieties.

FENDANT Unremarkable Swiss white wine made from Chasselas grapes grown in the Valais region.

FERMENTATION Process by which yeast converts the sugar in grapes into alcohol.

FIANO White grape from southern Italy. It produces white wines of good flavor for early drinking, especially in the region of Campania.

FIDDLETOWN AVA Wine region in Amador County, California, within the Sierra Foothills AVA, known for Zinfandel made in a ripe, concentrated style.

FIELD BLEND Once a common practice in California, this term refers to a vineyard where a number of different grape varieties are planted, harvested, and fermented together, thus the wine blend is made "in the field."

FILL LEVEL The level to which wine rises in the neck of the bottle; this provides a clue to the condition of the wine. A low fill level probably indicates oxidation of the wine and a faulty cork.

FILTERING Process by which solids are removed from wine by passing it through a filter. Many winemakers believe filtering limits a wine's ability to mature in the bottle. Some wines are labeled as "unfiltered."

FINE WINE Difficult to define, the term covers the wines of the world that wine merchants, writers, and consumers agree, on a pragmatic basis, to regard as better wines.

FINESSE Tasting term which implies that the wine is one of high quality with great balance and subtlety of flavor.

FINGER LAKES AVA Cool growing region in north central New York State, where the climate is moderated by a group of lakes. The best vineyards are on benchland above the lakes. The Pinot Noir, Chardonnay, and Riesling can be good.

FINING Process for clarifying wine, in which material added to the wine in barrel or tank causes particles in the wine (leftover bits of the winemaking process, dead yeast cells, etc.) to attach themselves to the fining agent and drop to the bottom of the barrel or tank. Fining material includes egg whites, isinglass, and gelatin. Fining is avoided by some winemakers who believe it strips away natural flavors. Some wine labels now state that the contents of the bottle are unfined.

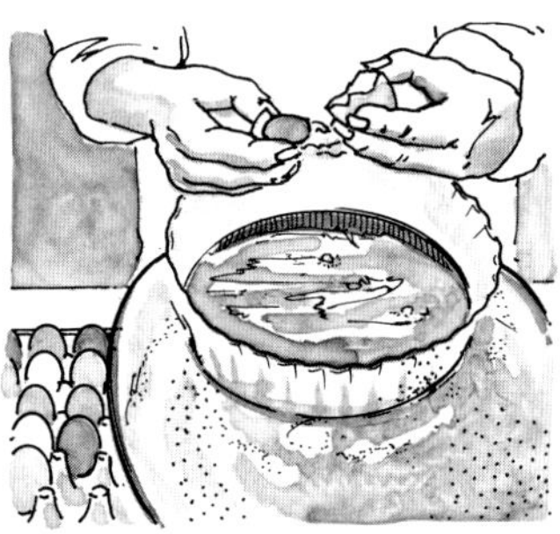

Real egg whites may be used as a fining agent to clarify wine

FINISH Tasting term for impressions left by a wine on the palate after swallowing.

FINO Style of Spanish sherry, always finished dry (except for a few export brands) and best served chilled.

FIRST GROWTH Direct translation of French term Premier Cru, usually used for the top category of classified wines of Bordeaux, France.

FITOU AC Red wine AC in Languedoc, southern France, making big, hearty wines, capable of at least short-term aging.

FIXIN AC French red wine AC in the Côte de Nuits, Burgundy. Its wines have never achieved the fame of nearby ACs such as Gevrey-Chambertin, but the style is similar.

FLEURIE AC One of the ten Cru Beaujolais of Burgundy, France, Fleurie is known for wines with an engaging, perfumy character.

FLOR Yeast that forms a film on the surface of wine following fermentation. The sherry wines of Spain are the best known flor wines.

FLORAL Positive tasting term used to describe aromas reminiscent of flowers, usually in white wines.

FLUTE Narrow wineglass best used for Champagne and sparkling wine, as it does not allow the bubbles to escape too quickly.

FLYING WINEMAKERS Term for Australian winemakers brought into France in the late 1980s to apply superior technical knowledge to wineries with large supplies of inexpensive grapes. The idea was a success, and a class of international winemakers has sprung up. Some critics have noted that the wines mostly taste the same—fruity and clean—with an international style that pays little attention to *terroir* and local grapes. The original "Flying Winemakers" were all from Australia, but now winemakers from California, France, and Italy are also involved. SEE ENOLOGIST.

FORTIFIED WINES Certain wines that have had alcoholic spirits (usually grape spirits) added to increase alcoholic content, or to stop fermentation while some grape sugars remain in the wine. Examples include port, Madeira, sherry, and Muscat de Beaumes-de-Venise.

FORWARD FRUIT Young wines where the fruit taste is the most dominant taste may be described as showing forward fruit.

FOXY Negative tasting term for wines made from native American grapes that have a distinctive musky aroma, which many people judge to be unpleasant.

FRANCE There is both a greater quantity and a wider variety of fine wine produced in France than in any other country in the world. These days the country has to fight harder to maintain its preeminent position in the wine world due to serious competition from New World wine producers. France's high reputation exists because it enjoys an abundance of suitable soils and climates for wine production, and it also has centuries of experience in producing fine wines and a long culture of drinking and exporting them. The wines of Bordeaux, Burgundy, and Champagne have set a standard of quality that much of the world seeks to emulate. The other important regions of the Rhône, the Loire, and Alsace are all capable of producing fine wines of individuality and high quality, and the vast Languedoc-Roussillon region has improved its standards dramatically in recent times. There is hardly a corner of France that does not produce good everyday table wine. France has set a standard, too, with its classification system, which guarantees origin and minimum standards for wines through the progression from Vin de Table, to Vin de Pays, VDQS, and Appellation Contrôlée, a model which has been followed by many other wine countries. However much good wine is made elsewhere, France remains the spiritual home for fine wine and one which winemakers around the world return to time and time again.

FRANCIACORTA DOCG About half of the wine production in this northern Italian winegrowing region in Lombardy is sparkling wine made from Chardonnay, Pinot Blanc, Pinot Noir, and Pinot Gris.

FRANKEN German wine region known for its dry white wines made from Silvaner and Müller-Thurgau.

FRANKLAND RIVER SEE GREAT SOUTHERN.

FRANSCHHOEK WO South African winegrowing valley region producing good white wines from Sémillon, a local specialty, and a promising range of reds.

FRASCATI DOC Well-known Italian white wine made in the hills of Lazio from Trebbiano and Malvasia.

FREE-RUN Juice that drains from the grapes without crushing.

FREISA Red grape variety grown in Piedmont, Italy. The typical wine made from Freisa is slightly fizzy with a hint of sugar, although the wine is also made in a dry style.

FRENCH COLOMBARD Name given in California to Colombard. It is a white wine grape originally brought to the state from France. Twenty years ago it was the most widely planted white grape in California, used mainly for cheap jug wines. SEE COLOMBARD.

FRENCH PARADOX The term refers to research showing that even though the French consume more fat than many people believe is good for them, they seem to be protected from many health problems usually associated with such a diet, possibly by the daily consumption of red wine.

FRESH Tasting term for youthful, usually simple wines.

FRESNO STATE UNIVERSITY Part of the California State University system, regarded as a "hands-on" school for winemakers and viticulturists. Fresno has its own vineyards and a commercial winery operation.

FRIULI GRAVE DOC Formerly Grave del Friuli, a DOC in northeast Italy making fresh, fruity wines, including Merlot and Chardonnay.

FRIULI-VENEZIA GIULIA Wine region in northeast Italy bordering Austria and Slovenia. It makes some of Italy's best white wines, mostly from Pinot Grigio, Pinot Bianco, Chardonnay, and Tocai. Red wines from Cabernet Sauvignon and Merlot can also be good. A specialty of the area is the light red Refosco.

FRIZZANTE Italian term for a semi-sparkling wine.

FRONSAC AC Small red wine appellation west of Pomerol in the Bordeaux region of France, where the wines have shown significant improvement in the past few years. The chief grape varieties are Merlot and Cabernet Franc.

FRUITY Favorable tasting term for a wine that has a distinctive fruity flavor, usually applied to young wines with some intensity.

FUMÉ BLANC Winemaker Robert Mondavi of California invented this term as part of a campaign to sell more Sauvignon Blanc wine in California. The name is taken from Blanc Fumé, a French Loire synonym for Sauvignon Blanc. The name caught on and, as Mondavi did not own the name, it became very popular on California wine labels. Recent U.S. regulations require Sauvignon Blanc to appear as a subheading on Fumé Blanc labels. SEE SAUVIGNON BLANC.

FURMINT White wine grape grown widely in Hungary. It is the main grape used to make the dessert wine Tokay.

GAILLAC AC Wine region in southwest France, producing fresh white wine from the Mauzac grape, which has a distinctive green apple flavor and makes some good sparkling wines. Gaillac red wines have greatly improved since Syrah has joined the vineyard mix.

GAJA, ANGELO Arguably the outstanding figure in Italian wine, for which he is an international ambassador, Angelo Gaja (1940–) is best known for his brilliant and very expensive single-vineyard Barbarescos from Piedmont, which rank among Italy's top investment wines. He also introduced international grape varieties to Piedmont.

GALESTRO Dry white wine from Chianti, Tuscany, Italy, based mostly on Trebbiano grapes, no longer wanted in Chianti wine.

GALICIA Green mountainous region in northwest Spain. Rainfall is high and grapes were traditionally trained to climb high up concrete posts to keep mildew at bay. The best wines are perfumed, crisp whites made from Albariño and sold under the varietal name.

GALLO, ERNEST AND JULIO Ernest Gallo (1909–) and his late brother Julio (1910–1993) have done more to make the United States a wine-drinking nation than anyone else. They started making and selling wine in Modesto, California, at the end of Prohibition in 1933, with

immediate success. The brothers—Ernest on the marketing side and Julio in the vineyards—were shrewd judges of public taste and gave the people what they wanted, including somewhat questionable sweet wines such as Thunderbird, and a wide range of red and white jug wines, identified with names such as Chablis Blanc and Hearty Burgundy. In the 1970s, seeing the move toward premium wines, the Gallos began introducing cork-finished, vintage-dated varietal wines, made from grapes grown on California's North Coast. These wines have met with critical and popular success. Today, one of every four bottles of wine sold in the U.S. is made by Gallo. The company, which is said to be the world's largest wine producer, owns more than 10,000 acres (4,047 hectares) of vineyards in California, many of them in premium Sonoma County AVAs.

GAMAY Red wine grape used to make the fruity, highy popular wines of Beaujolais, France. It is also widely grown in France's Loire Valley and in Switzerland. It was once thought to be the Napa Gamay of California, a grape variety now known to be Valdiguié.

GAMAY BEAUJOLAIS Grape originally thought by California growers to be a true Gamay, which is now believed to be a lesser version of Pinot Noir.

GARD, VIN DE PAYS DU French region west of the Rhône in Languedoc. The best wines are a light, fruity red and a fresh rosé.

GARGANEGA White wine grape from Veneto, northeast Italy, used in the production of Soave.

GARNACHA Spanish name for Grenache.

GARRAFEIRA Word used on Portuguese wine labels to denote a red wine from a good vintage, aged for at least three years, including one year in bottle, before release. A white Garrafeira must have one year of aging, including six months in the bottle.

GATTINARA DOCG Italian wine district in Piedmont, where Spanna (local name for Nebbiolo) occasionally challenges Barolo as one of Italy's great red wines, but is more often disappointing. The wines tend to be lighter, and should be drunk younger, than Barolo.

GAVI DOC Trendy, often quite good, dry white wine from Piedmont, Italy, made from Cortese grapes. It has a pleasing citrus quality when young, which deepens and ripens with a few years in bottle.

GEELONG Wine district in the Victoria region of Australia, showing good potential for Chardonnay, Riesling, Pinot Noir, and Shiraz.

GEISENHEIM Important center of wine and viticulture research in the German village of the same name in the Rheingau. Much work there is focused on eliminating the use of chemical sprays in the vineyard.

GELATIN Material used in fining wine. SEE FINING.

GENEVA The substantial vineyard area close to the city of Geneva in Switzerland produces increasingly good white and red wines, but most are consumed locally.

GEORGIA Historically important wine area on the Black Sea northeast of Turkey. Modern Georgian wines could play a larger role in the world wine market as technology catches up in the vineyards and in the wine cellars. There are 38 grape varieties allowed in Georgia, including new plantings of Cabernet Sauvignon, Chardonnay, and Pinot Noir. Growing conditions and wine quality vary tremendously.

GERMANY Country best known for off-dry or sweet wines made from Riesling, Gewürztraminer, Silvaner, and Müller-Thurgau, as well as for a little good dry red based largely on Pinot Noir and Blauer Portugieser. The top wines are the great dessert wines, or Trockenbeerenauslese wines. Sadly, German wine exports are mostly flabby, semi-sweet Liebfraumilch-style wines. However, many of the younger German winemakers are calling for changes in German wine laws which they feel would lead to improved quality, while market forces are pushing German winemakers toward fruit-driven, dry wines. Germany will be an exciting country to watch over the coming years.

GEVREY-CHAMBERTIN AC French appellation in the Côte de Nuits in Burgundy, known for its red wines from Pinot Noir. Quality has taken a turn for the better recently.

GEWÜRZTRAMINER White wine grape grown around the world, at its best in Alsace, France, where it produces a spicy dry wine that can be rich and delicious. It is also made in a dessert style, the lush late-harvest Vendange Tardive of Alsace. It tends to make better wine in cooler areas.

GHEMME DOC Good red wines from this DOC in Piedmont, northwest Italy, are based on Nebbiolo.

GIGONDAS AC Appellation in the southern Rhône region of France, producing ripe, sometimes concentrated red wines and fresh, fruity rosés, based chiefly on Grenache. They are often quite good value.

GISBORNE Warm winegrowing area on New Zealand's North Island. It has produced good Chardonnay.

GIVRY AC Red wine from Givry in the Côte Chalonnaise, Burgundy, France. It has rich fruit and, at its best, an intense flavor that makes it stand out from other Chalonnaise reds. Whites are also improving.

G

GODELLO White grape, probably native to Galicia, northwest Spain, which makes a good, perfumy white wine, especially in Valdeorras DO.

GOLAN HEIGHTS Within Galilee, Israel, the high-altitude vineyards of the Golan Heights have attracted foreign interest and the most exciting wines of Israel are made there. Red and white international varieties such as Cabernet Sauvignon and Chardonnay are produced using New World methods.

GONZALEZ BYASS Traditional sherry firm, from Jerez in Spain, long recognised as an uncompromisingly high quality producer, whose range includes the world's best-selling sherry, Tio Pepe Fino, and several outstanding old sherries such as Apostoles dry Oloroso and Matusalem sweet Oloroso.

GOULBURN VALLEY Area in Victoria, Australia, bordering the river of the same name, producing excellent white wines made from the Marsanne grape.

GRACIANO Spanish red wine grape grown in Rioja and Navarra, used to some extent in the blending of Rioja red wines.

GRAFTING Process of joining one part of a vine to another vine, of the same or different species, usually at root-level. In the 1800s, following the devastation of many of the world's vineyards by *phylloxera*, it was only by grafting a growing vine onto *phylloxera*-resistant rootstock that vineyards survived. This process continues today worldwide to keep *phylloxera* at bay. Grafting may also be used as a fast method of replacing one grape variety with another more fashionable one.

GRAN RESERVA Spanish term for a wine from an outstanding vintage. A red Gran Reserva must spend a minimum of two years in barrel and three years in tank or bottle. A white wine must spend four years in cask and bottle, including at least six months in cask.

GRAND CRU French term for great growth, reserved for the best vineyard sites in Alsace, Burgundy, Champagne, and parts of Bordeaux.

GRAND VIN In Bordeaux, France, the name refers to the principal wine made by a château.

GRANDE MARQUE French term meaning "big brand." The *grandes marques* of Champagne were firms that made Champagne to certain minimum standards. They belonged to a group called *Le Syndicat des Grandes Marques*, disbanded in 1997.

Bollinger Champagne's headquarters

GRANDS-ÉCHÉZEAUX Grand Cru in one of the prime vineyard areas in Burgundy's Côte de Nuits, France. Only red wines are made. The best can age for many years.

GRAPE SPIRIT Fortified wines such as port, sherry, and Madeira are made by adding grape spirit either before, during, or after fermentation. It is a neutral spirit that has been distilled from wine.

GRASSY Tasting term often applied to Sauvignon Blanc, referring to the herbaceous aroma of the wine.

GRAVES AC Bordeaux AC in France producing a good range of dry white wines and red wines.

GRAVES SUPÉRIEURES AC A minimum alcohol content of 12 percent is required for dry, medium, or sweet white wines from this AC in Bordeaux, France.

GRAY RIESLING Once-popular California version of the Trousseau Gris grape variety of France (not, in fact, a Riesling). It makes a medium-weight white wine, usually finished off-dry. Plantings are declining, and few producers still make the wine.

GREAT SOUTHERN Vast region in the southern part of Western Australia which includes Frankland River and Mount Barker, areas making wines of increasing quality. Shiraz, Chardonnay, and Riesling do particularly well.

GREAT WESTERN One of the oldest wine regions in Victoria, Australia, famous for sparkling wines. It has a growing reputation for whites.

GRECHETTO Italian white wine grape, widely grown in the regions of Umbria and Tuscany.

GREECE Expanding beyond the typical resin-flavored Retsina, Greece is striving to make serious wines of distinction. Several large producers are leading the quality movement, and smaller wineries are coming up fast.

GREEN Wines made from under-ripe fruit, often with a green, somewhat angular or hard flavor.

GREEN VALLEY AVA Cool sub-AVA of Sonoma's Russian River AVA in California. There is a second Green Valley AVA to the east, in a much warmer section of the state in Solano County. This latter AVA is rarely seen on a label.

GRENACHE Red grape which thrives in hot weather, widely cultivated in southern France, especially in the southern Rhône, and in Spain (where its local name is Garnacha), as well as in Australia, California, and elsewhere. At its best, it produces a rich, fruity red wine with intense flavors and some concentration. It is also a good grape for fresh, fruity rosés.

GRENACHE BLANC White wine grape found in southern France and Spain (where it is called Garnacha Blanca) making generally undistinguished wines.

GRIGNOLINO Grown almost exclusively in Piedmont, northwest Italy, this grape makes a light red varietal wine with good acidity for consumption while young. A small amount of Grignolino is also made in California.

GRILLO White grape variety grown on the island of Sicily, Italy, which has potential to make full-bodied white wines.

GROS MANSENG Found in southwest France, this white grape variety is used particularly for dry wines from Jurançon AC and from Pacherenc du Vic-Bilh AC. Not as fine as Petit Manseng.

GROS PLANT DU PAYS NANTAIS VDQS French white wine from the Atlantic end of the Loire Valley. Made from Folle Blanche, the wine has high acidity and goes well with the area's seafood dishes.

GROSSLAGE German term for a large group of vineyards.

GRÜNER VELTLINER White wine grape widely grown in Austria. At its best, it makes distinctive floral wines of good character.

GUENOC VALLEY AVA Appellation centered in southern Lake County, California, with a small part in extreme northern Napa County. It has only one winery, Guenoc.

GUIGAL Considered one of the best producers in the high-quality northern Rhône Valley, Marcel Guigal now commands a cult following for his single-vineyard Côte Rôties, such as La Turque. The firm is also a successful and reliable merchant offering a range of wines from the northern and southern Rhône.

HALBTROCKEN German word meaning half dry, an off-dry wine style between the dry *trocken* wines and sweeter wines. It is shown on the label in addition to the official German classification regulating how ripe the grapes were at harvest, which indicates both flavor intensity and alcohol levels. A Kabinett Halbtrocken will be relatively light, whereas a Spätlese Halbtrocken is likely to be higher in alcohol whilst remaining off-dry.

THE HAMPTONS AVA Warmer of two AVAs (the other being North Fork) on eastern Long Island, New York, producing good Merlot and Cabernet Sauvignon.

HARASZTHY, AGOSTON Originally from Hungary, Haraszthy (1812–1869) has been called the "Father of Modern California Viticulture." In fact, he wasn't and never claimed to be. But he did promote California wines and strive for improved viticultural and winemaking technology, which along with his entrepreneurial skills made him an important figure in the development of California wines. He also built Buena Vista winery in 1858, still in operation in Sonoma.

HARD Tasting term for wines that have a tough edge; they are not approachable when young, and are the obvious opposite of a soft wine.

HAUT-MÉDOC AC Appellation in Bordeaux, France, which includes the famous communes of Margaux, Pauillac, St-Estèphe, St-Julien, Listrac, and Moulis. The appellation is used for red wines made outside these communes.

HAUT-POITOU VDQS French Loire Valley appellation making red, white, and rosé wines. The reds, from Cabernet Sauvignon or Gamay, and the rosé, from Gamay, are best drunk young. The whites, from Sauvignon Blanc or Chardonnay, are crisp and delicious. There is also sparkling wine.

HAWKES BAY Winegrowing region on New Zealand's North Island, best known for Chardonnay, Merlot, Cabernet Sauvignon, and Syrah.

Te Mata winery, Hawkes Bay

HEAT SUMMATION SYSTEM System developed by researchers at the University of California at Davis to measure the amount of heat in degrees Fahrenheit available to the vine at a given location. Using this system, California vineyards are classified into five regions. Region I is the coolest, Region V the hottest.

HENSCHKE Family-owned winery in South Australia's Eden Valley, which owns some of the world's oldest vines, used for its flagship Hill of Grace Shiraz, one of Australia's most internationally coveted investment wines. The husband and wife team of winemaker and viticulturist makes an exemplary range of wines.

L'HÉRAULT, VIN DE PAYS DE Vast Vin de Pays covering the entire *département* of the Hérault in the Languedoc region of France. Large amounts of red wine are made from Carignan, Grenache, and Cinsaut, as well as some white and rosé. Most of it is sold in bulk, but hillside vineyards, overlooked in the past, show great potential.

HERMITAGE AC Some of the world's greatest wine comes from this northern Rhône AC in France. The best reds, made from Syrah, are capable of at least 20 years of aging. The white wines, made from Marsanne and Roussanne, are not so well-known but can be equally good and just as long-lived.

HESSISCHE BERGSTRASSE Small German wine region near Darmstadt. Riesling is the top grape.

HILLSIDES Grapes from hillside vineyards have long had a reputation for making higher-quality wines, possibly because hillside soils are typically thinner and better drained, putting more stress on the vines, which results in more intense fruit. In addition, in cooler climates, hillsides offer a better aspect toward the sun which favors ripening of the grapes.

HOCHHEIM Wines of this Rheingau village in Germany were once reputed to be the favorite of England's Queen Victoria. The Rieslings of Hochheim are some of the fullest from the Rheingau, especially from the best-sited vineyards of Hölle and Kirchenstück.

HOT Tasting term for wines that are out of balance, with high alcohol causing a burning sensation.

HOWELL MOUNTAIN AVA In this AVA in Napa, California, rugged vineyards planted at elevations of between 1,600 feet and 2,200 feet (488 m and 671 m) produce grapes for excellent Cabernet Sauvignon and Zinfandel wines.

HUGEL Based in the fairy-tale village of Riquewihr in France's Alsace region, the family-owned merchant Hugel, founded in the seventeenth century, remains the region's best known, and most widely distributed, producer. The sweet Vendange Tardive and Sélection de Grains Nobles wines are particular specialties. SEE VENDANGE TARDIVE AND SÉLECTION DE GRAINS NOBLES.

HUNGARY The years of state control saw a loss of quality in Hungarian wines; even the famed Tokay dessert wines deteriorated. However, things are now looking up for both Tokay and table wine as foreign interest in native Hungarian varieties has increased.

HUNTER VALLEY Region in New South Wales, Australia, best known for Sémillon and Chardonnay. Shiraz and Cabernet Sauvignon are among the best reds.

HYBRID Offspring of two vine varieties of different *Vitis* species, such as Seyval Blanc.

ICEWINE The name for Eiswein in Canada and the United States. These very sweet, very expensive wines are made by the same process as in Germany. Canada produces outstanding Icewines. SEE EISWEIN.

IDAHO There are relatively small plantings of wine grapes in the southwest corner of this state, on hillsides more than 2,000 feet (610 m) above Snake River. Because of the cool climate, ripening can be a problem, but Chenin Blanc and Riesling show promise.

IGT Abbreviation of *Indicazione Geografiche Tipici,* the Italian equivalent of the French Vin de Pays, now being used for many Super-Tuscan Vino da Tavolas.

L'ILE DE BEAUTÉ, VIN DE PAYS DE Area on the French island of Corsica which is showing remarkable improvement, especially with red wines made from Cabernet Sauvignon, Merlot, and Syrah, and whites from Chardonnay and Vermentino.

INAO Abbreviation of *Institut National des Appellations d'Origine,* the French government agency that is responsible for regulating France's appellation system.

INDIA Although much of India is unsuitable for growing wine grapes, there is new interest in wine production in certain areas. Plantings of several international varieties have shown promise. A good start has been made on sparkling wine production with the help of consultants from Champagne, and a joint venture with a California producer is encouraging.

INTERNATIONAL STYLE Since the rise in popularity of wines from the New World, there have been growing numbers of wines that taste more of a particular style of wine production than of the origin of the grapes. This is often referred to as an international style and is most prevalent among relatively inexpensive wines, especially those made by "Flying Winemakers" who make wines in several different countries. The wines are usually clean and fruity, often with some obvious oak aging, but without great complexity of flavors or the ability to age.

INZOLIA One of the most important grapes of Sicily, providing increasingly good whites with an aromatic flavor.

IPM Abbreviation of Integrated Pest Management, a complex system of insect and vine disease control using a minimal amount of agrochemicals, ideally none. It includes setting beneficial, or "good," insects against bad ones.

IPR Abbreviation of *Indicação de Proveniência Regulamenta,* the second level in the Portuguese wine classification system.

IRANCY AC French area near Chablis, Burgundy, making little known, delicate red wine from Pinot Noir with lean, lively fruit.

IROULÉGUY AC Area in the Basque Pyrenees of southwest France, making excellent red and white wines and a small amount of fruity rosé.

IRRIGATION The delivery of water to grape vines to supplement natural rainfall. This practice is widespread in New World wine countries, especially in Argentina and Riverland in South Australia, but it is not permitted in the classic European wine regions, such as Bordeaux and Burgundy in France.

ISO Abbreviation of International Standards Organization, an international regulatory body based in Switzerland. The ISO wineglass, made of very thin glass, is accepted throughout the world as one of the best wine-tasting glasses.

ISONZO DOC Region in northeast Italy, next to Collio DOC, making 20 different styles of red and white wine. Pinot Grigio and Chardonnay as well as Merlot are considered the best of these.

ISRAEL Not all of Israel's wine is sweet and not all of it is kosher. In the past 20 years there have been dramatic improvements in quality, particularly in the high-altitude Galilee district of Golan Heights. Here some excellent dry wines are being made from Chardonnay, Cabernet Sauvignon, and Merlot.

ITALY The past 20 to 30 years have witnessed remarkable changes in Italian wines, in terms both of production and of the styles and kinds of wine made. Italy's best-known wine, Chianti, has been virtually reinvented in a dramatic new style. Barolo, one of Italy's superstar red wines, is going through a period of change. All over Italy, modern technology and new vineyard plantings are leading to wines in a more modern style which is fresh, fruity, and clean. Many of the Super-Tuscans are being looked to as models around the world. In short, the image of Italy as a producer of cheap "spaghetti wines" is completely out of date. Indeed, Robert Parker has declared that Italy is now a serious rival to France.

JABOULET AINÉ, PAUL Internationally famous for Hermitage La Chapelle, which is legendary for its longevity in top vintages, Jaboulet specializes in both reds and whites from the northern Rhône, France.

JADOT, LOUIS Based in Beaune, Jadot is one of the leading merchants and vineyard owners in Burgundy,. France, with a wide and highly reliable range of both red and white wines with wide international distribution.

JAMMY Tasting term for wine with rich concentrated fruit and an intense grapy character, often applied to California Zinfandel and, sometimes, Australian Shiraz.

JAPAN Wines from Japan are rarely seen outside that country. There are a few good national wines, but most contain a large percentage of bulk wine that has been imported from other countries.

JARDIN DE LA FRANCE, VIN DE PAYS DU Covering most of France's Loire Valley, this Vin de Pays region produces large amounts of inexpensive white and red wine. The reds are usually light and the whites are often sharp and acidic.

JASNIÈRES AC French Loire Valley AC making very good dry white wines based on Chenin Blanc.

JEFFERSON, THOMAS The man who drafted the Declaration of Independence, and who later became U.S. president, Jefferson (1743–1826) was a noted wine connoisseur. He encouraged the wine industry in the new nation and urged that wine be taxed at a lower rate than spirits.

JEREZ Y MANZANILLA DO Spanish DO in Andalucía making several styles of sherry, from dry Finos to intensely sweet dessert wines. The wines are fortified (except for a few examples sold on the home market) and are based on the Palomino grape or, for certain sweet sherries, the Pedro Ximénez. The sherry district forms a triangle among the towns of Jerez de la Frontera, Sanlúcar de Barameda, and Puerto de Santa María.

JOHANNISBERG RIESLING One of the names, along with White Riesling and Rhine Riesling, applied to the Riesling grape in California and elsewhere outside Germany.

JOHNSON, HUGH English writer and educator, Johnson (1939–) has done much to popularize wine.

JUG WINE Term commonly applied in California to cheap wines bottled in oversized half-gallon and gallon jugs. They are usually sold with screw caps for stoppers. Quality is never high, but the wine is usually cleanly made and drinkable.

JULIÉNAS AC Beaujolais Cru of Burgundy, France, making relatively big red wines based on Gamay.

JUMILLA DO Appellation in eastern Spain, which has long had a reputation for big red wines with too much alcohol and tannin. These wines are still a major part of production, but there is a move toward a lighter, fresher style of fruity red wine, which is encouraging.

JURA Mountain region in eastern France, east of Burgundy and north of Switzerland. It is particularly renowned for its highly alcoholic *vin jaune*, a sherrylike wine from the local Savagnin grape, and for its *vin de paille*. The Burgundian grapes Chardonnay and Pinot Noir are also grown in Jura. SEE VIN JAUNE and VIN DE PAILLE.

JURANÇON AC Appellation in southwest France making excellent sweet white wine from late-harvest Petit and Gros Manseng grapes. A good-quality dry wine, Jurançon Sec, is also made.

K

KABINETT Term for German wines with the lowest ranking on the QmP ripeness (referring to the grapes) scale. SEE QMP.

KAMPTAL-DONAULAND Austrian region producing good dry whites from Riesling and Grüner Veltliner.

KNIGHTS VALLEY AVA Relatively warm AVA in Sonoma County, California, producing good Cabernet Sauvignon and Sauvignon Blanc.

KOSHER WINE Wine produced under the supervision of a rabbi to suit it for drinking by Jews observing the faith's dietary laws.

KREMSTAL Region in Donauland, Austria, making some of that country's best white wines.

KRUG Each of Krug's Champagnes, from the nonvintage Grand Cuvée to the single vineyard Clos du Mesnil Blanc de Blancs, is of prestige standard, sold at luxury prices. Grape selection is rigorous, the base wines are oak-aged, and the aging process is long. Krug is one of France's premier wine producers.

KUMEU/HUAPAI Viticultural area near the capital of Auckland, on the North Island of New Zealand. Much of the wine made in the local wineries is from bought-in grapes.

LACRYMA CHRISTI DEL VESUVIO DOC Southern Italian region improving the quality of its white wines.

LACTIC ACID Mild acid that may be present in wine; the same acid is present in yogurt. The secondary, or malolactic, fermentation in red and white table wines is designed to change harsher malic acid into softer lactic acid.

LADOIX AC Burgundian village in the Côte de Beaune region of France, producing mostly red wine which is somewhat light and best drunk young.

LAFON, DOMAINE DES COMTES Run by the dynamic Dominique Lafon, this highly fashionable Burgundy domaine produces some of the world's finest French Chardonnay, particularly top-quality Meursault and Le Montrachet.

LAGO DI CALDARO DOC Northeastern Italian appellation known for a light red wine made from the Schiava grape, which, at its best, makes delicious fruity wine for very early drinking.

LAGREIN Distinctive red wine grape from the Trentino-Alto-Adige region of Italy, which makes very fragrant, fruity wines.

LALANDE-DE-POMEROL AC Just north of the Pomerol AC, this French Bordeaux region makes good-value, good-quality red wine. It is drinkable when three to four years old but is also capable of longer aging.

LAMBRUSCO Style of wine made in Emilia-Romagna, Italy, best known in the United States as a slightly sweet, easy-to-drink red or white wine with a bit of fizz. The dry red version is consumed locally. There are various DOCs producing the same style of wine, usually of similar quality. All DOC Lambrusco wines are made from the very prolific red grape of the same name.

LANDWEIN German and Austrian equivalent of French Vin de Pays.

LANGHE DOC Hilly appellation near the town of Alba, in the Piedmont region of northwest Italy, making good-quality red and white wines from Nebbiolo, Barbera, and Chardonnay grapes.

LANGUEDOC-ROUSSILLON Wine area of southern France which, although historically the source of inexpensive table wines, has lately moved steadily up the quality scale and is now becoming one of the more exciting French wine areas. The new wines are the result of modern technology, which has helped tremendously, and also of a change in attitude. Some of these wines are made from new plantings of international grape varieties, such as Merlot and Cabernet Sauvignon, while others are made from traditional Mediterranean grapes.

Winery in Languedoc-Roussillon

LATE BOTTLED VINTAGE (LBV) Port taken from a single vintage and bottled from four to six years following the harvest. The so-called traditional style of LBV is bottled unfiltered, so that it will throw a sediment. This traditional style, when made using port from a good year, offers some of the pleasures of a vintage port. The modern style of LBV is filtered before bottling. Some believe this takes away much of the character of the port.

LATE-HARVEST Wine in which the grapes are picked several days, or perhaps even weeks, after the normal harvest is finished. The wine is sweeter due to the buildup of sugar in the grapes. Fermentation is stopped before all the sugar is converted to alcohol.

LAZIO Frascati DOC, the standard white wine served in the cafés of Rome, is produced in this central Italian region.

LEAF REMOVAL Summer practice of cutting away leaves near the grape bunches on the vines to expose the grapes to more sunlight, which decreases the chance of rot and mildew forming on the grapes.

LEBANON Historic wine-producing country that has recently given the world some powerful red wines. Château Musar makes lush, full wines based on Cabernet Sauvignon and Syrah.

L

LEES Sediment that settles to the bottom of barrels or tanks following fermentation. It consists mainly of dead yeast cells, with some pulp, grape stems, and seeds. Wines left in contact with the fine lees (mainly dead yeast cells) are relatively complex in flavor.

LEFLAIVE, DOMAINE The best-known producer of white Burgundy, now using biodynamic techniques, Domaine Leflaive produces top-class Chardonnay from some of the Côte de Beaune's very best Grand Cru vineyards. The related merchant business of Olivier Leflaive is one of the more reliable in the Côte de Beaune.

LEGS Tasting term for the tracks left on the inside of the glass by some wines; also called tears.

LEMBERGER Grown in Germany and Austria, where it is also known as Blaufränkisch, and in the state of Washington, this red grape variety produces distinctive wines with pleasing dark berry fruit.

LENGTH Flavor that lingers in the mouth after a wine is swallowed.

LEROY, DOMAINE Run by the indefatigable Lalou Bize-Leroy, this Burgundy domaine is farmed using biodynamic methods and grapes harvested at very low yields. The result is some of the best-quality, but highest-priced Pinot Noir in the world.

LICHINE, ALEXIS Russian-born wine merchant and writer Lichine (1913–1989) helped introduce a whole new generation of Americans to the fine wines of Bordeaux, France. Lichine liked to emphasize the romantic side of wine, and his first book, *Wines of France* (1951), was an exciting introduction to wine for many.

LIEBFRAUMILCH QBA Slightly sweet, unremarkable style of German white wine, usually from the Rheinhessen or Pfalz wine regions. It is an extremely popular export and is responsible for a great deal of prejudice against German wine.

LIGURIA Mediterranean coastal wine region running from Italy's French border down to Tuscany. It produces a wide range of white and red wines, mostly for local consumption. Liguria's most famous wine is the white Cinqueterre.

LIMOUX AC First appellation in the Languedoc region of southern France to insist on vinification in oak for Chardonnay and Chenin Blanc blends.

LIQUEUR MUSCAT Liqueur Muscat is made in Australia from very ripe, almost "raisined" Brown Muscat grapes that are partly fermented and then fortified with grape spirit. The wine is then matured for several years in old oak barrels. The best come from Rutherglen in the north of Victoria.

LIQUEUR DE TIRAGE Mixture of wine, sugar, and yeast, added to sparkling wine to begin the secondary fermentation.

LIRAC AC Appellation in the southern Rhône Valley of France, occasionally making quite good red wine of some intensity, as well as some white and rosé. They should all be drunk young.

LISTRAC-MÉDOC AC Appellation in the Haut-Médoc, Bordeaux, France, producing red wine with good fruit and distinct flavor.

LIVERMORE VALLEY AVA California AVA influenced by cool winds off San Francisco Bay. The gravelly soils are good for Cabernet Sauvignon. Sauvignon Blanc and Chardonnay also do well.

LOCOROTONDO DOC Area in Apulia, southern Italy, producing dry white wine for early drinking.

LODGE Term used by port and Madeira shippers for the building where wine is stored and aged.

LODI-WOODBRIDGE AVA Increasingly important, quality-oriented California winegrowing region between San Francisco and Sacramento, in the San Joaquin Valley. Once known for its cheap and hearty red wines, Lodi improved its wine quality in a very short time, beginning in the vineyards. Most of

the production is sold to coastal wineries, but the name is starting to turn up on labels as well. Most of the standard California varietals do well, with Zinfandel the best.

LOIRE Region of France embracing dozens of different soils and growing areas, from the Atlantic Ocean almost as far as Burgundy. The Loire is home to the famous wines of Sancerre, Pouilly-Fumé, Vouvray, Chinon, Anjou, and many others including Muscadet. Wine styles range from dry white, red, and rosé wines through marvelous and long-lasting dessert wines to sparkling wines. Quality is generally good and sometimes very impressive. The best white wines are based on Chenin Blanc and Sauvignon Blanc. The best reds are from Cabernet Franc, Gamay, and Pinot Noir.

LOMBARDY Rich, heavily populated north central Italian winegrowing region, with much of the crop used for spumante production. The region includes Lugana DOC and Franciacorta DOCG.

LONG ISLAND There are two AVAs on the eastern end of this island off New York City. The more heavily planted North Fork AVA has more ocean exposure, while The Hamptons AVA has a slightly warmer climate. Riesling and Chardonnay have done well, but there is increasing excitement over Merlot and Cabernet Sauvignon.

LOUPIAC AC Area of Bordeaux, France, making sweet white wines with limited aging potential.

LUGANA DOC White wines are made from the Trebbiano grape in this DOC on the shores of Lake Garda in Lombardy, Italy.

LUSSAC-ST-ÉMILION AC Bordeaux AC in France, making light, attractive red wines for early drinking.

LUTOMER LASKI RIZLING Semi-dry light white wine, once the biggest wine export from the former Yugoslavia, now in Slovenia. It is not made from Rhine Riesling, but from the lesser Laski, or Welschrizling.

LUXEMBOURG White wines of high acidity are made here from vineyards on the banks of the Mosel River. There is also a small amount of very light Pinot Noir.

M**ACABEO** Most widely planted white wine grape in northern Spain, also gaining popularity in southern France. The wines have a floral character and are somewhat low in acid. The grape is known as Viura in much of northern Spain.

MACERATION In red winemaking, the skins, pips, and pulp are left to soak, or macerate, in the fermenting must in order to impart color and tannins to the wine. Usually, the longer the maceration, the more deeply colored and tannic the wine will be. White wines may also be made with a few hours' skin maceration before pressing.

MACÉRATION CARBONIQUE See Carbonic Maceration.

MÂCON AC Basic AC in Mâconnais, Burgundy, France, producing red, white, and rosé wines that should all be drunk when young. The better white wines are usually labeled Mâcon-Villages AC.

Mâcon Supérieur is reserved for wines, usually red, with a slightly higher minimum alcohol level than the basic Mâcon AC.

MÂCON-VILLAGES AC More than 40 villages in the Mâcon area of Burgundy, France, are allowed to make white wine using this AC. Made from Chardonnay grapes, the wines are, at best, fresh and lively for everyday drinking. Among the best villages are Chardonnay (possibly the origin of the grape), Clessé, Lugny, and Viré.

MÂCONNAIS One of the largest wine districts in Burgundy, France. It is best known for white Chardonnay-based wines, particularly from Pouilly-Fuissé AC.

MADEIRA DOC Subtropical Portuguese island DOC where the fortified wine of that name is made. After *phylloxera* destroyed Madeira's vineyards in the nineteenth century, the inferior new vines that were

Madeira barrel, bottle, and glass

planted robbed the modern wine of some of its older power. In an attempt to restore quality, there is a move underway to replant the traditional vines—Malvasia, Boal, Verdelho, and Sercial. Madeira's typically burnt, tangy taste is achieved by heating the young wine. Some is still made and aged naturally in wooden casks. The best examples are capable of surviving for centuries.

MADERIZATION Process by which wine is oxidized, usually by heating it, to produce a particular style, such as a Madeira style. The wine should also be fortified to prevent it from becoming vinegary. The term is often used incorrectly as a negative tasting term for a wine spoiled by exposure to oxygen. In fact, such a wine will be oxidized.

MADIRAN AC Appellation in southwest France, which has greatly improved of late. Its red wine, made from the Tannat grape, can be soft and pleasing when aged in oak.

MAIPO VALLEY Important wine region in Chile's Central Valley making very good red wines from Cabernet Sauvignon and others.

MÁLAGA DO Fortified, usually sweet wine from Andalucía, southern Spain. Several grapes are used, including Muscat and Pedro Ximénez, which are dried in order to concentrate the sugars. The fortified wines are matured in old oak barrels. The best wines have intense flavors and are much underrated.

MALBEC One of the five red Bordeaux grape varieties, at its best today in Argentina, where it makes wines of complexity and power. Elsewhere, Malbec is almost always used for blending.

MALIC ACID One of the harsher-tasting acids in wine, it can give white wines an appley flavor. Malolactic fermentation converts malic acid into milder lactic acid. SEE MALOLACTIC FERMENTATION.

MALOLACTIC FERMENTATION Secondary fermentation, following the basic alcoholic fermentation, which converts harsh malic acid to mild lactic acid. It may occur spontaneously, be induced, or be prevented, depending on the style of wine desired.

MALVASIA Large family of grapes, both white and red, grown particularly in Italy but also all over Europe's Mediterranean vineyards.

The red Malvasia Nera is one of the grapes used in Apulia's red wines.

LA MANCHA DO Huge appellation in central Spain, which has seen vast improvements in wine quality. Red wines made from various grape varieties including Cencibel (the local name for Tempranillo) are fresh and fruity. Whites are also much better. With the introduction of new varieties such as Viura from Rioja, Chardonnay, and Cabernet Sauvignon, La Mancha's prospects for producing enjoyable everyday wines look good.

MANZANILLA Fino style of sherry made only in the seaside town of Sanlúcar de Barrameda, Andalucía, southern Spain. Compared to Fino, Manzanilla seems to have higher acidity and, somehow, a hint of the salt air from the sea.

MARANGES AC Pleasant, light red and white wines are made in this AC in Burgundy, France.

MARCHES Italian region bordering the Adriatic Sea, making good white wine in Verdicchio dei Castelli di Jesi DOC and fresh, inviting reds from Sangiovese and Montepulciano in Rosso Conero and Rosso Piceno DOCs.

MARCILLAC AC Appellation in southwest France making hearty, fruity reds from Fer, a local grape. The wines are best drunk young. Some rosé wine is also made.

MARGARET RIVER Western Australian wine region first planted in the 1960s. The most successful wines are Bordeaux-style reds from Cabernet Sauvignon. Ripe, concentrated Chardonnays are also good.

MARGAUX AC Lovely, balanced red wines from this French AC in the Haut-Médoc area of Bordeaux are characterized by medium fruit and can age for 10 to 15 years.

MARLBOROUGH Sauvignon Blanc is the best wine from this region on New Zealand's South Island. Also first-rate are its rich Chardonnays, mineraly dry Rieslings, and increasingly good Pinot Noirs.

MARSALA DOC Once a highly respected fortified dessert wine, this specialty of the Italian island of Sicily has lost some popularity. An attempt is being made to revive the tradition of Vergine, a dry Marsala made from indigenous grapes Grillo, Catarratto, and Inzolia.

MARSANNAY AC French appellation centered on the village of the same name in Burgundy. It makes a perfumed and pleasing red wine, a dry rosé, and a fine dry white wine. These are good-value wines that deserve more attention.

MARSANNE Increasingly important white wine grape in the Rhône region of France, also widely grown in Australia. At its best, it makes wine with a rich, nutty character.

MARTINBOROUGH Cool-climate winegrowing region on the North Island of New Zealand, known for its Chardonnay and Pinot Noir, although Cabernet Sauvignon can also be quite good.

MASSON, PAUL Born in Burgundy, France, Masson (1859–1940) went to California in the 1870s and became involved in the wine industry, both in production and in promotion. His greatest contribution was in setting high technical standards for California wines in the decades before Prohibition.

MASTER OF WINE Professional qualification, abbreviated to MW, granted to those who pass the rigorous examination set by the London-based Institute of Masters of Wine.

MATARO Red wine grape grown since the nineteenth century in California. When it and other Rhône varieties became popular, winemakers there started calling it Mourvèdre. SEE MOURVÈDRE.

MATURATION Once a wine has been fully fermented, it undergoes a period of maturation in tank or barrel before bottling. For an inexpensive white wine, this may be a matter of weeks; for better whites and reds it may be months or years, depending on the quality and style of wine. During this period, the wine should soften and develop complexity. After bottling, the winemaker may decide to mature the wine for a few further months or years before release. A wine will mature more slowly in bottle than in tank or barrel. Once the wine leaves the winery, it might undergo a further period of maturation, or aging in bottle, from six months for a simple red wine to 20 years for a Classed Growth Bordeaux, a top-quality California Cabernet Sauvignon, or a vintage port.

MATURE When a wine has reached a plateau in the aging process, it is said to be mature—that is, it will get no better.

MAULE Large vineyard area in Chile's Central Valley, south of Santiago, best known for white wines made from Sauvignon Blanc and Chardonnay. Many decent red wines are also produced.

MAURY AC French appellation in the Roussillon area producing red *vin doux naturel*.

MAZUELA SEE CARIGNAN.

MCDOWELL VALLEY AVA Relatively cool winegrowing area in Mendocino County, California, which has a good reputation for Syrah. Other Rhône varieties have also been planted in this AVA.

MCLAREN VALE Area of South Australia noted for powerful Shiraz, Cabernet Sauvignon, Grenache, and full-bodied Chardonnay.

Mechanical harvesting

MECHANICAL HARVESTING There is still some concern about mechanical harvesting's impact on grape, and therefore wine, quality, but it is becoming increasingly accepted, especially in large-scale viticulture. The latest machines are gentler and do not cause as much vine damage as older versions.

MÉDOC Some of the world's most famous red wines are made in this French AC in Bordeaux. Médoc is a district encompassing several ACs, and it is also an AC in its own right. Médoc AC is the northern part of the district with fewer great châteaux. The famous châteaux are in the southern part nearer the city of Bordeaux in the Haut-Médoc AC or in one of the smaller communal ACs such as Pauillac and Margaux. Four of the five First Growths are from the Médoc, which is dominated by Cabernet Sauvignon, backed up by Merlot and Cabernet Franc.

MELON DE BOURGOGNE White grape best known for the Muscadet wines of the Loire Valley, France.

MENCIA Red grape grown in northwest Spain, where many believe it is related to Cabernet Franc. At its best, in Rías Baixas and Ribeiro, it makes a charming, perfumed wine.

MENDOCINO COUNTY Most northern of California's coastal region winegrowing areas, with AVAs ranging from the cool Anderson Valley AVA near the Pacific to the warm interior Redwood Valley AVA. Wine varieties and styles vary with the microclimates, but in general, red grapes dominate in terms of quality, especially Cabernet Sauvignon, Zinfandel, and a few Rhône varieties. However, Chardonnay can also be good, as can Pinot Noir in the cooler areas.

MENDOCINO RIDGE AVA Relatively new AVA in the far west of Mendocino County, above the Anderson Valley AVA. The first U.S. AVA to be noncontiguous, Mendocino Ridge AVA is a series of mountain peaks, with vineyards planted at a minimum of 1,200 feet (366 m) above sea level, almost exclusively to Zinfandel.

MENDOZA Center of Argentina's wine industry, producing 75 percent of the country's wine. The best grapes, grown in vineyards in the Andes foothills, produce powerful, concentrated red wines, especially from Malbec and Syrah. There are also white wines made from Chardonnay and Sauvignon Blanc.

MENETOU-SALON AC French Loire AC making intense, inviting Sauvignon Blanc and fresh, fruity Pinot Noir reds and rosés.

MERCAPTAN Faulty wine emitting a skunklike odor may be affected by an excess of the sulfurous compound mercaptan, which can form after fermentation. The wine producer should have taken action to avoid this.

MERCUREY AC Wine village in the Côte Chalonnaise, Burgundy, France, making lovely, fruity red wines from Pinot Noir and a smaller amount of rich Chardonnay.

MERITAGE Members of this U.S. trademarked organization agree to make a wine only from the red or white Bordeaux varieties and label it Meritage. Further, the wine may be made in a volume of no more than 25,000 cases and must be one of the two most expensive wines made by the producer. The organization, formed in the 1980s, has had indifferent success in promoting its wines, although some of the wines have been outstanding and most are well above average.

MERLOT Long an important grape in Bordeaux, where it is blended with Cabernet Sauvignon and Cabernet Franc, Merlot is increasingly planted all over the world. At its best, Merlot is more supple and silky than Cabernet Sauvignon and matures faster. This approachability has fuelled its popularity, particularly in the United States. However, Merlot is fairly site-specific, and if it is grown in the wrong place or overcropped, the fruit is often thin and light. It was originally planted in California as a blending partner for Cabernet Sauvignon, but plantings have increased dramatically, often in the wrong sites. Some of the best North American Merlots are from Napa Valley, in California, from Washington State, and from Long Island in New York. Merlot has done well in Chile, can do well in Tuscany, Italy, and is now widely planted in southern France too. In its home in Bordeaux, some of the most sought-after wines from Pomerol, such as Châteaux Pétrus and Le Pin, are Merlot-dominated.

MÉTHODE CHAMPENOISE SEE CHAMPAGNE METHOD.

MEURSAULT AC Best known region in the Côte de Beaune, Burgundy, for Chardonnay-based whites. At their best, the wines are big and buttery with rich, long-lasting fruit. Quality has varied in recent years, due to intense worldwide demand.

MEXICO Oldest wine-producing country in the Americas, undergoing a renaissance of quality wine production centered in Baja California. For centuries, the majority of Mexico's grapes have been used for brandy distillation or for cheap table wines. Some forward-looking producers in Baja have invested in the necessary technology and vineyard replanting to produce some first-rate wines. Look especially for Zinfandel, Nebbiolo, Cabernet Sauvignon, and Chenin Blanc.

MICHIGAN Vines grow on Lake Michigan's eastern shores, in the United States, where the lake moderates the harsh climate.

MICROCLIMATE In the narrow sense, microclimate defines the climate within a very restricted area, perhaps within the canopy of a single row of vines. In a more general sense, it describes specific conditions within a small growing area where, for example, all the vines are subject to cool ocean breezes.

MIDI Imprecise geographical term for the region of southern France roughly between the Pyrenees and the Rhône Valley.

MINERALY Tasting term for both a wine with a prized, refreshing complexity in certain light whites, and a rather unpleasant tinny flavor.

MINERVOIS AC Area in Languedoc, France, making sound, good-value red, white, and rosé wines for drinking young. The best wines are red and are filled with ripe, pleasing fruit, sometimes on the jammy side.

MIS EN BOUTEILLE AU CHÂTEAU/ MIS EN BOUTEILLE À LA PROPRIÉTÉ These and similar French terms indicate that the wine was bottled at the property where the wine was produced rather than being bottled somewhere else.

MISSION Name used in California for the original wine grape brought to the Americas by the Spanish in the sixteenth century. Probably the same grape as the País in Chile and the Criolla in Argentina, it makes indifferent wine.

MITTELRHEIN Small German wine region along the Rhine, beginning just south of Bonn. The vineyards, planted largely to Riesling, grow on steeply terraced hillsides. Much of the wine is used to make Sekt, the German sparkling wine.

MOELLEUX French word for mellow, used to describe a slightly sweet wine.

MOËT & CHANDON The Brut Imperial Nonvintage Champagne from the large house of Moët & Chandon is by far the biggest selling brand of French Champagne worldwide. Moët was the first Champagne house to launch a prestige cuvée back in the 1930s. The very expensive Dom Perignon remains highly sought after.

MOLDOVA Former member of the Soviet Union showing great potential for quality wine. There are already decent examples of Cabernet Sauvignon and Merlot wines being made in a Bordeaux-like style as well as some excellent Chardonnay. As technology advances and winemaking practices improve, the wines should get better and better.

MONASTRELL Spanish name for Mourvèdre.

MONBAZILLAC AC Appellation in southwest France making some excellent, age-worthy sweet white wines in a Sauternes style.

MONDAVI, ROBERT Mondavi (1913–) is the key figure in California wine in the twentieth century. His family wines are, for the most part, superb; but it is Mondavi himself who has been so important in setting quality standards. He has traveled tirelessly around the world as an ambassador for California wine. With joint ventures in Chile, in Italy, and with France's Rothschild family at Opus One in Napa, he has advanced the cause not only of California wine, but of all wine.

MONTAGNE-ST-ÉMILION AC Excellent red wine is made in this AC in Bordeaux, France. The wine has a rich earthiness when young, but it also has aging potential.

MONTAGNY AC French AC in the Côte Chalonnaise, Burgundy, producing good, flinty white wines for drinking young.

MONTECARLO DOC Italian region of Tuscany producing a range of good red wines from Sangiovese and Syrah, often blended, as well as some good, fruity dry white wines from Trebbiano, Sémillon, and Pinot Grigio.

MONTEFALCO DOC Excellent red wines made from Sangiovese can be found in this Tuscan DOC in Italy.

MONTEPULCIANO Red grape, planted in east central Italy, which makes a spicy, lively wine. It has no connection with the great red wine Vino Nobile di Montepulciano.

MONTEPULCIANO D'ABRUZZO DOC Area in Abruzzo, Italy, which is the prime spot for the Montepulciano grape. The wines range from fairly simple to more complex wines of some distinction. Most are good-value wines for early drinking.

MONTEREY COUNTY Large county on California's Central Coast making a wide range of wines. The best

AVAs are Carmel Valley, Santa Lucia Highlands, Chalone, and Arroyo Seco. The best wines include Chardonnay, Pinot Noir, and Cabernet Sauvignon. Monterey has many different soils and microclimates; growers in the region are beginning to search out the best vineyard sites, suggesting that wines should continue to improve.

MONTHÉLIE AC Good-value, quite appealing red wine from the Côte de Beaune, Burgundy, France. The fruit is more forward than in many Burgundy wines.

MONTILLA-MORILES DO Area of Andalucía, southern Spain, producing hugely underrated (and underpriced) sherry-style wines. A rich intensity in the flavors can be astonishing, especially in the dry Oloroso and the sweet wines, enriched with Pedro Ximénez.

MONTLOUIS AC Chenin Blanc grapes in this appellation in France's Loire Valley make wines similar to those in Vouvray AC.

MONTPELLIER, UNIVERSITY OF The French national school of viticulture forms part of this university. It is the center of a great deal of important research on vine diseases and pests.

MONTRACHET AC The white wine of the Grand Cru Montrachet, in the Côte de Beaune, Burgundy, France, is considered by those who are lucky enough to taste it to be the best Chardonnay in the world. It is rich and concentrated, with

lingering flavors that are quite distinct and memorable.

MONTRAVEL AC Appellation in southwest France making dry white wine from Sémillon.

MOREY-ST-DENIS AC Both the red and white wines can be very good, as they should be with five Grands Crus in this AC in the Côte de Nuits, Burgundy, France. Most of the wine is red, with abundant fruit that takes on a velvety texture as it ages. There is a little white wine.

MORGON AC A great deal of the wine from this Beaujolais Cru, in France, has soft, light cherry fruit which is attractive when young. In a good year and from the right vineyard, Morgon takes on a darker, almost lush quality.

MORNINGTON PENINSULA Cool, fairly new wine region in Victoria, Australia, showing great promise for Chardonnay and Pinot Noir.

MOROCCO Once a major supplier of bulk red wines, the wine industry in Morocco has declined.

MOSCATEL Spanish word for Muscat (mostly Muscat of Alexandria).

MOSCATO Italian name for the Muscat grape.

MOSCATO D'ASTI DOCG A delightful, semi-sparkling white wine made from grapes grown in the hills around Alba and Asti in Piedmont, northwest Italy. The wine, made from Moscato Bianco, is a delicate version of Asti made for very early drinking.

MOSCATO BIANCO SEE MUSCAT BLANC À PETIT GRAINS.

MOSCATO DI PANTELLERIA DOC The Muscat of Alexandria grape is used in this rich, intensely flavored dessert wine, made in the *passito* style from sun-dried grapes on the small island of Pantelleria, southwest of Sicily, Italy.

MOSEL-SAAR-RUWER A collection of German vineyard areas along the Mosel River and its tributaries, the Saar and the Ruwer. The best wines come from the middle Mosel, where some of the world's top Rieslings are made in the wine villages of Piesport, Brauneberg, Bernkastel, Graach, Urzig, and Erden. They have mineraly fruit with a honeyed finish that lingers in the mouth. There are also steely Rieslings made along the Saar and softer wines from the Ruwer.

MOSSEL BAY Close to the Indian Ocean in South Africa, Mossel Bay has only recently been planted with vineyards. It is believed to have good potential for cooler-climate grapes, such as Chardonnay, Riesling, and Pinot Noir.

MOULIN-À-VENT AC Beaujolais Cru consistently producing red wines that offer flavors in the Pinot Noir spectrum rather than Gamay, from which it is made. After a few years of aging, the best take on a chocolate-spice flavor.

MOULIS AC Smallest of the ACs within the Haut-Médoc, Bordeaux, France. The wines, all red, are very attractive at four to six years, but better examples can age for at least 20 years. They are very good value.

MOUNT BARKER Vineyard area within the vast wine region known as Great Southern, Western Australia. SEE GREAT SOUTHERN.

MOUNT VEEDER AVA The best grapes from this AVA in the southwest of Napa County, California, are undoubtedly Cabernet Sauvignon and Zinfandel, although some excellent Chardonnay is also made. The Cabernet can be a little hard when young but is capable of long-term aging.

MOURVÈDRE French name for a red wine grape sometimes known as Mataro in California; also grown in Australia, southern France, and Spain (as Monastrell). SEE MATARO.

MOUSSEUX French word for sparkling; it may be applied to both Champagne-method and bulk-processed wines.

MUDGEE Area in New South Wales, Australia, adjacent to Hunter Valley, beginning to get the attention it deserves with new plantings of

Cabernet and Shiraz. The region is slightly cooler than Hunter Valley.

MÜLLER-THURGAU Cold-weather grape developed in the nineteenth century, long thought to be a cross of Riesling and Silvaner.

MURRAY RIVER One of Australia's most important rivers, the Murray provides a ready source of irrigation for the vineyards. In Victoria, the area around the river is one of several in Australia where vast quantities of everyday wine are made from high-yielding vineyards.

MUSCADELLE White grape best known in Bordeaux, France, used in blends with Sémillon and Sauvignon Blanc, especially for the sweet ACs such as Sauternes, Barsac, and Cadillac. It is also found in Eastern Europe and Australia.

MUSCADET Alternative name for Melon de Bourgogne, the grape variety used to make Muscadet AC in the Loire Valley of France. SEE MELON DE BOURGOGNE.

MUSCADET AC Basic French AC for all Loire Valley Muscadet. There are three higher-quality subzones within the region, which are, in increasing size: Muscadet des Coteaux de la Loire AC, Muscadet Côtes de Grand Lieu AC, and Muscadet de Sèvre-et-Maine AC. All must use lower yields than Muscadet AC and may make and label their wines *sur lie*. Most of the best domaines are in the large Muscadet de Sèvre-et-Maine AC, which is named after the Loire tributaries of Sèvre and Maine. Good Muscadet has a modest zestiness. Most Muscadet wines should be drunk young, but those made *sur lie* have a richer, creamier texture and can age for longer.

MUSCAT Many authorities believe Muscat may have been the world's first wine grape. There are over 200 different branches of the Muscat family, making dozens of different styles of wine from dry through sweet to sparkling. Muscat is grown everywhere that wine is made.

MUSCAT OF ALEXANDRIA One of many grapes of the Muscat family, grown around the Mediterranean and all over the world. It sometimes makes very good wine on its own, or it may be used as a blending wine for its perfumed, lively fruit.

MUSCAT DE BEAUMES DE VENISE AC The most famous French fortified Muscat comes from the southern Rhône Valley. A luscious dessert wine with a very grapy flavor, it is made from Muscat Blanc à Petit Grains.

MUSCAT BLANC À PETITS GRAINS Generally considered the best version of the Muscat grape, it appears all over the world under various names including Brown Muscat and Muscat Canelli. It is the only variety of Muscat allowed in such diverse wines as sparkling Asti from northern Italy (where it is called Moscato Bianco), Muscat from Samos in Greece, and Liqueur Muscat from Australia. It is widely grown for the sweet Muscats of southern France and is the most prolific Muscat in California, too. It is known for its distinctly grapy characteristics.

MUSCAT CANELLI See Muscat Blanc à Petits Grains.

MUSCAT DE RIVESALTES AC Made from a combination of Muscat Blanc à Petits Grains and Muscat of Alexandria, this wine from the Roussillon region, southern France, has full, rich fruit, which results to some degree from the technique of leaving the juice on the skins for a period of time.

MUSCAT DE ST-JEAN-DE-MINERVOIS AC Small AC high in the hills of Languedoc, southern France, offering a superior fortified Muscat Blanc à Petits Grains.

MUSIGNY AC One of the great Grands Crus of Burgundy, France. Its outstanding red wines offer rich, deep fruit combined with a silky elegance that can be breathtaking.

MUST The grape juice, along with bits of stems, seeds, and pulp, that comes out of the crusher and begins fermentation.

NAHE German wine region named after the Nahe River, making Rieslings that are considered to be among Germany's finest.

NAPA COUNTY One of California's prime counties for premium wines. Some of Napa's more important AVAs are Napa Valley, Rutherford, Stags Leap District, Oakville, Howell Mountain, Diamond Mountain, Mt. Veeder, and Carneros, which it shares with Sonoma County.

NAPA GAMAY Long thought to be the Gamay of France, this red wine grape, grown in California, is now known to be, and is labeled as, Valdiguié, a minor grape variety.

NAPA VALLEY AVA Arguably the most famous AVA in North America, embracing most of Napa County. In fact, it takes in so much territory as to be meaningless as an AVA, and a process is underway of dividing it into smaller sub-AVAs. In general, the valley's best wines are Cabernet Sauvignon and Merlot, with Chardonnay and Pinot Noir in the cooler Carneros district beside San Francisco Bay.

Beringer winery, Napa Valley

NATIVE AMERICAN VINES Although vine species such as *Vitis labrusca* are used to make very ordinary table wines in the eastern United States, native American species such as *Vitis riparia* and *Vitis* *rupestris* have played a crucial role in the wine world in the form of *phylloxera*-resistant rootstocks, which are grafted onto *Vitis vinifera* all over the world.

NAVARRA DO Long in the shadow of the neighboring region of Rioja, northern Spain, Navarra has been busy establishing its own reputation during the last few years. Growers are planting standard international grape varieties, and excellent wine is being produced from Cabernet Sauvignon, Merlot, and Chardonnay. However, traditional varieties have not been neglected. Ripe, juicy red wines are being made from Tempranillo and lovely full-bodied rosés from Garnacha. Navarra is playing a major role in Spain's wine renaissance.

NEBBIOLO One of the world's great red wine grapes, used to make Barolo, Barbaresco, and many other fine Italian red wines, including the sometimes underrated Gattinara. Oddly enough, Nebbiolo has failed to gain much of a foothold outside Italy, perhaps because it is at its best in the cool vineyards of Piedmont, where it is usually the last grape picked when the autumn fogs are thick on the ground. (The name comes from *nebbia*, the Italian word for fog.) Although Nebbiolo is grown in California and Australia, the best versions outside Italy have come from Mexico, where they are grown at high elevations in the coastal hills of Baja California.

NEBBIOLO D'ALBA DOC Appellation in Piedmont, northwest Italy, producing a light style of Nebbiolo, intended for early drinking.

NÉGOCIANT French word for a merchant, someone who buys (usually) finished wine for resale. A *négociant éléveur* adds finishing touches to the wine, including aging in barrel and/or bottle, before selling it.

NEGROAMARO Italian wine grape whose name translates as the "black bitter one." It is the most important red variety in Apulia, southern Italy, where it can produce intensely flavored, high-alcohol wines.

NELSON Region on New Zealand's South Island producing good Chardonnay, Riesling, and Sauvignon Blanc.

NEMATODE Tiny roundworm found in most soils. One kind feeds on the roots of grape vines, damaging the efficiency of the root system and, as a result, seriously damaging the vineyards.

NERELLO Italian red wine grape grown on the island of Sicily, mainly used in blends.

NERO D'AVOLA One of the better red wine grapes in Sicily. It has good aging potential.

NEUSIEDLER SEE-HÜGELLAND Austria's best dessert wines come from this region within Burgenland. The vineyards are situated on the shores of the vast, shallow Neusiedler Lake, which provides ideal conditions for the formation of

noble rot, the fungus that allows luscious sweet wines to be made from a variety of local grapes, such as Scheurebe and Bouvier.

NEW MEXICO One of the oldest wine-producing states in the U.S. There are a few wineries in the area now producing drinkable wine.

NEW SOUTH WALES Australian state producing much less wine than it consumes. Growing conditions are mainly hot, and the best areas are Hunter Valley, Mudgee, Orange, and Cowra.

NEW WORLD Informal category including the wines of North and South America, South Africa, Australia, and New Zealand. The term also refers to a style of winemaking, characterized by up-front flavor and fruit, which originated in California, then spread to Australia and New Zealand. Some winemakers in these regions and countries consider the term patronizing.

NEW YORK STATE Although wine grapes have been grown in New York State since the seventeenth century, it was not until the middle of the twentieth century that a serious effort was made to grow vinifera grapes. Since then, progress has been enormous. The weather can present challenges—from freezing temperatures to hurricanes on Long Island. The most important AVAs are Finger Lakes, Hudson River, and Long Island, which has two AVAs, North Fork and The Hamptons. The most successful grape varieties, depending on the exact site, are Cabernet Franc, Merlot, Pinot Noir, Chardonnay, Riesling, and a few hybrids, such as Seyval Blanc. Excellent Icewine is made in the Finger Lakes AVA.

NEW ZEALAND The wines of New Zealand are quite distinctive, with intense fruit on the nose and on the palate. However, there is great diversity due to different soils, microclimates, and winemaking approaches. On the North Island, both Gisborne and Hawkes Bay do well with Chardonnay. The best reds are also from the North Island. Bordeaux styles from Cabernet Sauvignon, Merlot, and Cabernet Franc can be of high quality from Waiheke Island in Auckland and from Hawkes Bay; Pinot Noir from Martinborough, not far from Wellington, is becoming world-class. The largest wine region, Marlborough, is on the cooler South Island, where the best wines are whites made from Sauvignon Blanc and Chardonnay. The Sauvignon has shown tremendously pungent varietal fruit and has become a wine style in its own right. Elsewhere on the South

Island, Nelson, Canterbury, and Central Otago also do best with whites, especially Riesling, but some increasingly good Pinot Noirs are also appearing.

NIAGARA PENINSULA One of Canada's best winegrowing regions, the peninsula juts out from the bulk of Ontario between lakes Erie and Ontario, creating the same conditions as a cool-climate maritime region. The most successful white grapes are Chardonnay for dry white wine, Riesling, and the hybrid Vidal, which makes a very good Icewine. The best red wine is far and away Pinot Noir, but Cabernet Franc is also good.

NIEDERÖSTERREICH Largest wine region in Austria, producing some of the country's finest dry white wines, especially from Riesling. The best vineyards are close to the Danube River.

NIERSTEIN Village in the Rheinhessen, Germany's largest wine region, which boasts some spectacular vineyards. These are sited on the steep banks of the Rhine and form part of the Rheinterrasse. Top vineyard sites include Ölberg, Orbel, and Hipping. Both Riesling and Silvaner can be superb. The Nierstein name is also used for many inferior wines from the flatlands behind the village, which are part of the vast Gutes Domthal Grosslage vineyard.

NOBLE GRAPES This term has a historical meaning in Alsace, France, where it refers to the eight major permitted grape varieties. It is also widely used to refer to potentially high-quality varieties such as Chardonnay, Riesling, and Sauvignon Blanc for whites or Cabernet Sauvignon, Merlot, Pinot Noir, and Syrah for reds, which have been grown for many years in traditional fine wine regions, but are now planted all over the world. In wine regions where local, lesser-known grape varieties have been grown for many years, the introduction of so-called noble grapes is likely to indicate an improvement in the fortunes of the wines.

NOBLE ROT English term for *Botrytis cinerea*, a fungus that attacks ripe white wine grapes and, if the weather conditions are right, dries them out, resulting in intensely concentrated sweet grapes. The rot does not spread evenly through a vineyard, or even through a single bunch, so careful handpicking is necessary. All this leads to some of the world's great dessert wines,

Grapes with noble rot

such as French Sauternes, German Trockenbeerenauslese Rieslings, and Hungarian Tokay.

NONVINTAGE Wine that does not give a vintage year on the label. A large proportion of sparkling wine is nonvintage (NV), and so is sherry. A great deal of inexpensive jug-style wine is also NV.

NORTH CAROLINA Because the climate of this state is hot and humid, most of the vineyards are planted with sturdy native American *Vitis labrusca* varieties, notably Scuppernong. *Vitis vinifera* varieties rarely survive.

NORTH COAST AVA Umbrella AVA for grapes grown in coastal and near-coastal counties north of San Francisco, California, including Lake, Marin, Mendocino, Napa, Solano, and Sonoma counties.

NORTH FORK AVA Cool maritime-influenced AVA on Long Island, New York State. The best wines are made from Merlot and Cabernet Franc grapes.

NORTHERN SONOMA AVA Blanket California AVA joining the AVAs of Alexander Valley, Dry Creek Valley, Knights Valley, Russian River Valley, and its sub-AVAs, Chalk Hill and Green Valley.

NOSE Term used as a synonym for aroma and smell in wine tasting.

NOUVEAU French word for new, referring to a style of wine intended to be consumed within weeks of its production. The classic example is Beaujolais Nouveau.

NOVELLO Italian word for new, used as *nouveau,* above.

NUITS-ST-GEORGES AC Mostly red wine is made in this Côte d'Or AC in Burgundy, France. Like all Burgundies, the wines are wildly variable and quality depends on the producer. They are not wines for early drinking, needing at least three to five years to open up.

OAK Although other wood has been used for wine barrels, oak is now the top choice for storing and aging wine, not only because it is watertight but because of flavor characteristics it gives the wine. Modern consumers have come to like, and expect, the taste of oak in Chardonnay, for example. There are hundreds of oak species, but the three most important ones for wine are *Quercus alba,* known as American white oak, and *Quercus sessiliflora* and *Quercus robur,* both European oaks.

OAK CHIPS An alternative, cheaper method for adding oak flavor to wine, oak chips can be added to the wine at fermentation or at a later stage in the winemaking process.

OAKVILLE AVA Southern Napa Valley AVA, home to several California wineries including Robert Mondavi.

OAKY Tasting term for a wine that has obvious oak flavors.

O

D'OC, VIN DE PAYS Vast Vin de Pays area in the Languedoc region of France, which has attracted interest with a new wave of red and white wines in the international style. "Flying Winemakers" from Australia, plus a few from England, have set the pace.

OECHSLE German system for measuring the sugar content of must, or grape juice, the basis of the QbA and QmP systems.

OESTE Portuguese word for west, used as a collective name for six wine regions north of Lisbon on the west coast of Portugal.

OFF-DRY Wine that is only slightly sweet—not a dessert wine. There is no official definition for the term.

OHIO With a long history of wine production, the state of Ohio produces a few decent wines from vineyards in the Lake Erie AVA.

OILY Tasting term denoting an oily, rounded, viscous feeling on the palate, commonly found in buttery Chardonnay wine.

OKANAGAN VALLEY Exciting, fairly new winegrowing region with great potential in British Columbia, Canada. The climate is moderated by Okanagan Lake, allowing Cabernet Franc, Merlot, and Pinot Noir grapes to ripen, resulting in wines with vivid, zesty fruit; the white wines are even better.

OLD VINES The theory goes that older vines produce more concentrated grapes because, as the vine ages, production declines. In many cases, the theory seems to have a firm basis in reality, especially in the case of Zinfandel. Leading Zinfandel producers, such as Paul Draper at Ridge Vineyards in California, are working to clone old-vine Zinfandel for future production. At this point, there is no legal definition of how old a vine must be before it merits this designation.

OLD WORLD Term used in contrast to New World. Old World includes Europe, North Africa, the Near East, and Russia—countries that obviously have little in common regarding wine.

OLIFANTS RIVER WO South African wine-producing region bordering the Atlantic, dominated by large cooperatives.

OLOROSO One of the two basic styles of sherry, the other being Fino. A true Oloroso is a fortified dry wine with a rich, nutty taste. However, many commercial Olorosos are sweetened.

OLTREPÒ PAVESE DOC Italian region in the hills around Milan, which is a major source of sparkling wine from Pinot Noir. There is also some light red made from Barbera, and a little white from Riesling and other grapes, which is drunk locally.

ONTARIO Canadian winegrowing region with a climate similar to the Finger Lakes AVA just across the border in New York State. The climate is moderated by Lakes Erie and Ontario, and the best vineyards are on the Niagara Peninsula between the two lakes. The best wines are Pinot Noir, Cabernet Franc, Riesling, and Chardonnay. Excellent Icewine is made from Vidal, a hybrid grape.

OPORTO Second largest city in Portugal, situated at the mouth of the Douro River. Traditional port shippers have their lodges, or port-aging houses, in the Vila Nova de Gaia suburb, on the opposite side of the river.

OPPENHEIM One of the best wine villages in Germany's large Rheinhessen region, best known for Rieslings from vineyards such as Kreuz, on the Rheinterrasse, which benefit from the reflected sunshine from the Rhine River.

OPUS ONE Napa Valley joint venture between Robert Mondavi and the late Baron Philippe de Rothschild of Bordeaux's Château Mouton-Rothschild, which received immense publicity when the first vintage was released in 1983. A blend of red Bordeaux grape varieties, Opus One is good but it has not yet reached the standards of Mondavi's own Private Reserve Cabernet Sauvignon.

ORANGE Small, fairly newly planted wine region in New South Wales, Australia, showing particular promise for Chardonnay.

OREGON Pacific Northwest state that can be a difficult place to grow wine grapes, not because of the cold winters but because of rainy summers and autumns. The hilly Willamette Valley AVA is the largest and best growing area, particularly known for its Pinot Noir and white varieties. Further south, the Umpqua Valley and Rogue Valley AVAs are warmer and drier, and suit Bordeaux varieties and Chardonnay. Oregon shares the Walla Walla Valley and Columbia Valley AVAs with Washington State. Pinot Noir received generous praise in the early days, but quality has never been consistent. There is excellent Chablis-style Chardonnay, good Riesling, and Pinot Gris in an Alsatian style. The first Oregon winemakers had more enthusiasm than technical skills, and they also lacked funds for proper equipment. As the second generation of winemakers takes hold and investments from California and elsewhere roll in, Oregon's potential for great wine may be realized.

ORGANIC The term organic refers to vineyards that are farmed without the use of chemical fertilizers, herbicides, pesticides, or other

In organic farming, sheep sometimes graze in the vineyards.

sprays. Much emphasis is placed on creating a healthy, living soil by adding natural compost and manure. This should produce healthy plants that are subject to fewer diseases, reducing the need for chemical sprays. It is proving to be a valid approach, with many growers pleased by the results. In many parts of the world including France and California, there are certification programs for organic viticulture. They regulate what treatments are allowed in the vineyard and recommend practices in the winery, limiting the use of sulfur dioxide and other additives.

ORNELLAIA Top Super-Tuscan red wine, a Cabernet-Merlot blend, made in the Bolgheri DOC, Tuscany, Italy, by a branch of the Antinori family.

ORVIETO DOC Popular white wine from Umbria, traditionally made in a sweet or off-dry style, now usually dry. The dry version, based on a blend of Trebbiano, Grechetto, and other local grapes, is a fairly neutral wine, though it can be agreeable if drunk young. There is also an Orvieto Classico, which doesn't differ greatly from the regular bottlings.

OVERBERG WO South Africa's coolest growing region, producing good to very good Sauvignon Blanc, Chardonnay, and Pinot Noir.

OVERCROPPING Viticultural practice of allowing the vine to set too large a crop, resulting in grapes (and wine) with diluted, thin flavors. SEE YIELD.

OXIDATION Wine that is overexposed to oxygen is oxidized. The term should not be confused with maderized. SEE MADERIZATION.

PAARL WO South African region accounting for just under 20 percent of all South African vineyards. There is wide variety in soils and climates, and wines range from sweet sherry styles to dry sparklers and full reds.

PACHERENC DU VIC-BILH AC Quite distinctive white wines are made in this AC in Madiran, southwest France, from a blend of intensely flavored local grapes. At its best, the wine (made in both dry and sweet styles) has a deep yellow color and lovely fruit.

PACINES AVA Warm growing region in San Benito County, in California's Central Coast AVA. There are some interesting old vineyards for red wine, but most grapes go into inexpensive commercial blends.

PADTHAWAY Relatively cool South Australian growing region making very good Chardonnay and better-than-average Sauvignon Blanc. Traditionally a white wine area, it is beginning to produce some Shiraz with great promise.

PAÍS Name used in Chile for the grape first brought to the Americas by the Spanish. SEE MISSION.

PALATE Term used to describe the reaction to tasting wine (and food) in the human mouth; often divided into front, middle, and back palate.

PALETTE AC In this tiny French AC in Provence, in the hills near Aix-en-Provence, vineyards are a mix of Mediterranean varieties. At their best, the wines can be very good. Reds are concentrated and rich, rosés are full-bodied, and whites have a distinct, long-lasting flavor.

PALO CORTADO Rare style of dry sherry with an intense, nutty flavor that lies somewhere between an Amontillado and an Oloroso.

PALOMINO Basic white wine grape of Andalucía, southern Spain, used in sherry production. The best version is called Palomino Fino. Basic Palomino is also grown in South Africa, South America, Australia, and California. It makes a neutral table wine of little interest.

PARELLADA Spanish white wine grape used in Cava production. If not controlled, it produces a huge crop, which makes a neutral still white wine. If grown in a cool region on poor soils, it makes wine with a pleasing floral character.

PARKER, ROBERT Parker (1947–) is arguably the world's most influential and controversial wine writer. Through his bimonthly newsletter, *The Wine Advocate*, and a series of books, he has communicated his passion for wine to the wine-drinking public. Some criticize Parker's use of the 100-point system, but he has always cautioned readers to use the numbers only as a supplement to his commentary. Others lament that he has had too much influence on wine style, believing that winemakers try to make the sort of big, round wines that he will like.

PARRINA DOC Italian coastal region in Tuscany making a hearty red with Sangiovese in the blend, and a white based on Trebbiano.

PASO ROBLES AVA Large AVA on California's Central Coast, expanding rapidly, with new plantings of Rhône varieties, especially Syrah, leading the way. Red wines, notably Cabernet Sauvignon and Zinfandel, are best, although Chardonnay does well in cooler sites.

PASSITO Italian term denoting wines made from dried grapes.

PASTEUR, LOUIS In the mid-nineteenth century, French scientist Louis Pasteur (1822–1895) analyzed the process by which yeast changes the natural sugars present in grape juice into alcohol and carbon dioxide, and showed that this process could be controlled, thereby ushering in the era of modern winemaking.

PATRIMONIO AC On the island of Corsica, France, this AC produces good red and rosé wines from the local Nielluccio grape, and a white based on Vermentino.

PAUILLAC AC Arguably the world's best Cabernet Sauvignon blends come from this AC in the Haut-Médoc, Bordeaux, France. The only possible challenge could be California's Napa Valley. There are three First Growths in Pauillac—Lafite-Rothschild, Latour, and Mouton-Rothschild—as well as 15 other Classed Growths. The wines at their best have intense fruit and a silky balance. They also age longer than other Bordeaux reds and can last from 20 to 30 years.

Château Latour, Pauillac

PÉCHARMANT AC Very good red wines are made from Bordeaux varieties, mostly Merlot, in this AC in Bergerac, southwest France. At best, the wines have medium body, with lovely ripe fruit, and are capable of aging for up to ten years.

PEDRO XIMÉNEZ Important grape in Andalucía, Spain, where it is used in sherry production, and in Montilla-Moriles DO, where it is the most planted variety. The grape, which ripens to extreme sweetness, can be dried and made as a rich, intense dessert wine. If not dried, it makes a fairly ordinary dry table wine. The sweet must of Pedro Ximénez is used to sweeten some Oloroso and cream sherries.

PEMBERTON Relatively new wine region in Western Australia with great potential for cool-climate varieties like Chardonnay and Pinot Noir. Shiraz also looks promising.

PENEDÉS DO Region in Catalonia, northeast Spain. It is the heart of the Cava industry. Good still red and white wines are also made. Several firms in the area have taken a lead in technological innovations and in experimenting with international varieties. Excellent red wines are made from Garnacha and Tempranillo, as well as from Cabernet Sauvignon and Pinot Noir. The best white wines include Parellada, when made by cold fermentation, and Chardonnay.

PENFOLDS Vast Australian winery, part of the giant Southcorp group, making a wide range of wines including what is arguably Australia's top wine, Grange (formerly Grange Hermitage), the ageworthy Shiraz. Penfolds has a reputation for reliability in all price ranges.

PENNSYLVANIA Lake Erie AVA stretches from Ohio through Pennsylvania to New York State, making it the only tri-state AVA. The lake moderates the climate, allowing reasonable wines to be made.

PÉRIGNON, DOM Benedictine monk Dom Pérignon (1639–1715) is credited with inventing Champagne. In fact, sparkling wine of one kind or another had been around for centuries before Brother Pierre Pérignon was laboring in the vineyards and cellars of Champagne. He did introduce many practices still followed today, such as pruning for low yields, and he also played a role in developing the art of blending wine from many different vineyards into a single cuvée, an important part of modern Champagne production.

PERNAND-VERGELESSES AC Relatively unknown village in the Côte de Beaune, Burgundy, France, producing both red and white wine. The reds have pleasing fruit and are capable of moderate aging. The whites have an attractive mineraly character and are a bargain.

PERRICONE Sicilian grape variety producing soft, red wines. It may also be called Pignatello.

PERU The first vineyards in Peru were planted under the direction of conquistador Francisco Pizarro in 1547. Most modern plantings are in the Ica Valley on the central coast, with much of the crop being used for distillation. Most standard international grape varieties are planted, producing some sound, drinkable table wines.

PESSAC-LÉOGNAN AC French AC in Bordeaux, created in 1987 out of the northern part of the original Graves AC. The new AC contains all of the Classed Growths of Graves. It is known for its fine red wines, but also makes some first-class whites.

PÉTILLANT French word for a slightly sparkling wine.

PETIT CHABLIS AC French AC in Burgundy, which includes vineyards on lesser soils and sites in Chablis. Its wines should be drunk young.

PETIT CHÂTEAU Informal grouping of Bordeaux wine producers, not included in any classification. The wines can be very good value.

PETIT MANSENG Low-yielding white grape variety which ripens late, drying on the vine. It produces highly concentrated grapes particularly used for the sweeter wines of Jurançon AC and Pacherenc du Vic-Bilh AC. It is now being planted elsewhere in France (in the Languedoc) and in California.

PETIT VERDOT One of the classic red wine grapes of Bordeaux, Petit Verdot is of particular importance in the Haut-Médoc, where it is used to add color and aroma to the blend. There is some Petit Verdot planted in California, Australia, and Chile; in all of these regions, it is almost always a blending grape.

PETITE SIRAH Red wine grape producing huge, deeply colored wines with a black-pepper character. Often part of a field blend with Zinfandel,

Petite Sirah may be added in small amounts to other red wines for color. It is widely planted in South America and California.

PEYNAUD, ÉMILE Few people have had a greater impact on modern winemaking than French enologist Émile Peynaud (1912–). From his base at the University of Bordeaux, Peynaud studied the winemaking process in painstaking detail. He always emphasized that good wine begins in the vineyard. Peynaud's influence has been spread by the many students he taught.

PFALZ German wine region, formerly called the Rheinpfalz, important both in terms of quality and quantity. Much of the wine is average or sub-average, but there are some high-quality wines. Excellent Riesling is produced around the villages of Wachenheim and Forst. In the warmer Südliche Weinstrasse, there is superb Pinot Noir, Pinot Gris, and Gewürztraminer.

PHYLLOXERA Root-eating louse that lives in the soil. It chews away at vine roots until the vine eventually dies from lack of water and nourishment. *Phylloxera* is native to the East Coast of the United States, where vine roots developed resistance to the tiny louse and managed to survive. The roots of the European vines, *Vitis vinifera*, were not resistant, and when *phylloxera* arrived in Europe in the late 1800s, and then returned to California via Europe, it devastated the vineyards. It took several years before viticulturists learned to graft vinifera vines

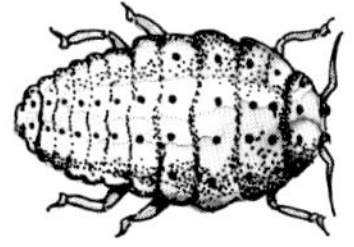

Phylloxera

onto resistant American rootstock. Recent devastating outbreaks of *phylloxera* in California have been caused by planting on rootstock that was not fully resistant.

PIC ST-LOUP AC Some of the best red wines from France's Languedoc region are made in this AC, from Syrah, Grenache, and Mourvèdre.

PIEDMONT Arguably Italy's most important region for quality red wines. Situated in the northwest, Piedmont is the home of the Nebbiolo grape which makes the great wines of Barolo and Barbaresco. Good, if somewhat lesser, wine is made from Barbera and Dolcetto grapes. Appealing white wines are based on the Cortese grape, and there are lively Asti sparkling wines made from Moscato.

PIERCE'S DISEASE Where this vine disease is endemic, it causes greater vine destruction than *phylloxera*. Native to North and South America, it is a bacterial disease spread by small insects called sharpshooters. Once a vine is infected, the leaves develop dead spots and drop off, and the entire vine dies within two to five years. The disease spreads rapidly, and at present there is no satisfactory chemical control, nor are there any resistant vinifera varieties.

PIGNATELLO See Perricone.

PINOT BIANCO Italian name for Pinot Blanc.

PINOT BLANC Although originating in Burgundy, France, Pinot Blanc's true home is in Alsace, where it is becoming increasingly important. It has been widely planted in Italy, where it is called Pinot Bianco, and is planted everywhere in central Europe. It is also proving popular in California and Oregon. The reason for the grape's success is simple: It has a clean, refreshing flavor with appley-spicy tones and good weight on the palate.

PINOT GRIGIO Italian name for Pinot Gris.

PINOT GRIS White wine grape producing fairly rich, slightly spicy wines with a fat mouthfeel. Probably the best Pinot Gris comes from Alsace, France, where it makes a deep golden wine. It is also very good in Oregon, where it is made in much the same style as in Alsace. In Italy, where it is called Pinot Grigio, Pinot Gris makes a good dry white.

PINOT MEUNIER Red wine grape used as part of the classic blend for Champagne. It is the most widely planted grape in the Champagne region of France.

PINOT NERO Italian name for Pinot Noir.

PINOT NOIR Grape yielding one of the world's most exciting wines. A difficult grape to grow, it can also be temperamental in the wine cellar. However, when successful, it can give great pleasure. At its best, Pinot Noir offers a light cherry-raspberry-strawberry range of fruit, with an inviting silky texture. The Pinot Noir of Burgundy, France, is generally cited as the best in the world, but outstanding Pinot Noir is also made in California and Oregon, and to some extent in New Zealand. These newer versions have, in general, a greater intensity of fruit than is typically found in Burgundy. For the most part, Pinot Noir does not age as long as Cabernet Sauvignon. Much of its charm is youthful and fruit-driven.

PINOTAGE Cross of Pinot Noir and Cinsaut. A specialty of South Africa, where it was developed in the 1920s, at its best it has rich fruit, a blend of tropical nuances, plum, and cherry, that is utterly different from any other wine grape.

PLONK Term used in England, and now being heard in the United States, which seems to be losing some of its negative meaning and now denotes a basic wine that is passable for everyday drinking.

POMACE Term for everything left over after pressing and fermentation: the skins, seeds, and pulp.

POMEROL AC Merlot-based wine in this AC in Bordeaux, France, has tremendous appeal and is much sought after. The wine is rich and velvety, with lingering flavors, giving immediate pleasure but also capable of some aging. Two of the

Château Pétrus in Pomerol, France

world's most expensive wines, Château Pétrus and Château Le Pin, are from Pomerol.

POMINO DOC Small Italian wine region near Florence, Tuscany, which has traditionally made red wine from Cabernet Sauvignon, Merlot, and Sangiovese and white wine from Trebbiano, Pinot Bianco, and Chardonnay.

POMMARD AC Red wine AC in the Côte de Beaune, Burgundy, France, producing wine with rounded, almost meaty flavors, capable of aging for a minimum of ten years.

PORT Fortified wine made by adding brandy or other spirit to the fermenting grape must to kill the yeasts and stop fermentation before the natural grape sugar has all been consumed by the yeasts. This makes a sweet, high-alcohol wine. True port is from Portugal's Douro Valley, but port-style wines are made in many other countries.

PORT DOC Region of port production, centered on the Douro River in northern Portugal, inland from the city of Oporto. There are more than 80 different grape varieties authorized for port production. Most vineyards contain a bewildering mixture of grapes. There are several different styles of port, but they can be divided into two basic types: the vintage, or bottle-aged ports, which are declared only in exceptional years and are bottled after two years in barrel; and the wood ports. Vintage ports are very long-lived, with 20 years of aging common. The wood ports are ready to drink when bottled.

PORTUGAL Portugal offers a wide variety of wines and wine styles. There are delicious, lively Vinho Verdes from the north; rich port wines and interesting table wines from the Douro; red wines from the center, Dão and Bairrada; rustic, hearty wines from Estremadura; and promising new red wines from Alentejo, in the south. In addition, one of the world's most respected fortified wines is produced on the island of Madeira. Growers and winemakers in Portugal have, for the most part, made the decision to stick to the native grape varieties,

Evolution of port bottle shapes

producing wines that truly exhibit the national character.

POTTER VALLEY AVA The most northerly of California's North Coast AVAs. Located in Mendocino County, it is a fairly hot region, yet some success has been achieved with Chardonnay, Riesling, and Pinot Noir by planting vineyards at higher elevations.

POUILLY-FUISSÉ AC Appellation in Mâconnais, Burgundy, France, making good Chardonnays, which are sometimes overpriced.

POUILLY-FUMÉ AC At their best, these Sauvignon Blanc-based white wines from France's Loire Valley have an attractive, flinty bite. If overcropped, which they too often are, the wines are thin and insipid.

POUILLY-LOCHÉ AC Village in the Mâconnais, Burgundy, France, near Fuissé, making Chardonnay-based white wine that is rarely as good as Pouilly-Fuissé.

POUILLY-SUR-LOIRE AC Wines for drinking young are made in this French Loire AC from Chasselas.

POUILLY-VINZELLES AC The village of Vinzelles, in the Mâconnais region of Burgundy, France, simply added the name Pouilly to its own in an attempt to cash in on the popularity of Pouilly-Fuissé.

POWDERY MILDEW One of the most widespread fungal diseases to attack the vine, powdery mildew originated in North America, from where it spread to Europe, devastating the vineyards in the nineteenth century. Today, attacks are prevented or controlled mainly through the use of chemical sprays, though modern planting methods can also help prevent its attack.

PRÄDIKAT Word denoting quality levels of wine in Germany and Austria, based on grape sugar levels. It assumes that the sweeter the juice, the higher the quality. SEE QMP.

PREMIER CRU Quality level just below Grand Cru for French ACs.

PREMIÈRES CÔTES DE BLAYE AC Appellation in Bordeaux, France, producing good Merlot-based red wines, enjoyable while young but capable of limited aging.

PREMIÈRES CÔTES DE BORDEAUX AC Traditionally this French Bordeaux region's reputation was based on its sweet whites, but there are now some very pleasing reds and rosés being made, based chiefly on Merlot.

PRESS Winemaking equipment that separates grape juice from grapes by using pressure.

PRESS WINE Red wine pressed from pomace by a wine press. This wine can be very tannic and is sometimes blended into free-run wine to add body and tannin.

PRIMEUR French word applied to new wine, as in Beaujolais Nouveau, which is known as a *primeur* wine. SEE ALSO EN PRIMEUR.

PRIMITIVO Grown chiefly in Apulia, southern Italy, this red wine grape is thought to be the same as the Zinfandel of California.

PRIORATO DO Almost-forgotten DO in northeast Spain, undergoing a revival. Garnacha and Cariñena, planted on rocky hillside terraces, produce a small amount of concentrated red wine, capable of extended aging. Despite the success of the native vines, at least one large Spanish wine company has bought land in the area and planted Merlot and Cabernet Sauvignon.

PRODUCED AND BOTTLED BY Phrase on a U.S. wine label meaning that the named winery crushed and fermented at least 75 percent of the wine in the bottle.

PROHIBITION A ban on alcohol consumption in the United States from 1920 to 1933. During that period, however, wine was allowed at religious ceremonies; it could be prescribed as a medicine; and households could make up to 200 gallons of wine a year.

PROSECCO DI CONEGLIANO-VALDOBBIADENE DOC Flavorful sparkling wine from the Prosecco grape, very popular in the cafés of Venice and Verona, is made in this appellation in northeast Italy. Small amounts of still wine are also made.

PROVENCE Ancient wine area of France best known for wines of the Bandol, Bellet, Cassis, and Palette ACs, although a vast amount of basic table wine is also produced.

PRUNING Viticultural practice of trimming the vine while it is dormant to prepare it for new growth.

PUGET SOUND AVA Many of Washington State's wineries are in this coastal area AVA, but few grapes are grown there. Most grapes come from east of the Cascade Mountains.

PUGLIA SEE APULIA.

PUISSEGUIN ST-ÉMILION AC Attractive red wines are made in this small AC in Bordeaux, France.

PULIGNY-MONTRACHET AC French AC in the Côte de Beaune, Burgundy, one of the finest in the world for Chardonnay. There are four Grands Crus—Le Montrachet,

Bâtard Montrachet, Bienvenues-Bâtard-Montrachet, and Chevalier-Montrachet—and several Premiers Crus. The wines, which are powerful and richly flavored, should be kept for three to five years before drinking and, if from a good vintage, can age for 20 years or more. A tiny amount of red wine is also made.

PUNT Indentation in the bottom of a wine bottle, originally designed as an area for sediment to collect.

PUPITRE Champagne and sparkling wines made by the Champagne method were traditionally stacked in wooden racks, called *pupitres*, where they underwent *remuage* to shake the yeast deposits down into the bottle necks for later removal. Today, mechanized metal cages called *giropalettes* are often used in place of *pupitres*. SEE REMUAGE.

PUTTONYOS Measure of sweetness for Hungary's Tokay dessert wines. Six *puttonyos* is the sweetest.

PYRENEES Named after the mountain range between France and Spain, this Australian wine district in the state of Victoria makes minty Cabernet and Shiraz and good Chardonnay and sparkling wine.

QBA Abbreviation of Qualitätswein betstimmter Anbaugebiete, a German quality wine from one of 13 designated regions. QbA is a lower category than QmP.

QMP Abbreviation of Qualitätswein mit Prädikat. A higher ranking than QbA, QmP indicates a quality wine of distinction.

QUARTS DE CHAUME AC Intense, rich, sweet wines are made from Chenin Blanc in this French Loire Valley AC. Production is small, but the wines are worth seeking out.

QUEENSLAND Hot eastern Australian state making small amounts of Cabernet Sauvignon, Shiraz, and Chardonnay for everyday drinking.

QUINCY AC French Loire Valley AC making intensely flavored dry white wine from Sauvignon Blanc.

QUINTA Portuguese word for farm or wine estate.

RACKING Refers to the process of moving wine off the sediment in the bottom of a barrel or tank into a clean empty barrel or tank.

RANCIO Word denoting a fortified wine that has been deliberately maderized by exposure to oxygen and heat. The wines have an intense nutty/buttery smell that can resemble rancid butter. The best come from southern France and from Catalonia, Spain.

RAPEL VALLEY Merlot, Cabernet Sauvignon, and other red varieties do best in this area south of Santiago in Chile's Central Valley.

RASTEAU AC Appellation in the Rhône Valley, France, known for fortified red or white wines, sometimes made in a *rancio* style. Red, white, and rosé table wine from the area is sold as Côtes du Rhône Villages. SEE RANCIO.

RECIOTO Sweet wine made from dried grapes in northeast Italy.

RECIOTO DELLA VALPOLICELLA DOC Very good sweet red wine made in the Veneto region of Italy from grapes that have been dried on straw mats from harvest until January. The wines have delicious fruit and are best drunk young. SEE AMARONE DELLA VALPOLICELLA DOCG.

RECIOTO DI SOAVE DOC A few producers in the Soave area in the Veneto of northeast Italy take the best Garganega grapes, in particular, to be dried after harvest for production of a delicate, honeyed sweet white wine, often with an almond flavor.

RÉCOLTE French word meaning harvest. A *récoltant* is a grower.

REFOSCO Refreshing red wine grape, at its best in northeast Italy, where it makes a lively, fruity wine. A small amount of Refosco is produced in California.

REGIONS I–V SEE HEAT SUMMATION SYSTEM.

RÉGNIÉ AC French Beaujolais Cru making light red wine.

REGUENGOS DOC Appellation in Alentejo, southern Portugal with good potential for fruity red wines.

REMUAGE Step in the production of Champagne-method sparkling wines that involves gently turning the bottles, stacked in racks called *pupitres*, to move the sediment left from secondary fermentation into the neck of the bottle for disgorging (*dégorgement*). Traditionally *remuage* is done by hand, but today the process is often mechanized.

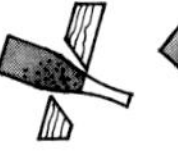

Bottles in *pupitres* at various stages of *remuage*

RESERVA Spanish and Portuguese word for wines of above-average quality that meet certain aging requirements. In Portugal, the wine must have an alcohol content of at least one-half percent above the minimum regional requirement. There is some regional variation in Spain, but a red wine should have a minimum of three years in cask and bottle, including at least one year in cask. White wines should have at least two years in cask and bottle, including six months in cask.

RESERVE U.S. term denoting a wine of exceptional quality. It has no legal definition.

RÉSERVE French term applied to a wine of high quality. There is no legal definition.

RESIDUAL SUGAR(S) Refers to the total amount of sugar remaining in a wine following fermentation, expressed as a percentage or as grams per liter.

RESVERATROL Natural antioxidant compound in red wine which may provide protection against heart conditions and other life-threatening diseases.

RETSINA Style of white and rosé wine common in Greece. At its best it is oily, with a refreshing crispness. The small amount of pine resin added to the wine provides a cooling effect on the palate. Drink as young as possible.

REUILLY AC Appellation in the Loire Valley region of France, producing very good Sauvignon Blanc and a small amount of Pinot Noir and Pinot Gris.

RHATSITELI White wine grape widely planted in Eastern Europe and in the former Soviet Union. There is also a little planted in China and in cooler regions of the United States. The wine has good fruit and acidity.

RHEINGAU German wine region noted for Riesling. There are a number of old, well-known estates, but younger winemakers are bringing new life into the area with some very stylish Rieslings and a small amount of Pinot Noir.

RHEINHESSEN Large German wine region producing wines of varied style and quality. The best wines come from the Bereich Nierstein district on the Rheinterrasse.

RHEINTERRASSE Best part of Germany's Rheinhessen, bordering the Rhine River. The vineyards face southeast and benefit from sun reflecting off the river's surface, an ideal situation for ripening Riesling grapes, in particular.

RHÔNE VALLEY One of France's most important wine regions. Vineyards follow the course of the Rhône River south of Lyon. In the northern reaches of the valley, the Syrah grape yields superb wine in the Côte-Rôtie, Hermitage, St-Joseph, Crozes-Hermitage, and Cornas. There are very few white wines, but superb wine from the Viognier grape is made at Condrieu AC and Château-Grillet AC. Farther south, the steep slopes of the northern Rhône give way to warmer flatlands, where great quantities of good red, white, and rosé wine are made under the Côtes du Rhône and Côtes du Rhône-Villages designations. Excellent red wines are produced in the south at the Châteauneuf-du-Pape AC. The great dessert wine Muscat de Beaumes-de-Venise AC is also from the southern Rhône.

RÍAS BAIXAS DO This appellation in Galicia, northwest Spain, makes some of the most exciting white wines anywhere, based on the Albariño grape. The best have rich, focused fruit and wonderful aroma.

RIBATEJO This large appellation on the Tagus River, inland from Lisbon, makes fruity reds which have improved in the past few years.

RIBEIRO DO The wines from this DO in Galicia, northwest Spain, have improved greatly recently, especially the whites, which have benefited from plantings of Torrontés and Treixadura grapes. The red wines are unremarkable.

RIBERA DEL DUERO DO Mainly a red wine appellation (there is also a little rosé) in the Castilla-León region of Spain. Based on Tempranillo grapes, locally called Tinto Fino or Tinto del País, the wines have a rich, velvety texture and warm fruit rivaling the best of Rioja. There is some Cabernet Sauvignon and Merlot, which is blended with the Tempranillo.

Vega Sicilia, Ribera del Duero

RICASOLI, BETTINO The Ricasoli family has long been important in the wine business. Bettino Ricasoli (1809–1880) was a dominant figure in Tuscany in the nineteenth century. An innovator in viticulture and enology, he invented the grape blend for Chianti, which remained unchanged until recently.

RICH Positive tasting term for a wine with great depth of fruit and a powerful, long finish.

RICHEBOURG AC Grand Cru in the Côte de Nuits, Burgundy, France, producing rich, deeply flavored red wine, which is capable of extended aging.

RIDDLING See Remuage.

RIDGE VINEYARDS Paul Draper, winemaker at Ridge since 1969, has established this Santa Clara, California, winery as one of the world's top estates. Over the decades, he has focused on the Monte Bello Cabernet Sauvignon from Ridge's own estate and on single-vineyard field blends based on old-vine Zinfandel. Ridge wines have great power, but are always balanced and representative of the *terroir*.

RIESLING This white wine grape is Germany's greatest contribution to the wine world. It excels in cool regions. The best Rieslings have a perfumed nose and lively acidity. The range is from bone-dry wines to rich, honey-sweet dessert wines. Excellent dry Rieslings are made in Alsace, France; in Oregon, in the Pacific Northwest; in New York State; and in Canada. Top Rieslings from Germany, Australia, and California are usually off-dry or sweet.

RIESLING ITALICO Grape variety widely planted in northern Italy, where it makes a dry wine. The grape is known as Welschrizling in central Europe. In Austria, it is used for a dessert wine.

RIOJA DOC At their best, the red wines from this appellation in northern Spain offer abundant fruit balanced with sweet oak and good tannic structure, although quality tends to be uneven. The main grape used is Tempranillo, but Garnacha, Mazuelo (the local name of the Cariñena grape, called Carignan in France), and Graciano, as well as the white wine grape Viura, can be incorporated as part of the blend. Barrel-aging is an important characteristic of Rioja red wines. Red wines with Crianza or Reserva on the label must spend at least one year in oak, while a Gran Reserva must spend two years. Rioja white wines are now based chiefly on the Viura grape, which is called Macabeo in the rest of Spain. Traditional Rioja white wine is also aged in barrels.

Remelluri estate, Rioja

RIPASSO Italian technique of adding the lees of Recioto wines to Valpolicella to give extra alcohol and flavor.

RISERVA Italian term applied to reserve, or special, wines. Each region has its own regulations.

RIVERINA Area in New South Wales making much of Australia's basic table wine and some good sweet wines from grapes affected by noble rot. Also known as the Murrumbidgee Irrigation Area.

RIVERLAND A large winegrowing region along the Murray River, in Australia. Inexpensive table wines are produced there.

RIVESALTES AC French AC in the Languedoc-Roussillon region, producing good fortified wine from the Grenache grape. It may also be made in a *rancio* style. SEE MUSCAT DE RIVESALTES.

RIVIERA LIGURE DI PONENTE DOC The best wine from Liguria, on Italy's Mediterranean coast, is a light, fruity white made from the Vermentino grape. There is also a good red wine made from Dolcetto.

ROBERTSON WO This warm inland area in the Cape Province of South Africa used to be known only for inexpensive wines. However, its soil has a high limestone content, which is proving ideal for growing Chardonnay and Sauvignon Blanc in particular. Good Champagne-method sparkling wines are made too. Quality is rising.

ROERO DOC Appellation in the Piedmont area of Italy, where fruity red wine made from the Nebbiolo grape has long been a favorite. A white, made from the Arneis grape, is also very appealing. The red wine is called Roero and the white is known as Roero Arneis.

ROGUE VALLEY AVA Recently planted, relatively warm AVA in Oregon, just north of the California border. Cabernet Sauvignon and Chardonnay look promising.

LA ROMANÉE-CONTI AC Probably the best red Grand Cru in Burgundy, France—certainly the most expensive—owned outright by Domaine de La Romanée-Conti. A tiny vineyard in the Côte de Nuits, only about 4.5 acres (1.8 hectares) in size, it produces incredibly rich, complex wines with pure fruit. This is a Burgundy that ages very well; in many vintages it does not reach its prime for 20 to 25 years.

ROMANÉE-ST-VIVANT AC Excellent French Burgundy Grand Cru in the Côte de Nuits offering balanced wines of great depth and power.

ROMANIA This country on the Black Sea can produce good wines from Cabernet Sauvignon, Merlot, and Chardonnay, but quality has fluctuated widely. With modernization, however, Romania's potential may soon be realized.

RONDINELLA One of three red grape varieties used to make Valpolicella and Bardolino wines in northeast Italy. Not as fine as the Corvina grape.

ROOTSTOCK Very few vines are now planted on their own roots because of the threat of *phylloxera*. Instead, vines are grafted onto resistant rootstock, either in the field or in nurseries.

ROSADO Spanish for rosé wine.

ROSATO Italian for rosé wine.

ROSÉ Rosé wines range in color from a very light pink to light red. The best rosés come from southern France and from Spain. There are two basic methods for making rosé. The first, and many believe the best, is to leave the fermenting wine on its skins for a very short time, just long enough to pick up the desired color, then to drain away the juice. The second method, used for cheap rosé wines, involves adding a little finished red wine to finished white wine. Rosé made in this way does not have the fresh, lively fruit of the former method. However, most rosé Champagne (even the best) is made by blending.

ROSÉ D'ANJOU AC French Loire Valley appellation making inexpensive rosé in an off-dry style.

ROSÉ DE LOIRE AC Fresh, lively dry rosé wine is made in this large AC in the Loire Valley of France.

ROSÉ DES RICEYS AC Dark, still rosé wine is made from Pinot Noir in this AC in Champagne, France.

ROSEWORTHY The Roseworthy Agricultural College, South Australia, has made important contributions to viticulture and enology in Australia. It is primarily responsible for the high technical standards of Australian winemakers. In 1991, it merged with the University of Adelaide.

ROSSO Italian word for red, as in *vino rosso.*

ROSSO CONERO DOC Much-improved Italian appellation in the Marches region on the Adriatic coast making a very good red wine from the Montepulciano grape. Sangiovese may also be used.

ROSSO DI MONTALCINO DOC Light and lively junior version of the famed Tuscan red wine, Brunello di Montalcino (a younger bottling of that Italian wine). Drink within three to five years.

ROSSO DI MONTEPULCIANO DOC A fruity, junior version of Vino Nobile di Montepulciano, made in Tuscany, Italy. It is bottled earlier and should be drunk younger.

ROSSO PICENO DOC Red wines from this Adriatic appellation of Italy are similar to Rosso Conero but based mainly on Sangiovese rather than Montepulciano. They lack the depth of fruit of Conero.

ROTHSCHILD, BARON PHILIPPE DE The Rothschild family has held property in Bordeaux since 1853, and Baron Philippe (1902–1988) greatly expanded the family's interests there. He was one of the most influential men in Bordeaux in the twentieth century, establishing the importance of château bottling, building the Mouton Cadet line into one of the world's most successful wine brands, adding Château d'Armailhac (formerly Château Mouton Baronne Philippe) and Château Clerc Milon in Pauillac, and establishing Opus One, an important joint venture in California with Robert Mondavi. However, the Baron is perhaps best known for his fight, which lasted decades, to elevate the flagship, Château Mouton-Rothschild, from Second to First Growth status in the 1855 classification, which he finally succeeded in doing in 1973, and for maintaining the high standard of quality for the wine. SEE OPUS ONE.

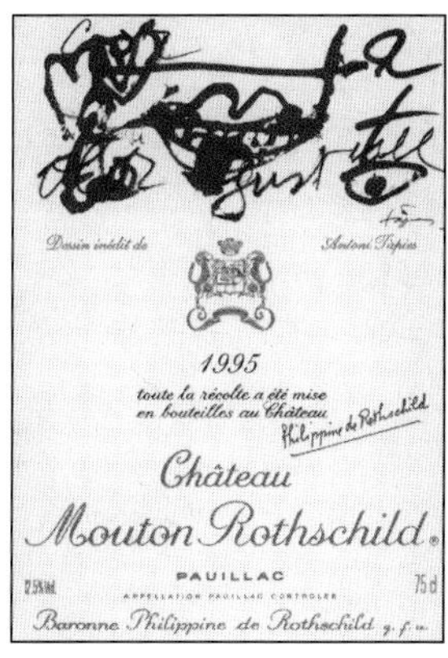

ROUGE French word for red, as in *vin rouge.*

ROUSSANNE At its best in France's Rhône Valley, where it is often blended with Marsanne, this grape makes perfumed, elegant white wine. Plantings of Roussanne are expanding into southern France, and there is a little grown in Tuscany, Italy, and also in California.

ROUSSILLON Usually seen as merely a suffix to Languedoc, this southern French region has a distinct personality and wine style. The best wines are red and are made from the standard Mediterranean varieties. There are good *vins doux naturels* too. White wine made from Macabeo is often blended into the red wines. There has been some interest in wines made from international varieties, mostly planted along the coast.

RUBY CABERNET Cross of Cabernet Sauvignon and Carignan developed in California in the 1940s. The idea was to combine Cabernet character with the productivity and heat resistance of Carignan. As a varietal, it makes a wine with good fruit but a rather short finish. The grape is now being grown in South Africa and Central and South America.

RUBY PORT Style of port left in barrel for two to three years. At its best, it should be juicy and fruity.

RÜDESHEIM Village in Rheingau, Germany, known for aromatic Rieslings from famous sites like Berg Schlossberg and Berg Roseneck.

RUEDA DO White wine appellation in Castilla-León, Spain, known for distinctive wines made from the Verdejo grape and for fruity and lively Sauvignon Blanc.

RULLY AC Much-improved AC in the Côte Chalonnaise, Burgundy, France, making good-quality white and red wine at a reasonable price.

RUSSIAN RIVER VALLEY AVA Many people believe that the best California Pinot Noir is produced in this cool winegrowing region in Sonoma County, California. The Chardonnay is also very good, and both grapes are used as a base for excellent sparkling wines.

Dehlinger wine estate, Russian River Valley

RUTHERFORD AVA World-class Cabernet Sauvignon comes from this appellation in California's Napa Valley. The best vineyards for Cabernet are planted on well-drained alluvial soils running along the western edge of the valley from Yountville in the south to St. Helena in the north. There is also good Merlot and exciting Sauvignon Blanc made from vineyards close to the Napa River. The best Cabernet Sauvignon wines produced in the Rutherford AVA are said to have a "dusty" taste.

RUTHERGLEN District in the state of Victoria, Australia, producing powerful, rich Cabernet Sauvignon, Shiraz, and delicious mouth-filling fortified dessert wines made from the Muscat grape.

SAALE-UNSTRUT When Germany was unified, the vineyards in this region of former East Germany were in a pretty poor state. However, things are now beginning to look up. The wines, which are made from Müller-Thurgau, Silvaner, and other grape varieties, are usually finished dry and, at best, have good fruit extraction.

SACHSEN Northernmost wine region in Germany making dry wines from Müller-Thurgau, Riesling, Pinot Blanc, and Pinot Gris.

SACRAMENTAL WINE Wine is integral to Judeo-Christian religious ceremonies. Rules for Christian altar wines, or wines for the Eucharist, vary from one denomination to another.

ST-AMOUR AC Soft and delightfully fruity red wines for fairly early consumption are made in this Beaujolais Cru in the Burgundy region of France.

ST-AUBIN AC There are reasonably priced and quite good red and oak-aged white wines made in this appellation in the Burgundy region of France.

ST-CHINIAN AC Wines from this AC in the Languedoc area of France are fruity, medium-weight reds with good spice and some intensity.

ST-ÉMILION In Bordeaux, France, dominant grapes in the St-Émilion ACs are Merlot and Cabernet Franc, producing wines with silky, inviting fruit. The higher St-Émilion wines are St-Emilion Grand Cru AC, which includes all the classified growths and many lesser wines. The latest classification listed 68 Grand Cru Classé wines, which tend to be good value compared to the Classed Growths of the Médoc. They are approachable when younger, yet can improve in the bottle for at least 10 to 15 years. St-Émilion Premier Grand Cru Classé is the appellation for the very best wines of St-Émilion. There is an "A" list and a "B" list. There are only two châteaux in the "A" level, Cheval Blanc and Ausone, and 11 "B" châteaux. The wines are superb.

ST-ESTÈPHE AC Wines from this AC in the Haut-Médoc, Bordeaux, France, have a reputation for fairly high tannin levels. That may be changing as more Merlot is being planted to soften the Cabernet Sauvignon. The wines can be drunk young, but they begin to open up with subtle fruit and good flavors after a decade.

Cos d'Estournel, a top château in St-Estèphe, Bordeaux

ST-GEORGES-ST-ÉMILION AC Fruity, approachable wines based mostly on Merlot are made in this AC in Bordeaux, France. They are drinkable young, but will improve in bottle for at least ten years.

ST. HELENA AVA Mid-Napa Valley, California, appellation producing good Cabernet Sauvignon on gravelly benchland on the western slopes, outstanding Chardonnay and Sauvignon Blanc on deep soils along the Napa River, and superb Zinfandel and Syrah on benchland on the east side of the valley.

ST-JOSEPH AC The top wines from this Rhône appellation, in France, are red and are based on Syrah. At their best, they have rich fruit and are a pure pleasure to drink.

ST-JULIEN AC French Bordeaux appellation in the Haut-Médoc making consistently well-balanced, elegant red wines, which are subtle and rounded on the palate.

ST-NICOLAS-DE-BOURGUEIL AC Small red wine AC within the Bourgueil AC in Touraine, in France's Loire Valley. The Cabernet Franc wines are intense yet refreshing, with fruit continuing to emerge even after ten years in bottle.

ST-PÉRAY AC French AC in the Rhône Valley, best known for sparkling wine from Marsanne and Roussanne grapes.

ST-ROMAIN AC Village appellation in the Côte de Beaune, Burgundy, France, making distinctive, mineraly white wines and good reds. The wines are capable of some aging and are good value for Burgundies.

ST-VÉRAN AC Pleasing, approachable Chardonnay is made in this appellation in Mâconnais, Burgundy, France. It is usually made without oak aging and should be drunk fairly young.

STE-CROIX-DU-MONT AC Sweet wines made in an aperitif style are produced in this appellation in Bordeaux, France.

SALICE SALENTINO DOC Appellation in Apulia, Italy, making good red wines from the Negroamaro and Malvasia Nera grapes, at their best after three to four years.

SALTA Small area in the north of Argentina with vineyards at very high altitudes, which have attracted foreign investment. There have been some good results with Cabernet Sauvignon and Torrontés.

SAMOS Greek island making lush, rich dessert wine from Muscat.

SAN LUIS OBISPO COUNTY Part of California's Central Coast AVA, this county contains several AVAs, the best being Arroyo Grande, Edna Valley, Paso Robles, and York Mountain. A small part of the Santa Maria AVA extends into the county. Leading wines are Cabernet Sauvignon, Zinfandel, Syrah, and Chardonnay.

SANCERRE AC French Loire Valley appellation making excellent white wines from Sauvignon Blanc and very good reds and rosés from Pinot Noir. The wines are very refreshing and should be drunk quite young.

SANGIOVESE One of the most widely planted grapes in Italy. There are many different clones of the grape, which is made in a wide variety of styles, from young wines with strawberry-cherry fruit to the top Chianti Riservas and the Super-Tuscans. Sangiovese blends beautifully with Cabernet Sauvignon in both Super-Tuscan and California wines. The grape also shows great potential in Argentina.

SANTA BARBARA COUNTY This Central Coast California county produces a wide range of excellent wines, including Chardonnay, Riesling, and Sauvignon Blanc, for white wines, and Pinot Noir and Cabernet Sauvignon for reds. Santa Ynez Valley and Santa Maria Valley are the top AVAs.

SANTA CRUZ MOUNTAINS AVA This Central Coast viticultural area runs from just south of San Francisco to south of the Santa Cruz area in the California Coast Ranges. The best wines are Chardonnay, Pinot Noir, and Cabernet Sauvignon. The area suffered severe setbacks in the late 1990s due to outbreaks of Pierce's Disease.

SANTA LUCIA HIGHLANDS AVA Appellation in Monterey County, California, which runs along the eastern slope of the Santa Lucia Mountains above the Salinas Valley. The best wines are Cabernet Sauvignon and Chardonnay, although new plantings of Syrah and Pinot Noir show great promise.

SANTA MARIA VALLEY AVA For many years, North Coast wineries bought grapes in this Central Coast appellation located in Santa Barbara and San Luis Obispo counties of California. Now this AVA is beginning to set forth on its own, with excellent Chardonnay and outstanding Syrah and Pinot Noir.

SANTA YNEZ VALLEY AVA Bounded by the Pacific Ocean on the west, this cool growing region in Santa Barbara County, California, has had excellent results with Chardonnay and Riesling, and Pinot Noir is showing potential.

SANTENAY AC This appellation in the Burgundy district of France makes good solid red and white wines, with the best coming from the Gravières Premier Cru.

SARDINIA This Italian island does not make much top-quality wine, although there have been some improvements, and a move toward lighter, more approachable wines is encouraging. The best whites are made from Vermentino. Cannonau makes the best reds.

SASSICAIA DOC Sassicaia was one of the first Super-Tuscan wines, made in a Bordeaux style from Cabernet Sauvignon and Cabernet Franc. The wine achieved international success and spurred the development of many more Super-Tuscans. The estate has played an important part in the Italian wine revolution since the 1940s, culminating in the creation of a separate appellation for Sassicaia within the Bolgheri DOC.

SAUMUR AC Chenin Blanc is the base for delicious white wines in this Loire Valley AC in France, although it is permissible to blend in 20 percent Chardonnay. Some reds and rosés are made from Cabernet Franc.

SAUMUR-CHAMPIGNY AC Loire Valley appellation in France producing superb red wine from Cabernet Franc. The wine is quite good when young, but in good vintages it can age for up to ten years.

SAUMUR MOUSSEUX AC French Loire Valley AC making drinkable Champagne-method sparkling wine from Chenin Blanc, with an occasional touch of Chardonnay and Cabernet Franc.

SAUTERNES AC One of the world's great dessert wines is made in this appellation in Bordeaux, France, from late-harvest Sémillon, Sauvignon Blanc, and Muscadelle, usually affected by noble rot. It has its own Cru Classé system.

SAUVIGNON BLANC Extremely versatile grape, which can be vinified in a number of styles. In France, it comes into its own in the Sancerre region of the Loire Valley, where it is cool-fermented in stainless steel and bottled fairly early. This captures its intense fruit and aroma perfectly. Even more pungent are the best New Zealand Sauvignons, which have forged their own distinctive style. In the Bordeaux region of France, where it has historically been blended with Sémillon, winemakers are increasingly using oak to add complexity to the wine. The same is true in California, South Africa, and Australia. Sauvignon Blanc is also used to make sweet wine, either on its own or as a blend with Sémillon (as in Sauternes). SEE FUMÉ BLANC.

SAVAGNIN Curious white grape grown in the French Jura region to make the sherrylike *vin jaune*.

SAVENNIÈRES AC Appellation in France's Loire Valley for wines made from Chenin Blanc, which range from dry and steely to rich and sweet, although there is much more of the dry style. At its best, the wine has great power and concentration and can age for ten years or more.

SAVIGNY-LÈS-BEAUNE AC The best wines in this French AC in Burgundy's Côte de Beaune are the reds, which are lean in style and should be drunk within ten years, since they lack the depth for longer aging. Only a small amount of white wine is made.

SAVOIE French alpine region on the border with Switzerland making white wines from the local Jacquère and Altesse (or Roussette). A few light reds are made from Gamay and Pinot Noir, and fuller reds are made from the local Mondeuse.

SAXONY SEE SACHSEN.

SCHEUREBE Cross of Riesling and Silvaner, widely planted in the Pfalz and Rheinhessen regions in Germany, and in Austria. It makes attractive sweet white wines and pungent dry ones.

SCHIAVA Red wine grape grown in large quantities in the Alto Adige DOC of northeast Italy, where it produces light, fruity wines.

SCHLOSS JOHANNISBERG Famous wine estate and vineyard enjoying one of the prime vineyard sites in Germany's Rheingau region. Exclusively planted with Riesling, it is one of the few simply labelled wines from Germany where vineyard name and estate are the same. The name Johannisberg Riesling, which is widely used in the United States and elsewhere to denote the true Riesling variety, took its name from this estate.

SCHLOSSBÖCKELHEIM Village in Nahe, Germany, making good wine, especially from the vineyard sites of Felsenberg and Kupfergrube.

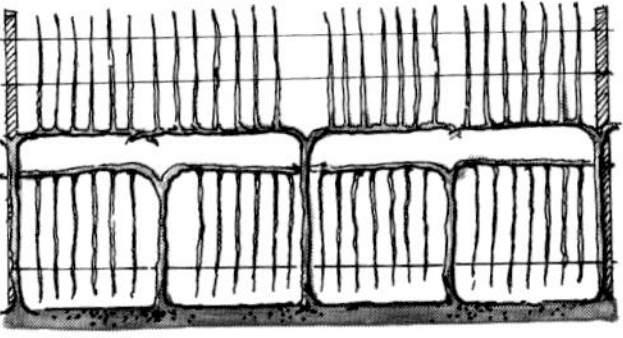

Scott Henry system

SCOTT HENRY System of vine training which divides the vine vertically into two curtains, one growing up and one down. The system dramatically increases production and grape quality. It is also compatible with mechanical harvesting. The system was developed by Oregon winery owner and grower Scott Henry.

SEC French for dry.

S

SECCO Italian for dry.

SECO Spanish and Portuguese for dry.

SECONDARY FERMENTATION Fermentation that occurs after the initial alcohol fermentation. It may be a second alcoholic fermentation that takes place in the bottle, as with sparkling wine, or a malolactic fermentation to convert malic acid to lactic acid in still wines.

SECOND WINE Many wineries produce a second wine from grapes and wine not considered of a good enough quality for the principal wine. The practice originated in the Bordeaux region of France. These so-called "second-label" wines are often made from lower-quality vineyards and are generally made for immediate drinking.

SEDIMENT The substance left after fermentation, consisting of dead yeast cells, bits of stem, and seeds.

SEKT German term for sparkling wine. The best of these are made in the classic Champagne method.

SÉLECTION DE GRAINS NOBLES Sweet wine made in Alsace, France, from late-harvest Muscat, Riesling, Gewürztraminer, or Pinot Gris. Ideally the grapes should be affected by *Botrytis cinerea*, or noble rot. The term is starting to be used in other regions, such as the Loire Valley.

SÉMILLON White wine grape grown in Bordeaux and elsewhere, notably for the great sweet wines of Sauternes and Barsac, in southwest France, Australia, New Zealand, California, and Washington State. In dry wines, the grape is often blended with Sauvignon Blanc or, in Australia and Washington, with Chardonnay. It makes a dry, complex wine and in Australia has shown great aging capability, especially in the Hunter Valley. Because it is a thin-skinned grape, it is easily affected by noble rot, making it a good choice for dessert wines, by itself or with Sauvignon Blanc.

SETÚBAL DOC Good fortified wine from south of Lisbon, Terras do Sado, Portugal, called Moscatel de Setúbal when made from mostly Moscatel grapes.

SEYSSEL AC Appellation in the Savoie region of France best known for a light sparkling wine.

SEYVAL BLANC A hybrid white grape with high disease resistance, Seyval Blanc has the ability to ripen in damp autumn weather. It is a desirable grape to plant in cool climates like those of Canada, New York State, and England. It makes an attractive wine, crisp and fruity.

SHENANDOAH VALLEY AVA California appellation in the Sierra Foothills AVA making very good Zinfandel in a jammy style. New plantings of Syrah show promise.

SHERRY SEE JEREZ Y MANZANILLA DO.

SHIRAZ Australian name for Syrah. A few Californians are also labeling the wine Shiraz. SEE SYRAH.

SICILY The traditional wines of this hot-climate Italian island are fortified, Marsala being the prime example; but increasing amounts of pleasing table wines are being made from grapes planted in cooler mountain vineyards.

SIERRA FOOTHILLS AVA Umbrella AVA covering vineyards in Amador, Calaveras, El Dorado, Mariposa, Nevada, Placer, Tuolomne, and Yuba counties near the Sierra Nevada range, east of California's Central Valley. Zinfandel is by far the best wine from the area.

SILVANER German spelling for the white grape Sylvaner. SEE SYLVANER.

SIN CRIANZA Spanish label term for young wines that have had little or no wood aging. SEE ALSO CRIANZA.

SKIN CONTACT/SKIN MACERATION SEE MACERATION.

SLOVAKIA Vineyards in this section of the former Czechoslovakia produce white wines from Pinot Blanc, Riesling, and Gewürztraminer.

SLOVENIA This country, which was formerly part of Yugoslavia, is working hard to revive its wine industry in order to compete with the rest of the world, especially its neighbors, northeast Italy, Austria, and Hungary. Part of the vineyard area is an extension of the Collio DOC in Friuli, northeast Italy, and has the potential to make red and white wines of equal quality. Further east, white grapes dominate; they do particularly well in the Lutomer region.

SOAVE DOC Italian DOC, near Verona, producing vast quantities of dry white wines of variable quality, primarily from Garganega grapes. Recently, DOC laws have been updated to allow up to 30 percent of Chardonnay, Pinot Bianco, or Trebbiano di Soave (a superior variety of Trebbiano) in the blend. When yields are kept low, wines from the Classico zone can be rich, nutty, and of excellent quality. A sweet Recioto di Soave is also made, from dried grapes.

SOFT As a tasting term, soft refers to a wine that is low in acid or tannins. Such a wine is generally for early drinking.

SOLAIA One of the best of the Italian Super-Tuscans, from Antinori, it rivals Sassicaia in this category of wines. A blend of Cabernet Sauvignon, Cabernet Franc, and Sangiovese grapes, Solaia is a rich wine of great complexity and depth from a vineyard next to Tignanello in Chianti Classico.

SOLERA Spanish system of aging and blending fortified wines, especially in the DOs of Jerez y

Manzanilla (the sherry region) and Montilla-Moriles.

SOMMELIER French word, used worldwide, for a waiter specializing in wine and wine service.

SOMONTANO DO Appellation in northeast Spain gaining attention for its excellent red and rosé wines made from Tempranillo and Moristel, an almost-forgotten local grape variety. There are also wines being made in a more international style from Chardonnay and Merlot.

SONOMA COAST AVA Catchall appellation on the North Coast of California covering all vineyards in areas that meet the cool Region I and Region II categories. It includes many existing AVAs and seems to have been created as a hedge against future plantings.

SONOMA COUNTY Coastal county north of San Francisco, California, the most heavily planted in the region. It is larger than Napa County to the east, with a greater variety of soils and microclimates. Excellent Cabernet Sauvignon, Merlot, Zinfandel, and Pinot Noir are made in Sonoma, as well as Chardonnay, Sauvignon Blanc, Viognier, and Gewürztraminer. Important AVAs include Alexander Valley, Carneros, Chalk Hill, Dry Creek Valley, Green Valley, Russian River Valley, Sonoma Mountain, and Sonoma Valley.

SONOMA MOUNTAIN AVA Viticultural area including mountain vineyards west and north of the town of Sonoma, with similar soils that are above the fog line and have the same overall climate pattern, a consistency not always found in U.S. AVAs. The best wines are Cabernet Sauvignon and Zinfandel.

Kunde Estate, Sonoma Valley

SONOMA VALLEY AVA Stretching some 40 miles (64 km) northward from the Carneros AVA on San Francisco Bay, this North Coast region has a varied mix of soils and microclimates. The best wines in the cooler areas are Chardonnay and Pinot Noir, while Cabernet Sauvignon and Zinfandel make the best wine on hillside vineyards on the east and west sides of the valley.

SOUTH AFRICA After years of stagnation, South Africa's wine industry

is going through a period of rapid improvement. Vineyards are being replanted to reflect international taste, and modern winemaking technology is in place in many wineries. There is no doubt that South Africa has potential to produce wine that can compete with any in the world—and in some cases it already does. It will be an exciting country to watch in the coming years.

SOUTH AMERICA All over South America, efforts are being made to improve wine production and join the international wine market, and to produce better wine for home consumption. In Brazil, Uruguay, Peru, Ecuador, and Colombia, vineyards are being replanted and modern technology is being installed in wineries. Argentina and Chile are already important producers. They began as shippers of inexpensive table wines but have made huge strides in the production of premium wines.

SOUTH AUSTRALIA Australia's largest grape-growing state, with a wide variety of wines made in many different styles, ranging from cheap bulk wines to some of the best wines anywhere. The best regions include Adelaide Hills, Barossa, Padthaway, Clare Valley, Eden Valley, McLaren Vale, and Coonawarra.

SOUTHWEST FRANCE Vast French region, home to a number of less-known, often good-value wines from between Bordeaux and the western Pyrenees. Look for wines from Bergerac, Cahors, Gaillac, Irouléguy, Montravel, and others.

SOUZAO A red wine grape used in the production of port in Portugal's Douro Valley, it is also planted in Australia and California by those wanting to make a port-style wine.

SPAIN In the last few decades, Spain has transformed its wine industry. Traditional regions are making important modifications in wine style to keep up with changing tastes. Rioja, for example, is offering many more young, fruity red wines for immediate drinking. The introduction of cold fermentation in stainless steel has revolutionized the style of white wine all over Spain. Heavier barrel-fermented whites have given way to fresh, lively, fruity wines.

SPANNA Synonym for Nebbiolo in Piedmont, Italy. SEE NEBBIOLO.

SPARKLING WINE Style of wine that usually undergoes a secondary fermentation. The Champagne method involves fermentation that takes place in the bottle; with other wines, the second fermentation may take place in a tank before bottling. Sparkling wines range in style from dry, or brut, to sweet, or doux, with several stages in between.

SPÄTBURGUNDER German name for Pinot Noir.

SPÄTLESE German term meaning late-harvested, the second rung in quality QmP wines. SEE QMP.

SPICY Tasting term for either a general or specific spice aroma or flavor in a wine.

SPITTOON Receptacle for wine that is not swallowed during a tasting. It may be small for individual use or large for a group.

SPRING MOUNTAIN DISTRICT AVA California AVA in the Mayacamas Mountains, on the west side of Napa. Soils vary within the AVA, but the most successful grapes are Cabernet Sauvignon, Petite Sirah, and Zinfandel.

SPUMANTE Italian for sparkling.

SQUINZANO DOC Appellation in Apulia, Italy, with good potential.

STAGS LEAP DISTRICT AVA California appellation on the eastern side of Napa Valley that extends up into the hills. It rivals Rutherford AVA as the best area for Cabernet Sauvignon in the Napa Valley. At their best, the wines are rich and supple, with deep fruit, and are capable of extended aging.

STEIERMARK Also known as Styria, the warmest wine region in Austria. The best wines are made from Chardonnay (made in an unoaked style) and Sauvignon Blanc.

STELLENBOSCH WO Considered the heart of the South African wine industry, this area is best known for outstanding red wines based on Cabernet Sauvignon, Merlot, Shiraz, and Pinotage. However, there have been great improvements recently in the white wines, and the area has produced some excellent Chardonnay and Sauvignon Blanc.

STILL WINE Wine that is finished without any bubbles.

STRUCTURE The structure of a wine is the sum of the relationship among all of the wine's elements—acidity, tannin, alcohol, sugar (if any), and oak. A wine's structure can be balanced or unbalanced, firm, sturdy, or weak.

SUGAR In relation to wine, this word refers to natural sugars in grapes. Fermentation converts these natural sugars into alcohol. Some of these sugars remain unfermented in nondry wines.

SULFUR Sulfur has been used for thousands of years to protect wine from spoilage and to protect grape vines from mildew. When elemental sulfur is burned it produces sulfur dioxide, used since the Middle Ages as a preservative. Sulfur dioxide is used, less often now, to kill wild yeast at the start of fermentation. In general, far less sulfur dioxide is used in winemaking today than in the recent past. It is almost impossible, however, to make a wine completely free of sulfur, since a little sulfur dioxide is produced naturally during fermentation.

SULFITES Since 1987, wines made in the United States have carried a label warning those who are allergic to sulfites, which are present in sulfur dioxide, that wine does contain sulfites. SEE SULFUR.

SULTANA SEE THOMPSON SEEDLESS.

SUPER-TUSCAN In the 1970s and 1980s, when huge advances were being made in the world of wine, younger Italian winemakers, led by the Tuscan Piero Antinori, realized that in many cases the Italian wine laws presented a handicap to their efforts to compete. They decided to direct their energies into making the best wine they could, regardless of regulations. These wines could be labeled only as Vino da Tavola, since they did not meet the regulations for classified wines. Eventually, the wines became so successful that in 1992 regulations were changed, allowing these so-called Super-Tuscans to be accommodated within the system. The first Super-Tuscan is generally considered to have been the Cabernet-based Sassicaia, which was followed by Antinori's Tignanello, the pioneering blend of Sangiovese with about 20 percent Cabernet Sauvignon.

SUPÉRIEUR French term applied to a wine that has a higher alcohol content than the minimum level required for the region.

SUPERIORE Italian term for wine that has a higher alcohol level than the minimum level required for the region.

SUPPLE Positive tasting term for a red wine with balance and a silky, smooth structure.

SUR LIE French term used around the world for a white wine left to mature in tank or barrel for a few months in contact with the sediment of dead yeast, or lees (*lies* in French). Wine matured in this way may develop more complex flavors. In Muscadet the use of the term on the label is strictly controlled, elsewhere it is left up to the producer to decide whether to use the term.

SÜSSRESERVE German term for sweet reserve, which is the unfermented grape must sometimes added to wine to make it sweeter. The wine is fully fermented to dryness, then the süssreserve is blended into the wine before bottling. This technique is used only for relatively inexpensive wines.

SUSTAINABLE AGRICULTURE Form of viticulture that tries to reduce the use of agrochemicals. It lacks the strict regulations of organic viticulture, but has the same goal: to increase soil fertility. For example, rather than use herbicides to control vineyard weeds, vineyard owners plant cover crops in the vine rows and plow them under for green manure.

SWAN VALLEY Very hot growing region in Western Australia producing largely unremarkable wines, except for some fortified bottlings.

SWEETNESS One of the four basic tastes that the palate perceives.

Most tasters can discern sweetness in wine at a level of roughly 0.5 percent residual sugar or higher.

SWITZERLAND Alpine country producing very good dry white wines of somewhat neutral character from the Chasselas grape and fruity red wines from Pinot Noir and Gamay in the French-speaking areas. There are some good light Pinot Noir reds and whites from Müller-Thurgau in the German-speaking areas and Merlot is made in the Italian-speaking area.

SYLVANER White wine grape widely grown in Germany (where it is called Silvaner), Alsace, and Eastern Europe. At its best, it makes a smoky, somewhat floral wine, but more often the wine is fairly neutral and is used for blending.

SYRAH Red wine grape making wines with a rich depth of fruit, good tannins, and a zesty spice in the finish which fills the mouth. It is the base for the great red wines of the northern Rhône in France. In Australia, where the grape and wine are called Shiraz, the fruit can sometimes be on the jammy side, but at its best it is superb, with brighter fruit than is commonly seen in the Rhône. In California, some winemakers use the term Shiraz to denote a wine that has lighter, drink-me-now fruit, and reserve the name Syrah for wines of greater depth. With plantings of Syrah now appearing in cooler coastal vineyards of California, the region is storing up great potential for this wine. Excellent young Syrah is also being made in the Columbia Valley, Washington State.

TABLE GRAPES Grapes grown for juice, jams, jellies, raisin production, or eating, such as Concord, a native American grape. Sometimes table grapes are used in wine or brandy production, as in California's Thompson Seedless variety.

TABLE WINE In a winemaking sense, table wine is wine of normal alcoholic strength. Under U.S. regulations, table wine is any wine with an alcohol content of between 11 and 14 percent, i.e., not a fortified wine. In Europe, table wine is the term for wine that does not meet quality classification requirements.

LA TACHE, AC Grand Cru in Burgundy, France, producing some of the greatest red wine in the world. The wine offers deep, layered flavors and should be kept for at least ten years before drinking. Not surprisingly, it is expensive.

TAFELWEIN German for table wine.

TANNAT Red grape from southwest France, usually blended with Cabernets Sauvignon and Franc and found particularly in the Madiran AC. It gives a rich but slightly tough red wine with a spicy, earthy character. It is also widely grown in Uruguay, where it produces some of the country's best reds.

TANNIN Prickly, harsh texture in red wine that comes from grape skins and from oak barrels. Young wines often have very heavy tannins which fade as the wine ages. Red wine needs to retain some tannin as it ages to maintain balance.

TARRAGONA DO An appellation in Catalonia, Spain, with a reputation for making dull, fortified wines, although this is changing. There is still plenty of wine for bulk production and for use by Cava (sparkling wine) producers in the Penedés region; but there are also deeply concentrated red wines based on Garnacha and Cariñena, made in a similar style to the wines of Priorato, which may, in the future, show Tarragona the way.

TART Generally negative tasting term for a highly acidic wine.

TARTARIC ACID The key acid in wine gives a tart, fresh flavor to the wine. It is important for the tartaric acid level to be balanced.

TARTRATES Crystalline deposits that form in wine, after fermentation, from the potassium salt of tartaric acid. They can be filtered out after the cold stabilization practiced by most large wineries.

TASMANIA Cool island off southeastern Australia attracting interest as a potential area for Pinot Noir and Chardonnay, for both still and sparkling wine production.

TASTEVIN Shallow metal tasting dish between 2.5 inches and 4 inches (6 cm and 10 cm) in diameter. Once used for tasting in France's wine cellars, *tastevins* are now mainly used for ceremonial purposes. Sommeliers sometimes wear small *tastevins* on cords around their neck.

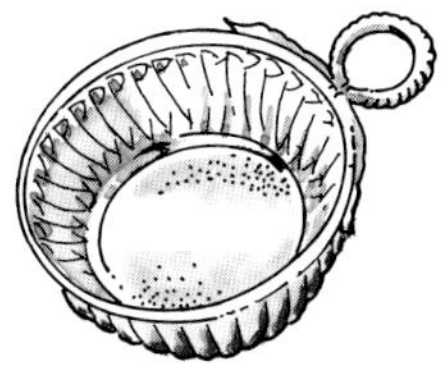

Tastevin

TAURASI DOCG Appellation in the Campania region of southern Italy, best known for its deep, rich red wine, made from Aglianico.

TAVEL AC Appellation in France's Rhône Valley making rosé with forward fruit and unusual complexity.

TAWNY PORT Style of port aged for several years before bottling. It has a deep, nutty flavor which lingers on the palate. The best are 10-, 20-, and 30-year-old tawny ports.

TAYLOR FLADGATE, AND YEATMAN This 300-year-old port house, owned by a British family, remains at the top of the tree in the Douro, Portugal. Their Quinta de Vargellas single-quinta ports are almost as highly regarded as the classic Taylor Fladgate vintage ports.

TCHELISTCHEFF, ANDRÉ Moscow-born Tchelistcheff (1901–1994) trained in agriculture in the former Czechoslovakia and in viticulture and enology in France. He set the style for Napa Valley Cabernet

Sauvignon. In 1937, he went to Beaulieu Vineyards, then owned by Georges de Latour, a French businessman. Tchelistcheff developed a Cabernet Sauvignon style emphasizing balanced fruit with a touch of sweet oak. He was a consultant for other wineries until just before his death and had a huge influence on California winemaking.

TEMECULA AVA Historic AVA south of Los Angeles in California, undergoing a revival. Several new wineries have been set up, with the best wine being unoaked Chardonnay.

TEMPRANILLO Spain's best red wine grape, Tempranillo is important in virtually every winegrowing area of central and northern Spain. The chief grape used in the traditional red wines of Rioja, it is also used in the new wave of unoaked Rioja red wines, which are becoming very popular for their youthful, zesty fruit. It is the most important grape in the Ribera del Duero, where it is called Tinto Fino or Tinta del País and makes a deeply flavored wine. In La Mancha, where it is called Cencibel, it makes a delicious, fruity young wine.

TEROLDEGO ROTALIANO DOC Red wine grape native to the Trentino region of northeast Italy. It makes a berry-fruity wine with light to medium flavors.

TERROIR French term for every aspect of a vineyard site, it includes soil, sun exposure, wind direction and velocity, vineyard microclimate, and any other natural element.

TÊTE DE CUVÉE French term for a producer's top wine, especially used for Champagne. The term has no legal significance.

TEXAS State showing great potential for winegrowing with plantings of Cabernet Sauvignon, Chardonnay, and Sauvignon Blanc.

THOMPSON SEEDLESS California white table and raisin grape, also called Sultana. It is the most planted grape variety in California. At one time, Thompson Seedless was used to fill out California's cheap jug wines, with E & J Gallo one of the main buyers. When Gallo stopped buying Thompson in the early 1990s, most other buyers followed suit. In South Africa, where it is called Sultana, this grape variety is also used in cheap table wines.

TICINO Italian-speaking area of Switzerland producing Merlot in a soft, seductive style.

TIGNANELLO After Sassicaia, this superb red wine set the style for the

Italian Super-Tuscans. Piero Antinori, following consultations with Émile Peynaud of Bordeaux, France, broke all the rules in Tuscany when he blended Sangiovese and Cabernet Sauvignon, aged it in new French oak barrels, and released it as an unclassified Vino da Tavola to popular and critical acclaim.

TINAJA Large earthenware vessel used to ferment and store wine in southern Spain. Some of the old clay *tinajas* are still in use, but there are also newer *tinajas* made from concrete, some of which hold thousands of gallons of wine.

Tinaja

TINTA CÃO Red wine grape used in port production.

TINTO Spanish and Portuguese for red, as in *vino tinto*, or red wine.

TINTO DEL PAIS/TINTO FINO In Ribera del Duero, these are local names for the Spanish red grape variety Tempranillo.

TOAST A process in barrel-making in which the staves (shaped wooden planks) are heated over flames so they can be bent into place. Barrels may be given a light, medium, or heavy toast, which affects the flavor of the wine.

TOCAI OR TOCAI FRIULANO White wine grape that makes distinctive wine with a nutty flavor in Friuli, northeast Italy, not related to the Tokay or Pinot Gris of Alsace.

TOKAY Dessert wine from Hungary, made from late-harvest white grapes affected by noble rot, the principal varieties being Furmint and Hárslevelü. An unusual feature of Tokay is that the wine is aged in long tunnels cut out of the hillsides. The tunnels are lined with a fungus which forms a film on the surface of the wine, similar to the flor of sherry. Some tasters have noticed a sherrylike taste in the wine. The sweetness level of Tokay is measured in *puttonyos*, with six *puttonyos* being the sweetest. Recent investment from some major wine companies has resulted in a more modern style with a fresher, less sherrylike taste.

The word Tokay is also used in Alsace as a synonym for Pinot Gris; this has nothing to do with the wine made in Hungary. The name may appear on labels in conjunction with Pinot Gris.

TORGIANO DOC Appellation in Umbria, central Italy, offering ripe red wine with deep black cherry and plum fruit. The Torgiano DOCG classification has been granted only to the reserve wines of a single producer, Lungarotti.

TORO DO Spanish appellation in Castilla-Léon, best for big, powerful red wines made from Tinta de Toro, a local name for Tempranillo.

TORRES, MIGUEL A. The president of Bodegas Torres, Catalonia, Miguel Torres (1939–) has had a major impact on modern Spanish winemaking. He was the first person in Spain to use cold fermentation techniques on a mass-distributed white wine, and Torres' Viña Sol has become one of the top inexpensive white wines in Spain. He has experimented with both native Catalonian varieties and international varieties and has introduced high vine density, mechanical pruning, and organic viticulture to Catalonia. He also established a winery some years ago in Chile and has been a leader in the quality drive there.

TORRONTÉS White grape variety of increasing importance in Argentina and Spain. It has great potential in Argentina, where it makes refreshing wines with good acidity, a pleasing aroma, and a slight Muscat taste. In Spain, Torrontés makes very good wines in the DO of Ribeiro, Galicia.

TOURAINE AC Umbrella appellation for the red, white, and rosé wines of Touraine in the Loire Valley region of France.

TOURIGA NAÇIONAL Portuguese red wine grape used in port production and now for excellent table wines, especially in the Dão DOC.

TRADITIONAL METHOD See Champagne method.

TRAINING SYSTEMS How the vine is trained to grow is an essential element in modern viticulture. The right training system for specific sites is important in terms of grape quality and productivity. There are dozens of systems in use around the world, ranging from simple head-pruned systems to complex systems requiring elaborate positioning of the vine shoots.

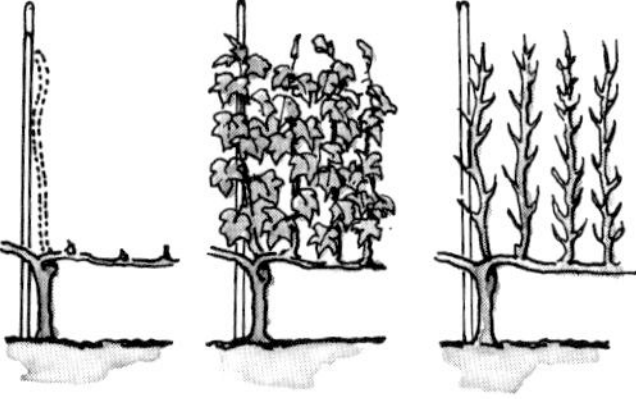

Vine-training system at different stages of growth

TRANSFER METHOD Method of making sparkling wine that involves a second fermentation and aging in the bottle, followed by transfer into pressure tanks for filtering and then re-bottling.

TRAS-OS-MONTES Province of northeast Portugal producing rustic red and white wines.

TREBBIANO Most planted white wine grape in Italy. In general, it makes a neutral white wine of no particular distinction, but it may be blended with other wines of more character. The grape is called Ugni Blanc in France, where it is used mostly for brandy distillation.

TRENTINO DOC Appellation in northeast Italy covering dozens of different wine styles from several varieties. Pinot Bianco and Pinot Grigio are the best whites. There are several good reds; one of the best is a Cabernet Sauvignon.

TRENTINO-ALTO ADIGE In the foothills of the Alps, this region in northeast Italy grows a vast number of grape varieties, both indigenous and international. Even its basic wines are of a very high quality.

TRITTENHEIM A German wine village on the Mosel River making well-balanced, fruity white wines with good acidity.

TROCKEN The German word for dry, *trocken* may appear on wine labels in addition to the official German classification. A simple QbA *trocken* is usually a light- to medium-bodied dry wine, whereas a Spätlese *trocken* or Auslese *trocken* is fuller in flavor and higher in alcohol, because the grapes have been harvested with greater ripeness.

TROCKENBEERENAUSLESE German word translating as "dried berry selected," meaning grapes affected by *Botrytis cinerea*.

TURKEY World's fifth-largest grape-growing country, although about 97 percent of the grapes are table grapes or grapes used for raisins. Very little wine is made, and it is of poor quality. There are plans to improve wine quality.

TUSCANY Leading wine area in Italy, home of the Super-Tuscan movement which began in the 1970s. Top appellations include Chianti, Brunello di Montalcino, and Vino Nobile di Montepulciano. White wines are not as important as reds, although the sweet Vin Santo is very good.

TYPICITY Tasting term indicating that a wine's taste is typical of the grape variety or region's character.

UGNI BLANC French name for the Italian white wine grape Trebbiano. SEE TREBBIANO.

UKRAINE The Crimea is the most important winegrowing region in this former member of the Soviet Union. Good-quality red and white table wines are made.

ULL DE LLEBRE Catalan name for Tempranillo.

ULLAGE The space in a bottle of wine between the cork and the wine level, also called fill space. A low wine level may indicate a leaky cork or some other problem, so the term is one to watch out for in catalogs for vintage wine auctions.

UMBRIA Over two-thirds of the wine produced in this Italian region is Orvieto. However, red wines from

Umbria, made in a fruity modern style, are of interest.

UMPQUA VALLEY AVA Appellation just south of the better-known Willamette Valley in Central Oregon. The best wines are made from Chardonnay and Pinot Noir.

UNITED STATES Wine is made in more than 40 of the 50 states from an astonishing range of grape varieties in more or less every style imaginable. California is the most important wine-producing region, but several other areas are also making excellent wines. Washington State is California's most consistent challenger, making wines of great fruit intensity and style. There are also fine wines being made in Oregon, New York, Texas, Michigan, Pennsylvania, Virginia, Missouri, Ohio, Idaho, and New Mexico. Unlike most of the European wine-producing areas, the appellation system is new to the U.S.A. The AVA (American Viticultural Area) designation has been far too inclusive for it to be meaningful, and at present it is not a reliable gauge of wine quality. As time goes on, the system may be fine-tuned, but currently it is simply a guarantee that 85 percent of the wine in the bottle is made from grapes grown in the named AVA.

URUGUAY Country with great potential for wine, although at this point very little has come forward. International consultants such as Paul Hobbs of California are working with local producers, and their efforts are encouraging.

ÜRZIG German wine village on the Mosel River known especially for the vineyard site of Würzgarten, which produces spicy Rieslings.

UTIEL-REQUENA DO Appellation in eastern Spain, inland from Valencia, making wonderful rosé from the Bobal grape. Red and white table wines are improving.

VACQUEYRAS AC French Rhône Valley AC making red, white, and rosé wines. The reds, made from a number of grapes led by Grenache, are rich and spicy.

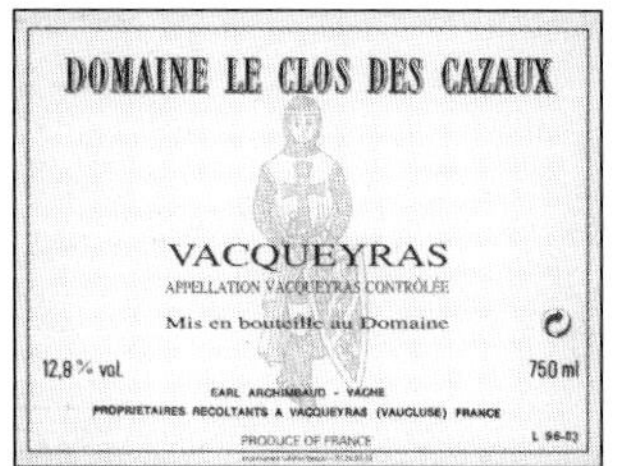

VALAIS Some of Switzerland's best wines come from this region. The whites are from Chasselas and several notable indigenous varieties. There are also light but good red wines from Pinot Noir and Gamay.

VALDEORRAS DO In Galicia, northwest Spain, this DO produces light, fresh styles of white and red wine from a range of varieties.

VALDEPEÑAS DO Appellation in Castilla-La Mancha, Spain, making a great deal of medium-quality red and white wine, much of it going to the Madrid market. A few reds from Cencibel (Tempranillo) can rival some of the wines of Rioja for a fraction of the price.

VALDIGUIÉ Unremarkable red wine grape, originally from France. It makes much better red wine in California, where it was known as Napa Gamay until the beginning of the 1990s, although it must now be called Valdiguié.

VALENCIA DO An enormous amount of wine is made in this Spanish appellation and the surrounding region. It is shipped in bulk from the port of Valencia. Most is best left untasted, however.

VALLE D'AOSTA Alpine region of Italy between Piedmont and France, producing good, light red wines from Nebbiolo and a fine dessert wine from Moscato.

VALLEJO, MARIANO GUADALUPE Military commander Vallejo (1808–1890) owned vineyards in Sonoma and Napa counties and gave cuttings of his vines to many pioneer American planters. Although his close friend Agoston Haraszthy is often called the father of California viticulture, Vallejo was much more influential in the development of commercial viticulture in northern California.

VALPOLICELLA DOC Appellation near Verona in Veneto, Italy, where red wine of highly varied quality is made from Corvina, Rondinella, and Molinara grapes. Styles range from simple wines for everyday drinking to rich, intense Recioto and Amarone Valpolicellas. The best Valpolicella table wine is made from the three above-mentioned grapes. Valpolicella Classico, from the hills is, at its best, a lovely wine with appealing cherry fruit, usually made for fairly early drinking. The sweet recioto wines, made from dried grapes, are very fruity with long-lasting flavors.

VALTELLINA DOC Italian red wine DOC in Lombardy, making mainly light red wines from Nebbiolo.

VARIETAL Term for a wine named after the single, or predominant, grape variety from which it is made.

VAT Large wooden, stainless steel, or concrete container for storing or aging wine. In the United States, if made of stainless steel, it will likely be called a tank.

Vats for storing or aging wine

VAUD Swiss winegrowing region to the north and east of Lake Geneva, where the best wines are white, made from Chasselas grapes. Red wines from Pinot Noir and Gamay are also made.

VDP Abbreviation of Verband Deutscher Prädikatsweingüter, an association of top German wine producers dedicated to improving the quality of the nation's wines.

VDQS Abbreviation of Vin Délimité de Qualité Supérieure, a French wine quality classification between Vin de Pays and AC.

VEGA SICILIA Spanish wine estate in the Ribera del Duero DO, the first in Spain to use French grape varieties. It makes Spain's most expensive red wines; the top wine is Vega Sicilia Unico.

VENDANGE TARDIVE Alsatian term for a late-harvest wine, increasingly used elsewhere.

VENETO Region in northeast Italy including Soave, Valpolicella, and Bardolino, as well as inexpensive but perfectly drinkable everyday wines made from a wide variety of grapes in many different styles. The bulk of them are fruity wines for early drinking.

VERDEJO White grape grown in northern Spain, best known for the dry, characterful whites of Rueda.

VERDELHO Originally from the island of Madeira, Portugal, where it is still grown, this white grape is also grown in Australia, where it produces full-bodied dry whites.

VERDICCHIO DEI CASTELLI DI JESI DOC White wine appellation in the Marches area of Italy producing very good fresh, fruity white wine from the Verdicchio grape.

VERMENTINO Attractive, floral white wine grape grown in Sardinia, Corsica, and in north central Italy.

VERMENTINO DI GALLURA DOCG White wine from Sicily, a newcomer to DOCG status.

VERNACCIA DI SAN GIMIGNANO DOCG Distinctive dry white wine made from the Vernaccia grape in Tuscany, Italy.

VICTORIA Growing conditions in this Australian state are varied, but there are a number of cooler areas suitable for Pinot Noir and Chardonnay, as well as dedicated winegrowers holding small estates who are determined to make world-class wines. Great fortified Muscats and some excellent Shiraz are also made. This region may have Australia's greatest potential for producing quality wines.

VIDAL White hybrid grape which makes intense, deeply flavored Icewine in Ontario, Canada.

VIEILLES VIGNES French term for old vines, although, as with the similar designation in California, the law does not specify a minimum age for vines classified as "old." In some areas, the term old vines refers to vines that are more than 20 years old, while in other areas the term is used to describe vines that are over 50 years old.

VIGNERON French for vine grower.

VIGNOBLE French for vineyard.

VIN DU BUGEY VDQS Wine area west of Savoie in eastern France, best known for sparkling wines.

VIN DE CORSE AC Umbrella AC for the entire French island of Corsica.

VIN DOUX NATUREL French term for a sweet fortified wine in which fermentation has been stopped by the addition of alcohol.

VIN GRIS Very pale rosé wine style made by pressing, but not macerating, red-skinned grapes.

VIN JAUNE White wine made in the style of a Fino sherry from the Savagnin grape. It is a specialty of the French Jura region.

VIN DE PAILLE Sweet wine from the Jura region of France, made from grapes that have been dried on straw mats before fermentation.

VIN DE PAYS Vin de Pays is distinct from Vin de Table in that it must come from grapes grown in a designated geographic area, which may be a *département* or a smaller area.

VIN SANTO Made in central Italy, this can be one of the world's great dessert wines. The wine is usually made from Trebbiano and Malvasia grapes dried on straw mats, fermented in small wooden barrels, and traditionally matured for several years in an attic. Temperature changes during storage give the wine a nutty, intense flavor with concentrated fruit.

VIN DE SAVOIE AC Catchall AC for the Savoie region of France, which borders Switzerland.

VIN DE TABLE French for table wine, the term denotes the lowest level of quality.

VINHO VERDE DOC Wine region and also a style of wine. In Portugal it is made in both a red and white style, but it is usually the white version that is exported. At its best, the wine offers lovely, slightly acidic fruit with a lower alcohol content than most table wine (often under 10 percent) and a hint of fizz. Verde (meaning green) in the name does not refer to the color of the wine, but to the fact that the wine is released in the spring, the greening of the year.

VINO COMARCAL Spanish classification category for wine from a large region. It is one step up in quality from Vino de Mesa.

VINO DE MESA Bottom rung on the quality scale for Spanish wines, equivalent to French Vin de Table.

VINO NOBILE DI MONTEPULCIANO DOCG Powerful red wine with deep, rich fruit, made from Sangiovese grapes in Tuscany, Italy.

VINO DA TAVOLA Italian term for table wine, although some Vino da Tavolas are not what they might seem. SEE SUPER-TUSCAN.

VINO DE LA TIERRA Spanish term for wines from a designated and specified region, roughly equivalent to France's Vin de Pays.

VINTAGE Wine grape harvest; denotes the year in which a wine was produced.

VIOGNIER Very fashionable wine grape, back from near extinction as one of the few white wine grapes in France's Rhône Valley. It makes a wine with lively peach-apricot fruit, which is very attractive for early drinking. Outside France, the best Viognier is made in California.

VIRGINIA Thomas Jefferson tried to plant a vineyard with European vine varieties in Virginia in the eighteenth century, but the climate was too harsh for sensitive vines to survive. With better vine selection today, this state is developing a significant industry. The white wines do best, with some surprisingly good Viognier.

VITICULTURE The farming of grapevines for wine.

VITIS LABRUSCA One of the native American grapevine species, mainly known in the form of Concord, grown particularly in New York State for indifferent table wine and for grape jelly.

VITIS VINIFERA Classic vine species of Europe and the Middle East, now grown all over the world and responsible for all the world's great wines.

VIURA Name used for Macabeo in northern Spain. SEE MACABEO.

VOLNAY AC There are lovely and elegant red wines made in this appellation in the Côte de Beaune, Burgundy, France. They are drinkable when young, but are also capable of aging for 10 to 15 years.

VOSNE-ROMANÉE AC Sacred territory for lovers of red Burgundy, this AC in the Côte de Nuits of Burgundy, France, contains six Grands Crus and more than a dozen Premiers Crus offering lovely wine with deep, rich flavors that can be aged for 15 to 20 years.

VOUGEOT AC Good-value red wine comes from this AC in the Côte de Nuits, Burgundy, France.

VOUVRAY AC French Loire AC offering Chenin Blanc wines, from dry to sweet to sparkling, all of good quality. The sweet wines, in particular, are worth noting and the dry wines have depth and richness.

VQA Abbreviation of Vintners Quality Alliance, a Canadian organization devoted to establishing and maintaining quality standards for Canadian wine.

This label appears on bottles of Canadian quality wine

WAIHEKE ISLAND Winegrowing area on a small island in Auckland harbor, on New Zealand's North Island, making very good Cabernet Sauvignon.

WAIRARAPA Alternative name for Martinborough in New Zealand.

WALKER BAY Southernmost South African wine region cooled by ocean winds and producing wines from Pinot Noir and Chardonnay.

WALLA WALLA VALLEY AVA Sub-AVA of the Columbia Valley AVA in Washington State. It is high desert country with vine quality very much controlled by irrigation. Merlot and Cabernet Franc are the best wines.

WASHINGTON STATE One of the most exciting new wine areas. The wines, characterized by intense varietal fruit, are well balanced and supple with engaging flavors. The Columbia Valley AVA, which covers almost all the vineyards east of the Cascade Mountains, includes both the Yakima Valley and Walla Walla Valley AVAs and several outstanding vineyard areas yet to be given AVA status, such as Red Mountain and Canoe Ridge. The few vineyards west of the Cascades come under the Puget Sound AVA. In general, after an early start with Riesling, the best wines now are Cabernet Sauvignon, Merlot, Cabernet Franc, Syrah, Sauvignon Blanc, and Sémillon, with some fair Pinot Noir from western Washington.

WEHLEN Wine village in the Mosel region of Germany, producing powerful wines of some intensity from Riesling grapes.

WEISSHERBST German rosé, particularly good from Baden.

WELSCHRIZLING White grape variety. SEE RIESLING ITALICO.

WESTERN AUSTRALIA Winegrowing regions are in the southwest corner of the state. Margaret River, Pemberton, and Great Southern are the most significant areas. The best wines from Margaret River include Cabernet Sauvignon and Sauvignon Blanc.

WHITE PORT Fortified wine made from white grapes in the Douro Valley of Portugal. It is enjoyed as an aperitif in Portugal and in France.

WHITE RIESLING Synonym for Riesling, used in California.

WHITE ZINFANDEL Pink, usually medium-sweet, blush wine, very popular in the United States in the 1980s; it spawned a flock of imitations such as White Merlot and White Barbera. None are white, but at the time Americans were drinking more white wine than red, so it was a good marketing tactic.

WIEN Small Austrian wine area inside the city limits of Vienna.

WILLAMETTE VALLEY AVA Most important appellation in Oregon. Pinot Noir is by far the prime grape, although Chardonnay and Pinot Gris also do very well. There has been a recent expansion of planting in the Eola Hills area of the Valley for further Pinot Noir production.

WINE THIEF Pipette used to extract a sample of wine from a barrel.

WINERY Facility where wine is made.

WINKEL Wine village in the Rheingau, Germany, where the famous Schloss Vollrads wine estate has been making outstanding Riesling for centuries.

WO Abbreviation for Wine of Origin, the basic wine classification system in South Africa.

WORCESTER WO Fertile, hot appellation in South Africa, with much of the wine produced going for distillation. There are a few floral white wines made from Colombard and Chenin Blanc and good fortified red and white wines.

WÜRTTEMBERG Fairly large southern German wine region on the Neckar River. About half the production is red, with some good wines made from Lemberger.

WÜRZBURG Wine city in Franken, Germany, making very good Silvaner and unremarkable Riesling.

XAREL-LO Spanish white wine grape important in the Penedés region, where it is used for Cava.

YAKIMA VALLEY AVA The most densely planted of Washington State's AVAs, the Yakima Valley is a heavily irrigated, semi-desert area. White varieties such as Riesling, Sémillon, and Sauvignon have done well for some time, but with huge increases in plantings over the past few years, certain sites are proving excellent for reds such as Merlot, Cabernet Sauvignon, Cabernet Franc, Syrah, and Grenache.

YARRA VALLEY Cool-climate area in the state of Victoria. It may be Australia's best area for Pinot Noir. Chardonnay is also important.

YEAST These one-celled organisms exist naturally on grape skins and are responsible for converting the grape sugars into alcohol. Many winemakers prefer to kill the natural yeasts with sulfur dioxide and add a cultured yeast to enable them to control the fermentation process more easily. A few winemakers are returning to the traditional use of natural yeasts, believing that they impart better flavors to the wine.

YECLA DO Red wine dominates this DO inland from Valencia in eastern Spain. Powerful, somewhat alcoholic wines are made from Monastrell and Garnacha. Some producers ferment part of the wine by carbonic maceration, which gives a lighter, more agreeable quality to the wine.

YIELD The amount of grapes produced per unit of area, usually expressed as tons per acre or tonnes per hectare. Although a commercial yield is essential for all producers, a relatively low yield is desirable in making fine wines because the grape flavors are more concentrated in a low yield. When the yield seems too high, the vineyard is said to be overcropped, leading to grapes (and wine) with diluted, thin flavors.

YORK MOUNTAIN AVA One of California's smallest viticultural areas, on an eastern slope of the coastal range in San Luis Obispo County. It is almost entirely planted to red grapes, with Zinfandel and Pinot Noir being most important.

ZELL German village on the Mosel River, best known for cheap wines called Schwarzer Katz (meaning "Black Cat").

ZINFANDEL Red grape variety found mostly in California, used to make wine in many styles from rosé (blush), as in White Zinfandel, through red wine with pleasant fruit and good structure to powerful late-harvest port-style beauties. The best AVAs for Zinfandel are Dry Creek Valley, Mendocino Ridge, Sierra Foothills, and hillside AVAs above Napa Valley.

CHAPTER 4

Choosing & Using Wine

How to match food and wine, decipher wine lists in restaurants, organize cocktail parties and wine tastings, and buy and store wine.

Matching Food & Wine

Pairing the right wine with food creates something greater than the sum of the parts. A complementary wine can enhance and add new dimensions to food, and vice versa. Matching food and wine is a fairly recent concept. In the past, people simply served the local foods with whatever wine was available, especially in wine-producing areas—an evolutionary, though not conscious, pairing. Over the years, the teaming of good food with fine wine has become an art form. This chapter explains the basic principles, and suggests specific wines to accompany foods in a range of categories.

BASIC PRINCIPLES

There are two fundamental ways to approach pairing wine and food: either match a rich, strongly flavored dish with an equally rich, powerful wine, or set off a strongly flavored, spicy plate of food with a light, acidic wine.

ACIDITY The acids in wine and the natural acids in food must be considered when making a match. Acidity in a wine is very helpful in food pairings. An acidic wine, such as Sauvignon Blanc, is useful in balancing a rich or spicy chili-based dish.

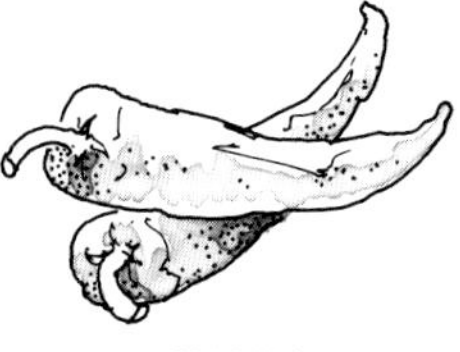

CHILIES
Acidic Sauvignon Blanc balances the hot taste of chilies.

AGE/MATURITY An older wine may be overwhelmed by strong flavors. Let the complex flavors of the wine shine on their own against a simpler dish—for example, a grilled steak with an aged Bordeaux.

BODY It is important to keep the body, or weight, of the wine in mind. A heavy, full-bodied wine will match well with a rich dish such as *boeuf bourguignon*.

OAK A young wine that still tastes of oak tannins tends to obscure subtle foods. That is one reason why young, oaky Chardonnay is often best served as an aperitif with a salty snack. A subtle oakiness in wine is not a problem.

SWEETNESS A sweet wine is best matched with a high-acid food, such as a blue cheese. Sweet foods tend to distort wine flavors and make dry wines taste flat and insipid.

FISH AND SHELLFISH

The old rule was white wine with fish. Today, anything goes, and red wines are often a good complement, especially with meaty or oily fish. It isn't so much the fish as the sauce it is in that makes the difference. White wine is still often the best choice with simple, unsauced grilled or broiled fish, with the notable exception of Pinot Noir with salmon.

ANCHOVIES With fresh grilled anchovies, try Sauvignon Blanc from California or the Loire Valley in France, or a Spanish Manzanilla sherry.

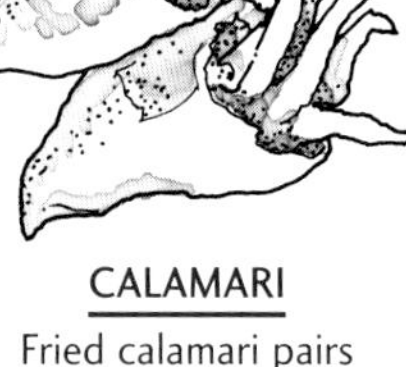

CALAMARI

Fried calamari pairs well with California Chenin Blanc.

CALAMARI (SQUID) For fried calamari, choose a fruity Chenin Blanc from California or an Italian Pinot Grigio. For calamari cooked in tomato sauce, try a pungent Sauvignon Blanc from New Zealand or California.

CAVIAR Serve Champagne, top-quality dry California sparkling wine, or unoaked French Chardonnay from Chablis.

CEVICHE Fino sherry, dry rosé from northern Spain, or unoaked Chardonnay from Chile or California are good choices.

CIOPPINO Serve a big, oaky Chardonnay from California or Australia. If you prefer red, try a medium-weight California Pinot Noir from Carneros or the Central Coast.

CLAMS For simple steamed clams, serve a white Bordeaux, Sauvignon Blanc from the Loire, or a dry rosé. For clams in cream sauce, try a mid-range white Burgundy from France or a medium-oaked California Chardonnay. Clams in tomato sauce require an acidic Sauvignon Blanc from New Zealand or Muscadet from the Loire in France. For clams in wine sauce, drink a better version of the wine used in the sauce.

FISH

White wine is often the best choice with simply cooked fish.

COD With broiled cod, try Pinot Blanc from California or a white Bordeaux from France. With dried cod (Bacalão), serve Pinot Gris from Oregon or Sauvignon Blanc from California.

CRAB Chardonnay from California or the state of Washington are both superb matches with fresh boiled crab or mild crab cakes.

FISH TERRINE An oaky Chardonnay from Australia or California, or a good quality German Riesling are good choices.

FLOUNDER Serve an unoaked Sauvignon Blanc from California, or Chardonnay from the Finger Lakes region of New York.

HALIBUT Try an Italian Pinot Grigio, a California Pinot Blanc, or a lightly oaked Chilean or California Chardonnay with broiled halibut.

LOBSTER For boiled lobster, buy the best white Burgundy from France or California Chardonnay you can afford. For lobster Newburgh, open a crisp Chardonnay from New York, or a light Pinot Noir from Oregon or the Russian River Valley in California.

MACKEREL Try a California Viognier or an Oregon Pinot Gris with broiled mackerel.

MONKFISH Serve a lightly oaked Chardonnay or Pinot Noir from California, or a fresh and fruity French Beaujolais.

MUSSELS For plain steamed mussels, choose a dry Riesling from Alsace, or an unoaked Sauvignon Blanc or Pinot Blanc from California. With mussels in cream sauce, try a lightly oaked California Chardonnay or a German Riesling; in tomato sauce, serve an herbal, high-acid Sauvignon Blanc, and for wine sauce, open a better version of the wine used in the sauce.

OYSTERS Serve Chablis from France, dry Riesling from Alsace, a good California sparkling wine, unoaked Sauvignon Blanc, or a light California Pinot Noir with raw oysters.

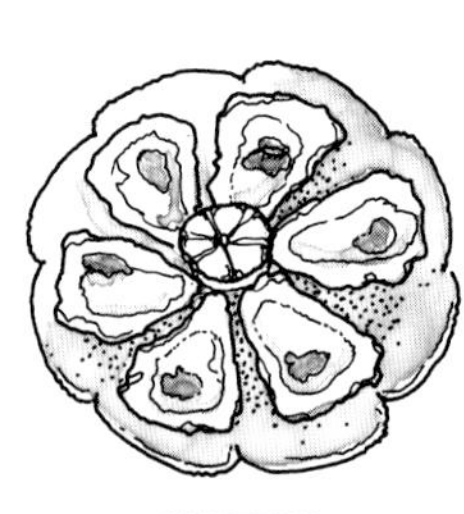

OYSTERS

French Chablis is a good match with a plate of oysters.

RED SNAPPER Try Pinot Noir, or a light Merlot from California with grilled snapper.

SALMON Salmon is a red-wine fish. Serve with California or Oregon Pinot Noir, a good red Burgundy, or a Beaujolais from France. If you prefer a white wine, choose a subtly oaky, elegant Chardonnay from California.

SARDINES Try grilled or baked sardines with a Spanish Albariño or a dry Orvieto from Italy.

SCALLOPS Serve a buttery California or Australian Chardonnay, or a young Merlot from the state of Washington with scallops.

SEA BASS White Bordeaux from France or Sauvignon Blanc from California, or a Chilean Chardonnay all pair well with this fish.

SCALLOP

You could try this shellfish with a California Chardonnay.

SHARK This dense, meaty fish calls for a Pinot Noir from New York State or a Merlot from the state of Washington.

SHRIMP AND PRAWNS For shrimp in garlic sauce, serve a light to medium-weight red such as a Merlot from Washington State. For fried or grilled shrimp (or prawns), try Sauvignon Blanc from the Loire in France, or from California.

SMOKED FISH Serve Gewürztraminer, Pinot Gris, or Riesling from Alsace, or a grassy Sauvignon Blanc from California or New Zealand.

SOLE French Chablis or a lightly oaked California Sauvignon Blanc makes a good pairing with this delicate fish.

SWORDFISH Serve grilled swordfish with California Chardonnay or French white Burgundy.

TROUT Freshwater trout is rather delicate. Serve with an unoaked Chardonnay from California or Oregon, an Albariño from Spain, or a Pinot Grigio from Italy. Sea trout can take Chardonnay or Viognier from California.

TUNA This fish has red wine potential. Try a southern Rhône from France, young Zinfandel, Pinot Noir, or Merlot from California. For whites, open a big, buttery Chardonnay from California or Australia.

MEAT, POULTRY, GAME

Red wine with meat is still a useful rule. However, when you add sauces or other flavorings, you need to consider them as well. Some types of meat seem to have a particular affinity with wines made from certain grapes—lamb goes well with Cabernet Sauvignon or Rioja reds, for example, while pork and rabbit taste good with Pinot Noir or Rhône wines. For game, and for most poultry dishes, the sauce and herbal flavorings make a considerable difference when choosing wine. White wine, or even dry rosé, will be the right choice with poultry on occasion, but red wine can work well too.

Tannin Tip

Steak and other red meats match well with highly tannic wines such as young Cabernet Sauvignons. The astringent quality of the wine cuts through the richness of the meat, and the richness of the meat softens the harsh tannins in the wine.

BEEF

There are many wines that taste good with beef. As a general rule, good red wine goes well with plainly cooked beef. By experimenting with sauces and flavorings, you can choose from powerful Cabernets, Zinfandels, Barolos, and Super-Tuscan red wines from Italy, or lighter reds such as Merlot and Pinot Noir.

BARBECUE Grilled beef is a good excuse to bring out hearty, full-flavored red wines such as Zinfandel or Syrah/Shiraz from California or Australia; southern Rhône, Languedoc, or Provençal French red wines would also be good.

CURRY An off-dry Riesling, unoaked Sauvignon Blanc from California, or even a young Zinfandel will work well with beef curry.

HAMBURGER An intriguing wine challenge, a hamburger often comes with catsup, pickles, onions, and perhaps mayonnaise. The temptation is to go for something cheap, but a Syrah, a young Cabernet, or a fruity red Zinfandel (all from California) can work well.

LIVER With calves' liver, try a red Rioja from Spain, a lighter Pinot Noir from Oregon, California's Russian River Valley or Anderson Valley, or a young Merlot.

MEAT LOAF With this American classic, try a young Cabernet Sauvignon from Chile, or a fruity Merlot from Washington State.

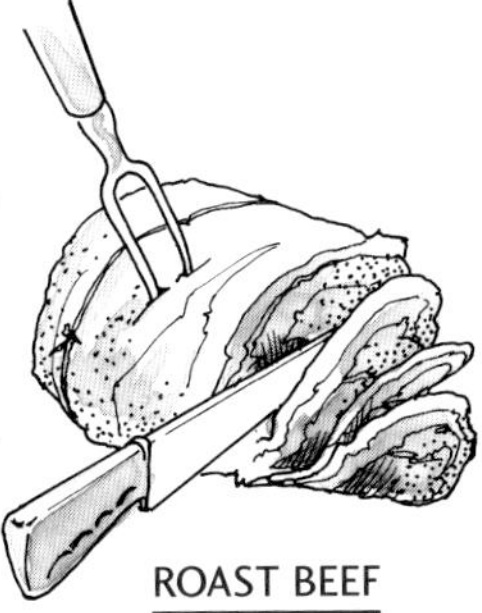

ROAST BEEF

If your budget can stretch to it, try a top French red Bordeaux with this rich meat.

ROAST Rich roast beef calls for the best. Pull the cork on a top red Bordeaux from France, a good California Cabernet Sauvignon, or one of the better French Rhônes or Italian Barolos.

STEAK Steak is always a red wine dish. The seasoning used will determine which red wine, but you can't go wrong with a good French red Bordeaux, a California or Australian Cabernet Sauvignon, a Washington State Merlot, Argentine Malbec, or a Spanish Rioja.

STEW Beef-based stews, from classic French *boeuf bourguignon* to homely beef goulash, are rich dishes that demand an equally rich wine, but one with some elegance and acidity. A good red Burgundy from France, a California Pinot Noir, a Spanish Rioja, an Australian Shiraz, or a big California Zinfandel would all be good partners with a rich beef stew.

ROAST DUCK

You could match this flavorful dish with a Syrah from the Rhône in France.

GAME

Red Burgundy from France is the classic match with game. Below are a few more suggestions for specific types of game.

DUCK Serve wild duck with a Syrah, from the Rhône in France, or from California, or with a Washington State Merlot.

QUAIL Oregon Pinot Noir, Beaujolais from France, or Washington State Merlot would all work well with quail, depending on the stuffing or sauce. If you prefer a white wine, choose an elegant Chardonnay with some oak.

RABBIT With this fairly mild-flavored meat, try an Italian Chianti, a light red Burgundy, or a good Beaujolais from France. For the classic rabbit in mustard sauce, you might like to try a white, such as a Pinot Gris from Oregon or a grassy Sauvignon Blanc from California.

VENISON You need massive red wine with this rich, flavorful meat. Open a cru classé French Bordeaux, a California Cabernet Sauvignon, or a top French Rhône.

LAMB

Lamb has a great affinity with the Cabernet Sauvignon grape, used in red wines from Bordeaux and California. In Spain, Rioja is often served with lamb. California Zinfandel, Washington State Merlot, and Australian Shiraz, Rhône reds, and good Chiantis also work. In general, lamb is a very wine-friendly food.

BARBECUE Zinfandel, young Cabernet Sauvignon, Merlot from California, or Rioja are good choices with broiled lamb. For a Middle Eastern–style kebab with spicy sauces, reach for the brighter flavors of Cabernet Franc, Syrah from California, or Shiraz from Australia.

CROWN OF LAMB

Roast lamb tastes delicious with a red Bordeaux from Pauillac, in France.

CHOPS Serve a mature Spanish Rioja, a Cabernet Sauvignon from California, or a Washington State Merlot with lamb chops.

ROAST A classic match would be a mature red Bordeaux from France (traditionally Pauillac), a first-rate California Cabernet Sauvignon, or a red Rioja Reserva from Spain. Steer clear of the classic mint sauce with lamb—the vinegar in the sauce will spoil the taste of the wine.

SHANKS This richly flavored dish is perfect with Spanish Rioja, a Rhône red from France, Syrah/Shiraz from California or Australia, or a big Zinfandel.

STEW The wine choice will vary with the stew. A stew with big flavors needs a wine to match it, such as a reserve Chianti from Italy, a California Cabernet Sauvignon, or a Zinfandel. With a more subtly flavored stew, try a Merlot or Syrah from Washington State or California.

PORK

Pork, with its underlying sweetness, is a more difficult match than beef or lamb, and is often cooked with spices that are not wine-friendly. The best bet is usually a younger low tannin wine (white or red)

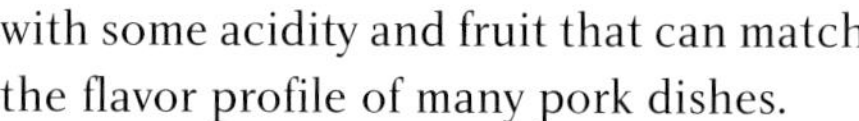
with some acidity and fruit that can match the flavor profile of many pork dishes.

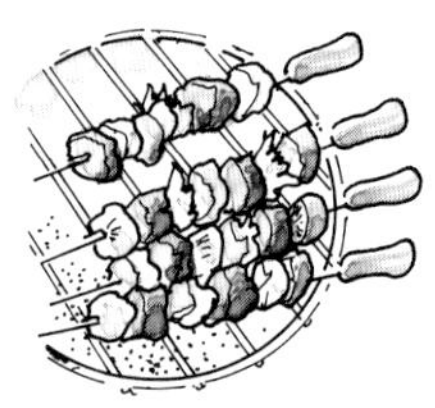

PORK KEBABS
Marinated in a hot sauce, pork kebabs go well with a chilled white Zinfandel.

BAKED HAM Side dishes apart, an Alsatian Gewürztraminer, an off-dry Riesling from Washington State or Germany, or a fruity young California Merlot will work with baked ham.

BARBECUE Some of the hottest barbecue sauces are lavished on pork, which can make choosing a wine hard. Try a semi-dry California Riesling or a chilled white Zinfandel.

CHOPS A full-flavored Pinot Noir from California's Central Coast is a good choice, or a spicy Australian Shiraz.

DRIED HAM With Italian or Spanish ham, dry rosé or a juicy young Grenache-based red from the south of France would work well.

ROAST A good match for roast pork is Pinot Noir from California, red Burgundy from France, red Ribera del Duero from Spain, or a full-bodied red from the Rhône in France.

POULTRY

Some meat flavors match perfectly with certain grape varieties. In the poultry category, duck and chicken are a great match with Chardonnay.

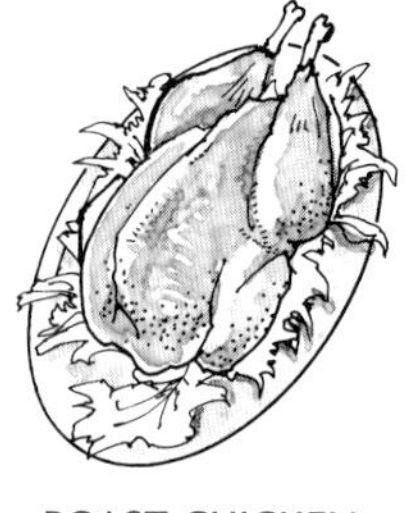

ROAST CHICKEN
You can serve simple roast chicken with red or white wine.

CHICKEN Simple roast chicken goes with anything from Chardonnay to Pinot Noir. It won't take a big red, but a roast bird seasoned with rosemary and garlic pairs well with Merlot,

French Beaujolais (not nouveau), or a light Australian Shiraz. With curried chicken, try an Alsatian Gewürztraminer or a dry California sparkler; chicken in tarragon or mustard sauce is fine with a light red such as Cabernet Franc, or an oaky Chardonnay from California or Australia. Fried chicken calls for a dry rosé from Spain or southern France, or a fruity California Sauvignon Blanc. With *coq au vin*, serve a better version of the wine it is cooked in.

DUCK Domestic duck is milder and sweeter than wild duck. Try it with a Washington State Merlot, an Italian Chianti, a California Syrah, or a buttery California Chardonnay.

GOOSE The richness of goose demands a good wine, for example a top red French Burgundy. However, it is often served with sweet side dishes, in which case a sweetish German Riesling might be a good option. In the mid-range, you could try a California Pinot Noir, a good red Rhône, or an Australian Shiraz.

TURKEY The first choice with this slightly sweet meat is a fruity California Zinfandel, which can handle any of the traditional turkey stuffings and pairs well with the meat itself.

VEGETABLES

Matching wines with vegetable dishes follows the same general principles as matching wine with fish and meat—whether the vegetable is an appetizer or the centerpiece of a main-course dish.

Difficult Vegetables

Asparagus and artichokes are especially hard to match with wine, since they make almost any type taste metallic. Asparagus might work with an oaky Chardonnay or Sauvignon Blanc. Any wine pairing with artichokes will be imperfect.

ARTICHOKE

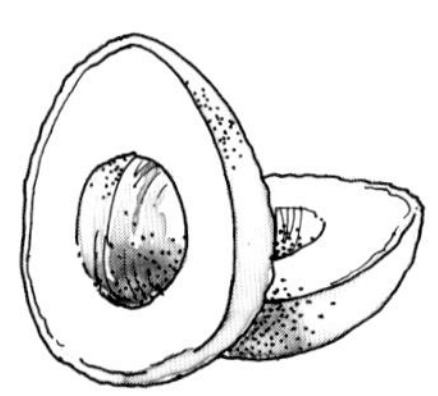

AVOCADO

Counteract the richness of this fruit with a grassy Sauvignon Blanc.

AVOCADO To cut through the fatness of avocado, try a grassy Sauvignon Blanc from New Zealand or California, or an Italian Verdicchio.

BEANS AND LENTILS Serve a fruity young red such as Syrah/Shiraz, a top French Beaujolais, or a California Merlot. For white, try an Alsatian Riesling or an Italian Pinot Grigio.

CORN Serve a buttery California Chardonnay.

EGGPLANT Serve a dry rosé or a light red wine such as a Dolcetto from Italy, or a medium-weight Chianti.

HUMMUS This chick-pea dip is best with a crisp, acidic wine, perhaps a dry Chenin Blanc from California or an Albariño from Spain.

MUSHROOMS Serve with Pinot Noir from California, Merlot from New York State, or a good French Beaujolais.

Snacks

Most snack food is salty, sweet, or both. Salted nuts can be served with a dry sparkling wine or a Fino sherry. Sweet snacks, such as raisins, pair well with Oloroso or one of the better cream sherries. A more substantial snack, such as pizza or quiche, tastes delicious with a young Zinfandel, a Beaujolais, or a Chianti.

OLIVES As an appetizer, try a glass of slightly chilled Fino sherry from Spain or a California sparkling brut rosé with olives.

ONIONS An onion tart or onion soup is perfect with an unoaked white wine such as Oregon Pinot Gris, Sauvignon Blanc from the Loire, or even a mid-range Chablis from France.

TRUFFLES With black truffles, open a top quality Champagne, a California sparkling wine, or a Syrah from California or the Rhône in France; with white truffles, serve a good French red Burgundy or an Italian Nebbiolo such as Barolo.

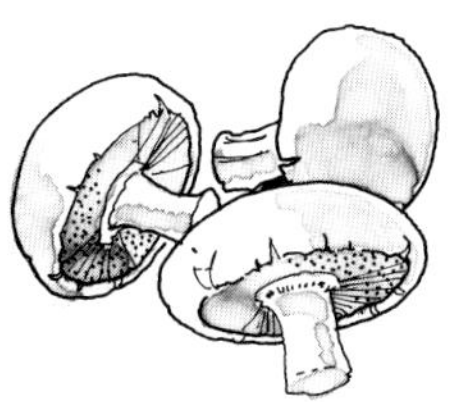

MUSHROOMS

One option with mushroom dishes would be a French Beaujolais.

PASTA

The wine selection for pasta dishes will depend on the sauces and flavorings.

CHEESE SAUCES The range of options is wide, but aim for a red or white with good acidity.

CREAM SAUCES A buttery California Chardonnay matches strength to strength; for contrast, try a zingy Sauvignon Blanc.

PESTO SAUCE Serve a young red wine such as a Dolcetto from Italy, a Beaujolais from France, or a Zinfandel from California.

TOMATO SAUCE Counter the acidity of the tomatoes with an acidic white wine. If the sauce has garlic and meat, however, you could go for a fruity red wine such as an Australian Shiraz or a young red Rioja from Spain.

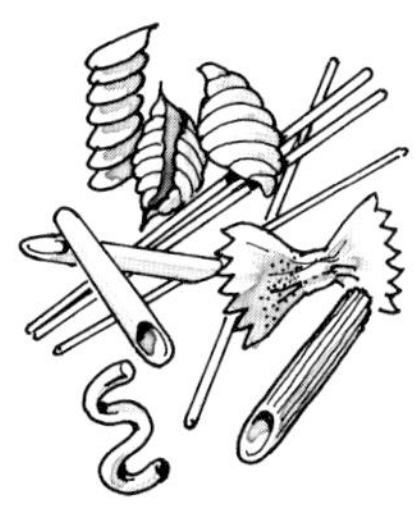

PASTA

Concentrate on the sauces and flavorings accompanying the pasta when making your wine choice.

GREEN SALAD

If you are drinking wine with a green salad, don't put a vinegar-based dressing on the salad—it will make the wine taste vinegary. You can use wine instead of vinegar in the dressing.

SALADS

A simple green salad with an oil and vinegar dressing, or any vinegar-based dressing, neither requires wine nor can it really be usefully paired with wine. There are a few salads, however, that can be matched with wine.

CAESAR A California sparkling wine will go nicely with a Caesar salad.

NIÇOISE This tuna-based salad is perfect with a dry rosé from southern France.

SEAFOOD You could serve a California Chardonnay with a seafood salad, or a mid-range white Burgundy from France.

SPINACH A grassy Sauvignon Blanc from California or New Zealand, or a brut rosé sparkling wine from California, will work well.

ETHNIC CUISINE

Much could be written about the explosion of interest in matching wine to ethnic cuisines such as Chinese, Mexican, Indian, and Pacific Rim. These cuisines did not evolve with wine and, for many years, no one really bothered to experiment and find out which wines worked. For the most part, ethnic food outside its country of origin was served with beer or soft drinks, not with wine. Now, however, some of the most imaginative food and wine pairing is happening in this area.

CHINESE Within China itself there are four basic cuisines, each of which has several sub-cuisines, so Chinese food cannot be dealt with in detail here. In general, look for a big spicy wine such as a Gewürztraminer, a grassy Sauvignon Blanc, or an off-dry Riesling; an unoaked Australian or California Chardonnay will also work. With pork and chicken dishes, a fruity young Zinfandel or Beaujolais from France can be a surprisingly good choice.

CHINESE FOOD

Spicy wines such as Gewürztraminer will pair well with Chinese food.

FUSION OR PACIFIC RIM A popular approach to creative cooking in countries bordering the Pacific, from the western United States to eastern Australia, this dynamic blend of Asian, Pacific island, and European-influenced styles is evolving into what some people are calling the first truly international cuisine. Because of the eclectic selection of spices and other seasonings, wine selections should be made on a dish-by-dish basis. Let your imagination run wild and consider seldom-met wines such as Vinho Verde from Portugal, Viognier from Virginia or California, and acidic and delicious Finger Lakes Riesling from New York State.

INDIAN As with China, there are several different Indian cuisines. In general, the more aromatic wines are best. For whites, try Gewürztraminer, off-dry Riesling, or Pinot Gris. A sparkling brut rosé, if not too dry, would also be a good choice. Red wines, such as an Australian Shiraz or California Syrah, can work well against the strong, spicy flavors of many Indian dishes. A young, zesty Zinfandel would also be a good choice.

Switching from Beer

There is an assumption that some foods go better with beer. Chili-based dishes, in particular, are often considered to be "beer foods." However, with the proliferation of different styles of wine, and the recent emphasis on fresh, fruity flavors, you can find a wine to match almost any type of food.

GLASS OF BEER

JAPANESE The cuisine of Japan doesn't have the massive heat of some Asian cuisines, which makes it seemingly more open to wine pairings. However, the subtle, often salty sauces and flavorings can be a problem. Go for off-dry Rieslings from Washington or California, semi-sweet white Zinfandel, or sparkling wine.

MEXICAN True Mexican food (not the searingly hot border food) is more open to wine pairings than many people believe. Red wines are often a good choice with Mexican food, especially young Zinfandels and Merlots from California. Light Pinot Noir from Oregon or the Carneros region of California can be quite pleasing. With *mole* chili-based sauces (with a hint of chocolate), try a young Cabernet Sauvignon or Merlot.

SOUTHEAST ASIAN (Cambodian, Malaysian, Indonesian, and Vietnamese) With the exception of Indonesian, these cuisines have fairly subtle seasonings, with rare explosions of heat. Unoaked Chardonnay, Sauvignon Blanc, young Zinfandels, and Merlots are good choices.

SOUTHWESTERN U.S./TEX-MEX The spicy Tex-Mex style of cooking can be tricky to match with wine, but classic Southwestern cuisine is full of complex flavors. In general, the same choices as for Mexican food apply here.

THAI Growing in popularity, Thai food features such exotic seasonings as lemongrass, galangal (a relative of gingerroot), hot chilies, and rich coconut milk, which make it one of the most difficult of Asian cuisines to match with wine. However, an Oregon Pinot Gris, a spicy Alsatian Gewürztraminer, fresh unoaked California Sauvignon Blanc, or an Italian Pinot Blanc would be a good place to start.

CHEESES

There's more to matching cheese and wine than you might think. Many cheeses are too strong to match with fine or mature red wine. In fact, white wines are often better with cheese than reds. Sweet white wines, in particular, taste good with sharp, salty blue-veined cheeses.

BLUE CHEESES The great blue-veined cheeses, such as French Roquefort, are a classic with Sauternes or a late-harvest California Sauvignon Blanc. Stilton is good with a mature tawny or vintage port. Spain's Cabrales matches well with dry Oloroso sherry or a mature red Rioja. Gorgonzola calls for a big red wine, such as a Barolo from Italy or an Australian Shiraz.

BRIE/CAMEMBERT A younger tawny port is a good match with these velvety, soft-ripened and triple-cream cheeses, as are fruity young red wines such as Pinot Noir from California's Russian River Valley or a good Beaujolais.

CHEDDAR This type of firm, often sharp cheese pairs well with late-harvest Sauvignon Blanc, Oloroso sherry, or a good vintage port. Red Bordeaux wine and cheddar is a combination to be avoided.

CHEDDAR

Mature cheddar tastes good with a glass of vintage port.

GOAT'S MILK CHEESES There is a wide range of goat cheeses, but in general they have strong flavors and are well paired with Sancerre from France, late-harvest Sauvignon Blanc from California, Sauternes, and mature tawny ports and lighter vintage ports.

SOFT CHEESES

Strongly flavored soft cheeses pair well with port.

GOUDA An aged gouda matches very well with a mature Bordeaux wine or California Cabernet Sauvignon.

MANCHEGO This classic Spanish cheese makes a good combination with vintage port, sweet Muscat, or even a fruity Zinfandel.

BRAND OF PARMIGIANO-REGGIANO Match this strongly flavored cheese with a big Italian red wine, such as Barolo or a reserve Chianti, or try a mature California Cabernet Sauvignon.

PECORINO Match the nutty flavor of this firm Italian cheese made from sheep's milk with Zinfandel, a lighter Rhône red wine, or sherry.

DESSERTS

There is a respected school of thought that believes a good sweet wine—what the Australians call a sticky—is dessert, and anything more is too much of a good thing. To get the best flavors from a great dessert wine, whether a Sauternes, Madeira, old sherry, or port, it is best to taste it on its own, or perhaps with a simple cheese course. However, the general rule if you want to drink wine with dessert is to choose a wine that is slightly sweeter than the dessert. Fruity desserts need a sweet wine with acidity. Some chocolate desserts can go well with port.

CHEESECAKE Oloroso sherry, Madeira, or ruby port would all be good choices.

CHOCOLATE Serve a tawny port, or go for a different approach and try a mature California Cabernet Sauvignon (a wine that often has chocolate traces in the flavor).

CRÈME BRÛLÉE Serve cream sherry, Madeira, or a sweet Muscat—for example, Muscat de Beaumes de Venise from France.

FRESH BERRIES Try Monbazillac from France or a semi-dry German Riesling.

FRESH FRUIT Serve a dry sparkling rosé, dry Alsace Riesling, or a fruity young white such as Viognier from California or an Italian Frascati.

FRUIT PIES An off-dry Riesling from Washington State or Oregon should work.

TIRAMISÙ Serve a sweet sherry or ruby port with this Italian dessert or, alternatively, try a sparkling Asti from Italy.

ZABAGLIONE Serve sweet Marsala (the wine used to make the dessert) or sweet Riesling from Germany or Washington State. Ruby port would also work well.

DESSERT

The sweetness of a dessert generally requires an even sweeter wine.

Wine in a Restaurant

There are many things to consider when ordering wine in a restaurant, such as the individual tastes of your guests, the types of dishes being ordered, and the number and sequence of courses, all while trying to sort out a wine list that may be unfamiliar to you. Bear in mind that the size of the list is not necessarily an indication of the quality of the wines—many restaurants have a huge wine list simply because it looks impressive. This section contains useful tips on how to decipher the wine list and choose your wine, what to do when it arrives, and how to deal with problems that may arise.

THE WINE LIST

If the wine list is not offered with the menu, ask for it immediately. It should include several selections from the world's major winegrowing regions, and even a short list will take some time to study.

There are several ways to organize a wine list. In the United States, the wines are usually organized by grape variety, while in Europe they are often grouped together by region. Either way, the wines are usually listed by price, with the least expensive wines at the top. However, an increasingly popular alternative is to list the wines by weight, with lighter wines at the top of the list—a lighter Cabernet Sauvignon, for example, would lead the list, even if it was more expensive than some of the wines that followed.

Wines should ideally be identified not only by variety, but also by region, vintage, and producer—for example, Cakebread Cellars Cabernet Sauvignon, Napa Valley, 1995, $55. This gives you enough information to make a satisfactory judgment on a price/value basis.

If you are unfamiliar with a wine on the wine list, ask the wine waiter for some help. To test the waiter's knowledge, ask first about a wine you do know. If the answer seems reasonable, then ask for a recommendation. In order to give the best advice, the wine waiter will need to have some idea of how much you want to pay, what sort of food you will be ordering, and your preferred style of wine.

WINE LIST

In good restaurants, the wine list is a self-contained book. Less expensive restaurants often include their wine selection at the front or back of the food menu.

WINE IN ICE BUCKET

At the table, white wine is kept cool in a bucket containing ice and water. The water should cover much of the bottle.

Flexible Wines

There is no universal food wine, but certain wines are reliable and flexible enough to go with a wide range of dishes. Versatile red wines include Beaujolais, Merlot, and young Zinfandel. For whites, it is hard to go wrong with a lightly oaked Chardonnay, Sauvignon Blanc, or sparkling wine.

ORDERING THE WINE

When you come to order the wine, you may find that your dining companions have ordered different dishes that may not all match well with a single wine. If, for whatever reason, you are limited to one bottle, order a versatile wine that will suit a wide range of food, such as a French Beaujolais, a California Sauvignon Blanc, an Alsace Riesling, or some other wine with good acidity and lively fruit. If you want to order more than one bottle to drink during the course of the meal, you can ask for the wines to be brought to table with the appropriate course, in general moving from white wine to red wine. A third alternative, which is increasingly popular both with consumers and restaurants, is to order wine by the glass, so each diner can drink a wine that complements his or her individual food choice. A restaurant that takes wine seriously will offer a selection of wines by the glass to pair with major items on the menu.

WHEN THE WINE ARRIVES

The wine waiter should present the bottle to you before opening. Check the producer and the vintage on the label to be certain the wine offered is the same as that on the list. The wine capsule and cork should be in place, and the bottle should be opened at the table.

First the waiter should offer the cork to you. Take a good look at it, since the producer's name is often listed on the cork. Even if you are not familiar with the particular vintage or producer, a sniff of the cork may alert you that the wine is corked (see page 36) or has some other moldy or unpleasant odor. Then taste the wine. If it meets with your approval, nod to the waiter, who will then pour wine for your dining companions at the table.

Backup Choice

When you are making your wine selection from the list, it's a good idea to choose a backup selection. If the waiter then says your first selection is out of stock, or if you reject it for some reason, you can quickly order another wine without having to return to the wine list.

PROBLEMS

The business of tasting and approving wine is more than just a charming ritual. By examining the color of the wine, you should be able to detect if a white wine is oxidized (its color will have brownish-yellowish tones), or if a red wine is over the hill, which can give the wine an unattractive brown edge. If the wine is corked, sniffing should reveal an unmistakable smell of wet cardboard. Another sign of a corked wine is a flat dullness on the palate when you taste it. At this point, any fault should be brought to the waiter's attention. In a reputable restaurant, the bottle will be replaced.

Occasionally, you may detect a fault that was not apparent at first sniff or tasting. If this happens, immediately call the waiter back and explain the situation. Again, the bottle should be replaced. It also happens that sometimes you simply do not like the wine, even though you cannot detect a fault. In most cases, the restaurant will not replace a wine simply because you do not care for it.

Parties & Wine Tastings

Parties planned around wine can range from an open house where several different wines or wine-based drinks are served, to a dinner party where the selection and sequence of wines are important considerations, to a large gathering such as a cocktail party. If you are planning a party where everybody brings a bottle of wine, it is helpful to decide in advance what wines you would like to serve. Then ask each of your guests to bring a different wine until all the wine slots are filled. If you have friends who are interested in wine, you might even want to hold an informal wine tasting.

DINNER PARTIES

The first consideration for a dinner party is whether to plan the wine around the food or vice versa. In most cases, the menu usually comes first, but if you want to show off a special wine or series of wines, then work forward from the wine.

PLACE SETTING

There are various ways of arranging place settings for a dinner party. This setting would suit a fairly informal occasion.

PLANNING THE MENU

In general, it is most satisfactory to move from lighter to heavier foods and wines. Plan the menu course by course—or wine by wine—and decide which wines will work best with each dish (see Matching Food & Wine, pages 260–279).

HOW MANY WINES

For a simple dinner shared with good friends, you might prefer to open only one wine and serve it right through to the dessert, or cheese and fruit. If the wine is to be in the spotlight, however, you could serve a different wine with each course, in which case you will need to consider glassware. If you do not have enough glasses for each course, and want to avoid washing them between courses, there is a trick that many wine professionals know: when you are finished with one course and wine, pour a small amount of the next wine into the glass, swirl it briefly, then empty it into a pitcher or dump bucket. This works perfectly well going from white to red wine, but less well going from red to white.

WINE IN ICE BUCKET

You can keep white or sparkling wine cool by placing it in an ice bucket filled with ice and water.

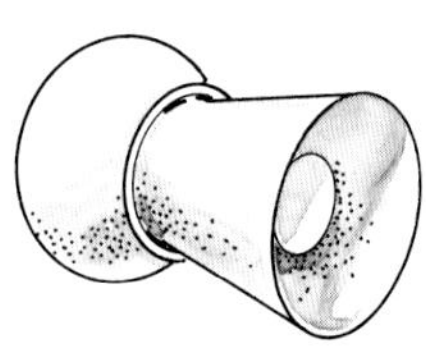

CHAMPAGNE STOPPER

If you have leftover sparkling wine, it will keep a little longer if you close the bottle with a Champagne stopper. It is not possible to reinsert a Champagne cork after it has been popped.

DECANTER

A decanter looks elegant on the dinner table, and the process of decanting helps to aerate a young wine, or to get rid of sediment in an older wine.

APERITIFS

Before you sit down to dinner, a glass of sparkling wine is always a welcome aperitif. Alternatively, you could serve a white wine such as Chardonnay, Mosel, or a light Alsace wine. A classic aperitif is a well chilled Fino or Manzanilla sherry. The distinctive flavor of sherry, combined with its delicate aromas, makes it a memorable welcoming drink. It is always a good idea to serve appetizers with the opening drinks. Olives or salted nuts go particularly well with a glass of dry sherry.

LINKING WINES

Wines that can segue from one course to the next should also be considered. For example, you might start the meal with a soup of clams and garlic, served with a medium-weight California or Australian Chardonnay. The next course could be grilled ahi tuna, which would also pair well with the Chardonnay. A mature red Bordeaux or Cabernet Sauvignon would be a good choice with a grilled steak in red wine sauce, and could be continued into the cheese course to follow.

DESSERT WINES

The choice of a dessert wine depends on the meal preceding it. If it has been an extensive and heavy meal, you might want to serve a lighter, less alcoholic wine, such as a sweet Riesling or Muscat. For serving after dinner, the classic digestif is a tawny or vintage port.

OTHER PARTIES

Many occasions lend themselves to sharing wine with friends, such as a wedding, a birthday celebration, or a simple open house. The kind of party you are planning will, to some degree, determine the type of wine you offer, but there are several other points to consider as well.

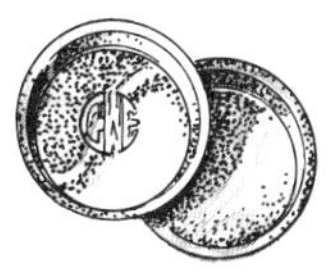

WINE COASTERS

Coasters will save your table surfaces from unsightly ring marks.

TIMING AND FOOD

How long will the party last, and what sort of food, if any, will be served? These are the two most important considerations when planning how much wine to serve and in what order.

Imagine, for example, that you are planning an open house from 2 P.M. until 6 P.M. This gives you a definite time frame of four hours. If you are serving wine, it would be a good idea to provide food as well. Eating slows down the drinking to some degree, and the alcohol in wine is

BAR TOOL

This implement is useful for opening wine bottles and cans at a drinks party.

Drinking the Wine the Guests Bring

At informal gatherings, it is fine to open wine brought by a guest. However, if you have planned a dinner party, the guest's wine may not fit into the wine sequence. In such a case, thank the guest and say that you will save the wine for another time.

Sangria

To make a simple sangria, dissolve ½ cup (4 fl oz/ 120 ml) sugar in ½ cup water. Slice and add 1 orange, 1 lime, and 1 lemon, then pour in a bottle of ordinary dry red or white wine. Add some ice cubes, stir, then add 1 cup (8 fl oz/ 250 ml) sparkling water. For larger quantities, add 1 cup of sparkling water and more fruit for each additional bottle of wine.

absorbed more slowly if it is taken with food. Finger foods, such as pâté with a sliced baguette or chips with salsa, can be prepared in advance and are easy for guests to eat while talking and circulating with glass in hand.

CHOOSING WINES

If a meal is not being served, the order in which the wines are served is much less important than at a dinner party. However, you should consider what types of wine would be appropriate for a cocktail party. Choose wines that emphasize fruit and full flavors without being too heavy.

For white wines, avoid anything too oaky, as oak tannins dry out the mouth. For reds, go for softer wines with low grape tannins for the same reason—a young Zinfandel or fruity Merlot would be a good choice. The aim is to serve a wine that is balanced and easy to drink. A Beaujolais from France, a fresh and fruity Pinot Grigio from Italy, or a Pinot Gris from Oregon would be ideal party wines.

If you decide to serve Champagne or sparkling wine, try to strike a middle range between a very dry brut and a cheap sweet fizz. A midrange Californian or Washington State sparkler, or a Spanish Cava is ideal. Cava, in particular, offers very good value. A less expensive sparkling wine can become more presentable when mixed with a little freshly squeezed orange juice and an optional splash of Cointreau—the classic Mimosa.

WINE-BASED DRINKS

You can stretch the wine budget and offer guests a refreshing variety by serving wine-based drinks such as sangria—always popular on a hot summer afternoon—or mulled wine, a favorite at winter holiday parties. These drinks, along with various hot and cold wine punches, are not only economical but make it easier to control the amount of alcohol consumed, an important consideration if guests are driving home. Remember to provide fruit juices, mineral water, or a nonalcoholic punch for nondrinkers.

ESTIMATING QUANTITIES

For a four-hour party with a few nondrinkers, most caterers recommend one-half to three-quarters of a bottle of wine per person. Of course, your knowledge of your guests may alter your rule of thumb. Most hosts would prefer to have wine left over than to run out before the guests leave. Many wine merchants will let you return unopened bottles.

WINE TASTING

A wine tasting is very different from a party, where the wine is there to be drunk. In fact, the main rule at a wine tasting is that the wine is not drunk—at least until after the tasting is finished. The point of a tasting is to assess a number of wines in a more or less formal setting with people whose judgments and palates you respect.

Mulled Wine

Put 1 cup of sugar, 2 cups of water, 3 or 4 cinnamon sticks, and 3 or 4 cloves in a pan and bring to a boil for about 5 minutes. Add 2 sliced lemons, cover, and let stand for 10 to 15 minutes. Strain out the cinnamon and cloves with a slotted spoon. Add a bottle of cheap, full-bodied red wine and reheat—do not boil. Pour into a pitcher or bowl for serving.

Tasting Times

The time of day is critical for formal tastings. Professionals and winemakers often taste first thing in the morning, while the palate is clear and not clogged with other flavors. At home, try to organize tastings before lunch, or in the evening before predinner drinks.

WINE-TASTING GROUPS

If you are learning about wine, or are a seasoned veteran, belonging to a wine-tasting group is a good way to increase the number of wines you taste. If you do not know of a group in your area, your local wine shop should be able to put you in touch with one.

ORGANIZING A TASTING

To set up your own wine tasting, you will need to provide some equipment: a spittoon for each taster, which may serve as a dump bucket for pouring away or spitting out wine; and some paper napkins. You should also provide sliced baguette or unsalted crackers, some water, score sheets, and sharpened pencils.

The wine should be poured in clear glasses before the tasters sit down. Pour each glass roughly one-third full so there is enough room for vigorous swirling.

All tasters should use the same scoring system. If you use a numerical system, make a few notes to back up your score and to help you remember the wine later.

Limit the number of wines to be tasted, since more than a dozen can fatigue the palate and subtle nuances may be lost. Even professional tasters restrict the number of wines they taste per session.

FORMAL TASTINGS

At very formal tastings, any conversation between the tasters is discouraged until the scores have been added up. At more informal tastings—including many professional tastings and wine competitions—tasters discuss the wines freely, but only after all participants have tasted and noted down their impressions.

VERTICAL AND HORIZONTAL TASTINGS The two most common tastings are the vertical and horizontal tastings. For a vertical tasting, different vintages of the same wine—for example, a Laurel Glen Cabernet Sauvignon from each of the 1990–1995 vintages—are tasted.

For a horizontal tasting, wines from the same vintage but different producers are assembled and tasted together—for example, all 1995 Zinfandels from producers in the Dry Creek Valley of Sonoma County, California. A horizontal tasting should be held blind.

BLIND TASTINGS Most professional tastings, and tastings at wine competitions, are blind tastings. The wine bottles are placed in bags to conceal the labels and anything else that might reveal the identity of the wine. Each bag is numbered and tasting notes are made based on the number on the bag. At the end of the tasting, all is revealed. The main point of a blind tasting is to keep knowledge of the producer or wine region from unduly influencing the taster.

BLIND TASTING
Wine bottles are put in paper bags to disguise their shape and hide the labels.

Blind tastings are most effective when a number of wines from different producers, and sometimes even different regions and vintages, are being tasted—for example, Pinot Noirs from Burgundy and Oregon, or several vintages of Chardonnays from Sonoma County, California.

Cooking with Wine

Wine is an important ingredient in many recipes, contributing flavor, body, and sometimes color to dishes as varied as the French chicken stew coq au vin; beurre blanc, a classic butter-and-shallot sauce for poached fish; and the frothy Marsala-spiked zabaglione. In marinades, stews, and braises, it can also enhance texture, tenderizing meats in dishes such as boeuf bourguignon. For pan-fried foods, wines can create a quick sauce when used to deglaze pan deposits, as in veal Marsala. However you use wine in cooking, a few simple guidelines can help you get optimum results.

BASIC PRINCIPLES

Whenever you cook with wine, consider four basic principles: the quality of the wine, how much to use, when to add it, and at what temperature to cook with it.

QUALITY Ideally, the wine you use in cooking should be of good quality because it will impart its complex flavor to the final dish. Never cook with a wine you wouldn't drink.

QUANTITY A little good wine goes a long way. When choosing to add wine to a recipe that does not call for it, substitute the wine for some of the other liquids rather than overwhelming the dish with it.

TIMING Wine may be added at various stages of cooking. For the boldest impact, add it at the end, reducing the wine to evaporate some of its water and alcohol; this concentrates acidity, residual sugar, and stronger flavor components, yielding intense results. By contrast, add wine to stews and braises early on to allow it time to permeate the other ingredients.

TEMPERATURE High temperatures can cause subtle aromatic flavor elements to disappear from wines; to preserve these qualities, limit cooking time and temperatures. Bear in mind, too, that alcohol boils away at 172°F (78°C), a much lower temperature than the boiling point of water. However, contrary to popular belief, not all the alcohol is eliminated quickly by cooking. Even after two hours of simmering, a small amount still remains.

POACHED PEARS
Pears poached in dry red wine stay firm and acquire a deep ruby hue.

WHICH WINES TO USE

Wine for cooking should generally be dry, because the higher residual sugar in sweet wines can alter the balance of flavors. In desserts, however, it is often better to use sweet wines or fortified wines, which impart deeper, more harmonious flavors.

Follow these suggestions for styles of wine to try in your own cooking:

DESSERTS Port, sweet sherry, Madeira, and Marsala are basics. Dry red wine is used with fresh strawberries or to poach pears.

MARINADES Red or white wine can be used as an ingredient in a marinade. The wine's acidity has a tenderizing effect.

MEAT AND GAME Red wine best suits meat's hearty taste and texture. The strong flavor of game also generally calls for robust reds.

POULTRY Cook with either dry white or dry red wine, depending on the other ingredients and desired effect. Red wine will impart color.

SAUCES Use dry red or white wine, depending on the sauce and its application. If the wine will be reduced, avoid highly acidic wines, as the acidity will grow more intense.

SEAFOOD Dry white wines go best with seafood.

SOUPS Use a dry or medium sherry or an off-dry white wine, usually added at the end.

SOUP

You can make a simple soup such as consommé taste extraordinary by adding a splash of dry sherry just before serving.

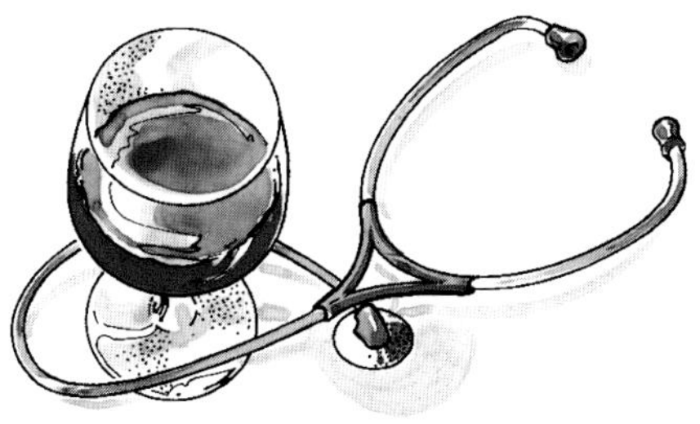

Wine & Health

The history of medicine shows us how attitudes toward wine and health have changed over the centuries throughout the world. Today, particularly in Mediterranean countries, it is generally accepted that moderate wine consumption can be good for one's health. To help define "moderation," and to make clearer who should drink and who should abstain, government health departments in many countries issue guidelines for a healthy intake level of wine, as well as for a maximum intake level of alcohol. They also issue warnings about the health risks associated with alcohol.

WINE AS MEDICINE

Wine has played an important part in medicine since ancient times. In those days, not only was wine often a safer option than the dirty drinking water, but its alcoholic and acidic properties were believed to help combat the germs that cause disease in humans.

As long ago as the fourth century B.C., the Greek physician Hippocrates urged the use of wine as a disease-preventative. Ancient Jewish and medieval Arab doctors also recognized wine's medicinal properties. Its use as a medicine in Europe continued throughout the Middle Ages.

At the end of the nineteenth century, medical attitudes toward wine changed. Excessive use of alcohol was recognized as a disease, and wine was not considered healthy for almost a century.

HIPPOCRATES

The famous Greek physician Hippocrates (460–377 B.C.), often called the father of modern medicine, advocated the consumption of wine for both the sick and the healthy.

THE FRENCH PARADOX

In the late 1980s and early 1990s, medical researchers found that certain compounds in red wine lowered low-density lipoprotein, the "bad" cholesterol that forms deposits in the arteries, and raised high-density lipoprotein, the "good" cholesterol that clears away the "bad" cholesterol. They also realized that wine contains strong antioxidants and acts as an anticoagulant. These properties reduce the risk of arterial blockage and death from coronary thrombosis. The phenomenon came to be called the French Paradox because it stemmed from the observation that the natives of southern France had a low death rate from heart disease, despite a high-fat diet. Numerous medical studies since then have reinforced the original observations.

DIETARY GUIDELINES

The U.S. government now lists wine as an element in its standard *Dietary Guidelines for Americans*. Wine producers are permitted to make a statement on bottle labels referring consumers to a telephone number or Web site that gives balanced information on the healthful effect of wine as a part of the daily diet. The label also carries a government health warning against drinking alcohol before driving a car or during pregnancy.

BACK LABEL

All American wine labels carry a government health warning.

Wine's positive effect on health is based on the assumption of moderate wine consumption, which U.S. guidelines define as one drink per day for women and two drinks per day for men. One drink is 5 fluid ounces (142 ml) of wine.

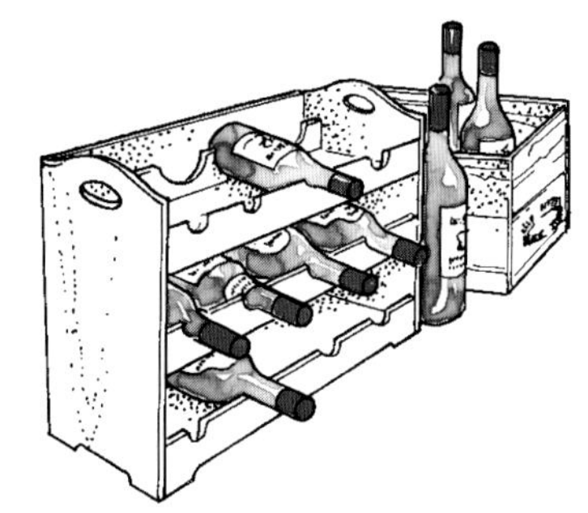

Collecting Wine

Most ordinary table wine is consumed within a few days, or even hours, of purchase. Some wines, however, are made to continue improving in the bottle and will taste better after several years than on the day you buy them. To enhance your enjoyment of the wines you buy, it helps to know not only how to select bottles that will be good to drink today, but how to store them in ways that will help them improve for tomorrow. This section presents the basics of buying and storing wine, as well as the factors that contribute to a wine's ability to age gracefully.

STORING WINE

Temperature is the most important consideration in wine storage. The ideal temperature for storing wine is between 50°F and 55°F (10°C and 13°C); the lower the temperature, the more slowly the wine matures. Up to 68°F (20°C) is fine, provided it is constant—fluctuating temperatures are particularly bad for wine. Light and humidity are also critical. Strong light will damage wine, especially white wine in clear glass bottles. Very dry storage conditions will cause the cork to dry out and allow air to enter the bottle. High humidity doesn't affect wine, but it will damage the labels. Wine is best stored in a quiet place, since even slight movement (such as vibrations from heavy street traffic) can disturb its sediment.

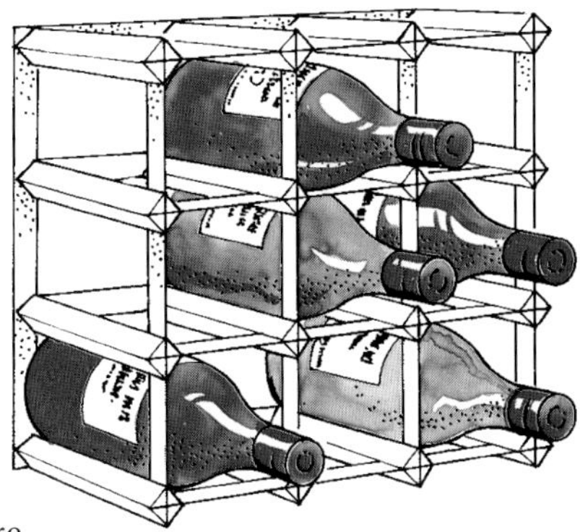

BASIC WINE RACK
This type of rack can be freestanding or fixed to a wall. You can add further racks as your wine collection grows.

FINDING STORAGE SPACE

You can create a wine storage space at home by insulating a small closet or an area under stairs. Avoid storing wine in attics and garages because of the extremes of heat. If you live in a hot climate, you will also need an air conditioner.

Having found a suitable space, the next step is to store the wine correctly. Bottles should be stored on their sides in wine racks so the corks stay in contact with the wine and remain moist. There are

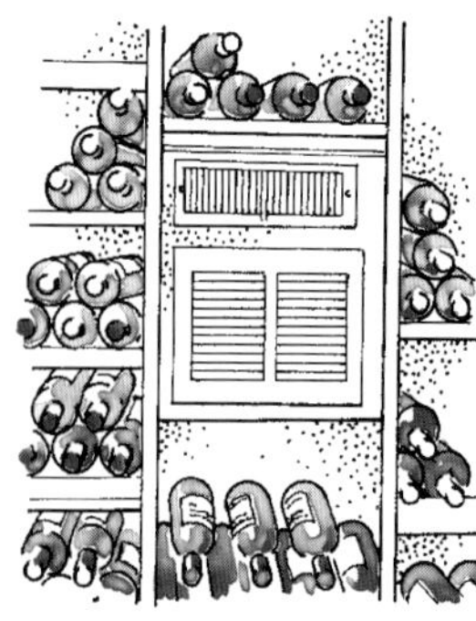

COOLING SYSTEM
Some wine racks have integrated air-cooling systems to keep the wine at a constant temperature.

many different wine racks available, made of wood, metal, plastic, and even concrete.

BASIC WINE RACKS These racks are designed to hold one wine bottle in each slot, and can be added to as your wine collection grows.

BIN-STYLE RACKS Often made to order, these racks are made up of bins which hold from 6 to 12 wine bottles each.

TEMPERATURE-CONTROLLED CABINETS These come in different sizes, from small display units to large cabinets that hold hundreds of bottles. They provide ideal temperature and humidity conditions for storing wine. The cabinets can be freestanding or built-in.

COMMERCIAL CELLAR SPACE You can rent commercial cellar space in most large cities. Ask your specialist wine merchant.

BIN-STYLE RACK
With room for a dozen bottles in each bin, this type of rack is useful if you buy your wine by the case.

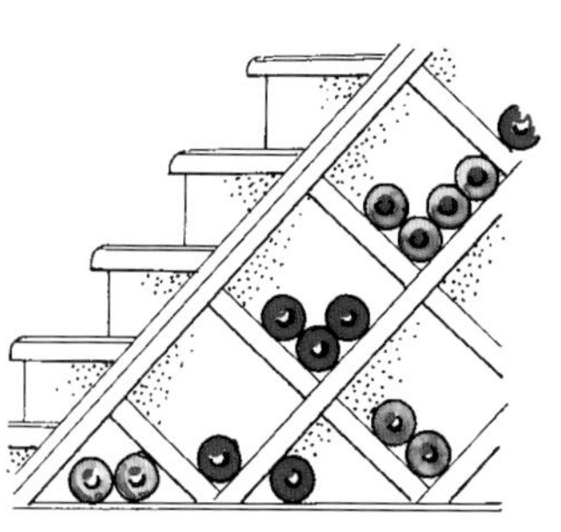

CELLAR RECORDS

It is easy to lose track of a wine and keep it past its prime, which is why keeping cellar records is important. A cellar book should contain the name of the wine, the location in the cellar (bin number or position in the wine rack), and space to make notes when the wine is drunk. If you know when you would like to drink the wine (perhaps based on a tip from the winemaker or your wine merchant), then note this down, too. You could also include the provenance of the wine: where you bought it, and something of its history if it has been resold several times. You should also make a note of how much you paid for the wine.

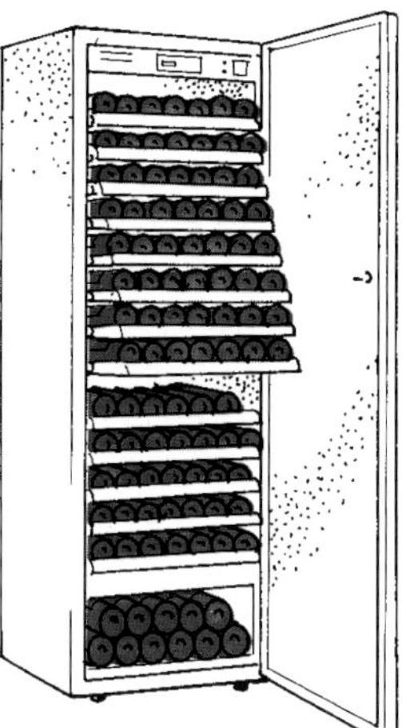

TEMPERATURE-CONTROLLED CABINET

A heating and cooling system maintains a constant internal temperature in this movable unit.

LAYING DOWN WINE

Most wine is made for drinking while it is young. However, there are some wines that will improve with additional aging time in the bottle and merit putting away for a few years. Any fine red wine you buy should be held for at least a month before opening, since freshly bottled or recently shipped wines need time for their sediments to settle.

Just how long you keep a wine depends on several factors. For red wines, all but the cheapest will benefit from a year or two of bottle aging. Some will age for decades, and it is a shame to consume such wines too young. As a general rule, red wines from a well-regarded region and producer are made with some aging potential. Red wines that can age longer than a few months include Cabernet Sauvignon, Merlot, and Pinot Noir.

By contrast, the majority of white table wines are not likely to improve with extended aging. There are, of course, a few exceptions, including several Rieslings and Chardonnays (particularly white Burgundies).

SPIRAL CELLAR

A concrete cellar can be sunk in a pit beneath a building.

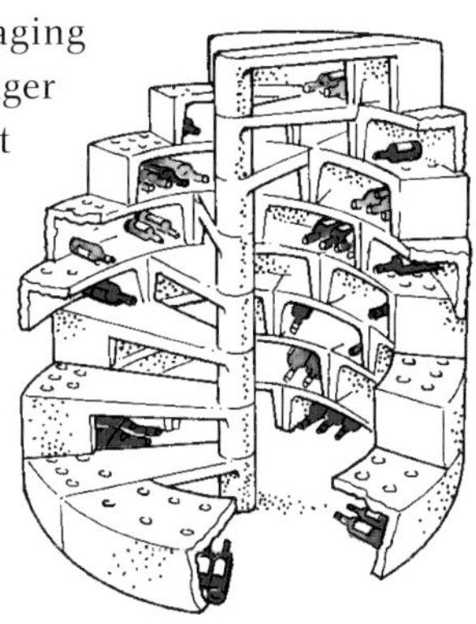

AGING PROCESS

The process by which red wine ages begins during fermentation and involves changes in phenols, a group of compounds that includes those responsible for color, tannin, and certain flavors in wine. These phenols react to the presence of oxygen during the winemaking process. The aging process continues in the bottle, where trace amounts of oxygen remain, left during the bottling process.

BOTTLE AGING

In the winery, bottles of wine are laid on their sides in cool, dark cellars for aging.

Depending on how the wine was made, the phenolic color compounds may drop out and settle as sediment around the raised punt in the bottom of the bottle. This then leads to changes in the color of the wine. Over varying amounts of time, usually several years, the brilliant red of a young wine will fade into the dusty, or brick-red, color of an older wine, with some browning evident.

As tannins continue to oxidize and soften, other factors come into play. The wine undergoes further changes, again usually over several years, with the obvious, fruity aroma of young wine giving way to the more complex bouquet of older wine. At this point, the wine is said to have developed “bottle bouquet.”

The aging process could be described as a flattened bell curve, with the young wine at the bottom of the curve moving slowly up toward a plateau that may hold for several years, depending on the wine, then gradually dropping away as the wine moves “over the hill.”

Exactly when the wine reaches full maturity is something that even winemakers cannot predict with absolute accuracy. There are simply too many variables, even unknown factors, involved in the aging process. Wine is, after all, a living thing.

Some white wines are also worth laying down. The concentration of phenols is lower in white wine than in red wine; in fact, phenols do not seem to play a dominant role in the aging of white wines. For example, Riesling is lower in phenolic material than Chardonnay, yet can age longer. Higher acidity in white wines certainly plays a role in the aging process. Barrel fermentation also adds to the aging potential of white wines, while malolactic, or secondary, fermentation seems to decrease aging potential. Sweet white table wines made from grapes affected by *Botrytis cinerea* will also age longer.

The pace of change in the wine can be influenced by factors outside the bottle, of course. As mentioned earlier, how the wine is stored has a critical influence on its development. Temperature is especially crucial, since wine stored at higher temperatures ages faster. The size of the bottle also plays a part. Wine in larger bottles ages more slowly than wine in small bottles. This probably has something to do with the smaller proportion of oxygen in the bottle, but no one is really certain.

Fortunately, in judging when a particular wine is ready to drink, various forms of guidance are available. Many major

Drinkable Old Wines

The oldest wines still drinkable are the great fortified wines—port, Madeira, and sherry. Madeira, in particular, seems to have a very long life, with drinkable examples well over a century old. The fortification with additional alcohol helps stabilize these wines.

wine publications have charts showing how particular wines develop. Another good source of information can be the individual winery, or, of course, your wine merchant. After all, it is in their interest that you enjoy their wine at its peak.

Wines with high tannin levels develop at a slower rate than those with lower tannin levels. It should be noted, however, that the presence of high tannins alone is not an indication that a wine will age. Above all, a wine must be balanced, with its tannin component (both from the grapes and from the barrels, if used), alcohol content, acidity, and residual sugar (if any) in harmony.

If in doubt, it is probably better to drink a wine slightly too young than to open it when it is past its prime. The young wine will still possess fruit and agreeable flavors, while a wine that is too old will have lost its charm and taste dull. Some general suggestions for deciding when to drink wines follow.

MATURITY CHART

The curved line on the chart below shows the development of a 1995 vintage of Cabernet Sauvignon from the Napa Valley. The wine is at the peak of its maturity after 12 years.

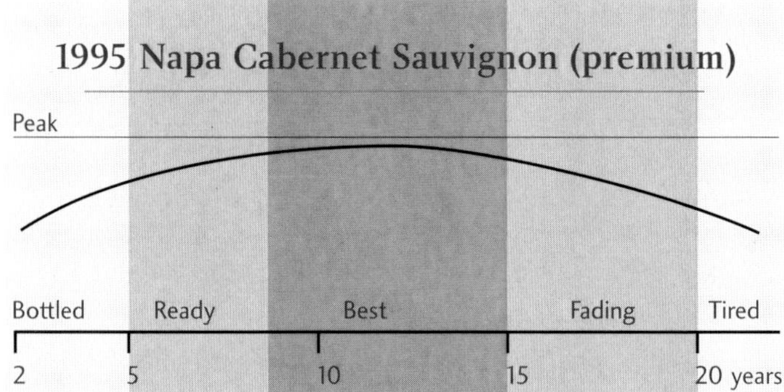

WINES TO DRINK YOUNG

Inexpensive wines are, with few exceptions, best consumed young. To make wines worthy of age, extra attention or special treatment in the vineyard and in the winery are required, and this is costly. The following wines, not an inclusive list, are suitable for early drinking.

REDS From France, Beaujolais (except for some of the Cru Beaujolais in very good years) and basic red Burgundy; from Veneto, in Italy, Chile, or Eastern Europe, inexpensive red wines, including Merlot and some unoaked Cabernet Sauvignon; from the Spanish regions of Castilla-La Mancha, Navarra, and Rioja, young red wines; from California, young Zinfandel.

WHITES Virtually any inexpensive white wine, including basic white Burgundy from France; Vinho Verde from Portugal; fresh, young white wines from the Penedés, in Spain.

WINES TO KEEP

Bear in mind that wines, even those made from the same grape variety, will age differently, depending on the region, producer, and vintage. The following is a selection of wines for keeping.

REDS From France, all Bordeaux and Burgundy Premiers Crus and Grands Crus, most Rhônes, a few other southern French wines based on Grenache and/or Syrah; from Italy, Barolo, Barbaresco, Brunello di Montalcino, Chianti Riserva, Super-Tuscans, Recioto di Valpolicella;

Tips on Drinking Old Wines

Old wines should be decanted gently (see Serving Wine, pages 42–43), as they are likely to have a lot of sediment. Since the bouquet of older wine is likely to be fleeting, only a short period of breathing is recommended. Older wines are best when drunk on their own, as their delicate flavors could be masked by food.

from Spain, top reds from Penedés, Priorato, Ribera del Duero, and Rioja; port and Madeira from Portugal; from the United States, top Cabernet Sauvignon and Merlot from California and Washington, Zinfandel and top Pinot Noir from California; Cabernet Sauvignon and Shiraz from Australia.

BAROLO
Made from Nebbiolo grapes grown in the region of Piedmont, in Italy, this famous red wine is best kept for about ten years to show its style.

WHITES From France, Sauternes from Bordeaux, Burgundy Premiers Crus and Grands Crus, Alsace Grands Crus and *vendange tardive*, and some sweet Loire wines; from Germany, top Riesling; from California and Australia, the best barrel-fermented Chardonnay, and Hunter Valley Sémillon from Australia.

VINTAGES

Give a wine grape everything a plant wants—sunshine, plenty of water, and lots of fertile soil—and it will probably make only average wine. High crop levels dilute the flavor, leading naturally to wines of less intensity. On the other hand, vines under stress, whether from poor soils or climate, tend to produce smaller crops, resulting in fruit—and wine—with more concentrated flavors.

MODERN VITICULTURAL TECHNIQUES

Many of the techniques of modern viticulture are aimed at imitating the marginal growing conditions found in classic regions such as Burgundy and Bordeaux in France. Growers choose rootstock with low vigor to reduce growth; the vine is pruned and the leafy canopy system is managed to reduce crop level. In the best vineyards, irrigation is limited and used as a tool to control vine growth. In many countries, irrigation is not allowed at all. If all else fails, growers sometimes send crews into the vineyard to take a "green harvest," cutting away a percentage of unripe grape bunches several weeks before the crop reaches maturity.

CROP LEVELS

There is no one ideal crop level for all wine grapes. It depends on the grape variety and the vineyard site. Worldwide, yields have been increasing due to healthier vines and improved farming. Still, the best growers aim to produce smaller crops. In California's warm Central Valley region, for example, Chardonnay vineyards often yield 12 to 14 tons an acre (30 to 35 tonnes per hectare). With proper care, an acceptable everyday table wine can be made from such high tonnage. In the coastal regions of Sonoma and Santa Barbara, yields of more than 5 tons an acre (12.5 tonnes per hectare) are considered on the high side. An extreme example is old-vine Zinfandel from the Sierra foothills and California coast, which often yields less than 1 ton per acre (2.5 tonnes per hectare).

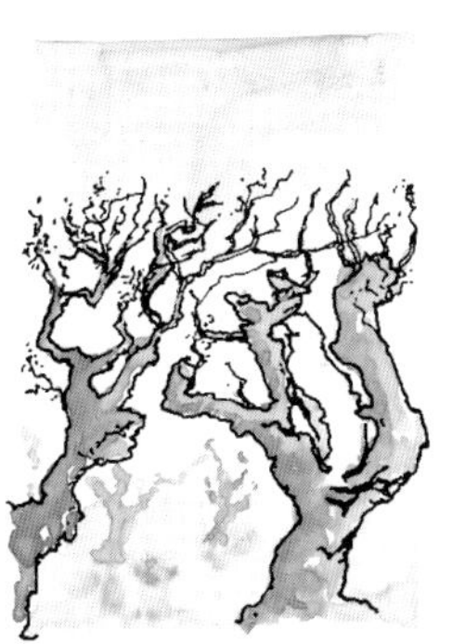

OLD VINES

Old Zinfandel vines produce lower yields that may result in wines with a more concentrated flavor than younger, higher-yielding vines.

THE WEATHER'S INFLUENCE

In the end, like all farmers, the grower is at the mercy of the annual weather cycle.

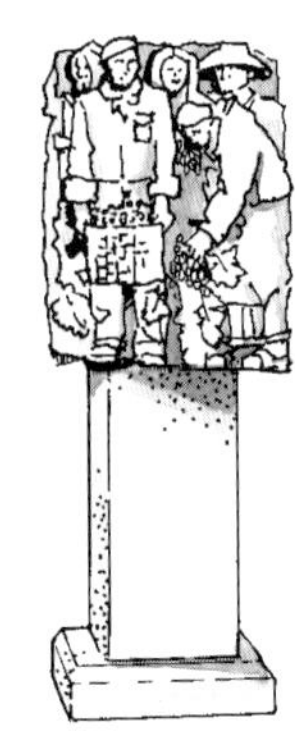

WINE HARVEST STATUE

A carving depicting the wine harvest stands in the town of Cenicero, in the Spanish winegrowing region of Rioja.

Since the soil is a constant, weather is responsible for vintage variations.

The growing season begins with bud break in spring. The time of bud break varies with area and grape variety. A cold spring can delay bud break, which in turn delays the maturity of the grapes later in the fall, increasing the threat of damage to the grapes from rains. If the spring is unusually warm, bud break comes early, leading to the danger of a late spring frost or freeze that could damage the vines.

The next critical step in the development of the grapes is flowering, which is followed quickly by fruit set. Flowering in California normally takes place sometime in May, depending again on vineyard location and grape variety. Rain or hail during flowering can be devastating to the vine, leading to a much reduced crop or increased danger of mildew.

What the grower hopes for next is a long, even growing season. If the summer is hot, the grapes ripen too fast and lose acidity, which leads to wines that taste flat and one-dimensional. However, there should be enough sunshine and heat to ripen the grapes, but at a slow, steady pace, so that acidity and grape sugars remain in balance.

Ideally, the harvest should be dry. Rain at harvest can cause mold and mildew. A cold rain at harvest also lowers sugar levels in the grapes. Too much heat at harvest can lead to a rapid increase in sugar levels and a drop in acidity and loss of flavor in the grape. The importance of when grapes are harvested cannot be overestimated. Veteran winemakers will agree that the most critical decision in winemaking is when to pick the grapes.

A winery may make outstanding wine from a rainy, cold harvest if the grapes are carefully selected before they are crushed, and rotten or moldy grapes are discarded. In larger growing areas, such as California, microclimates within the region may have a greater impact on wine quality than the overall regional weather.

Weather conditions throughout the growing season have a direct effect on the overall quality of the vintage, and more particularly on what might be called the personality, or style, of the vintage. Wines from a consistently cool growing season will show stylistic differences compared to wines from a season marked by, for example, a warm spell at harvest.

SMUDGE POTS
In California, kerosene-burning smudge pots protect vines from spring frosts by raising the overall temperature in the vineyard.

VINTAGE QUALITY

Vintage quality has a profound effect on a wine's aging potential. Wines from the best vintages tend to have the longest aging potential. Wines from poorer vintages have less aging potential, but can still develop character and style over a shorter time span, and may also represent good value.

VINTAGE CHARTS

Vintage charts can be useful in assessing particular wine vintages. They are meant to apply to the best wines from the top growing regions, wines that are worth laying down for a few years. They are not, however, fail-safe. For example, an important and frequently overlooked point concerning the whole question of vintage quality and aging potential is variation within regions, and among producers within a single region. Wine critics tend to talk about good or bad vintages in, say, Bordeaux or California, but the question of vintage quality is becoming more and more site-specific as viticulturists and winemakers learn to cope with what would have been regarded as very unfavorable vintage conditions only a few years ago.

The more detailed a vintage chart is, the more useful it can be. A simple chart might, for example, rate Washington Chardonnay in a given year on a numerical scale, usually a 10-point scale. More detailed charts would break down

VINTAGE CHART

The simple chart below gives average ratings of the vintage years from 1988 to 1998 in Oregon and Washington. The numbers represent marks out of 10 for each vintage.

Vintage Chart

OREGON	98	97	96	95	94	93	92	91	90	89	88
Pinot Noir	9	8	6	6	9	7	9	8	9	8	8
Chardonnay	8	7	7	7	8	7	8	7	8	8	8

WASHINGTON	98	97	96	95	94	93	92	91	90	89	88
Cabernet (or Merlot)	8	8	8	7	9	7	9	8	7	9	7
Chardonnay	7	7	8	8	8	7	8	7	6	9	8

KEY needs more time · ready but will improve · at peak · fading

Washington Chardonnay into regions, or AVAs, such as Yakima Valley and Walla Walla Valley. A vintage chart should also give some indication of wine maturity—is it ready to drink now? In five years? Ideally, the chart should be updated each year. Most annually updated wine guides contain vintage charts.

BUYING WINE

You can buy wine directly from the winery, or from a wine store or supermarket. Wine can also be ordered by mail or via the Internet, and fine wine can be purchased at auction.

If you are able to buy directly from the producer, you will have the advantage of knowing that the wine has been properly stored at the source. Most reputable wine merchants also store wine correctly, but often they have little control over how the wines are shipped. You should also be able to obtain from the producer sound advice on the current drinkability of the wine and its aging potential. If you don't live near a winery, you could make a combined wine buying and wine touring trip, visiting and shopping at several different wineries. This also gives you the opportunity to taste the wine in advance.

Establishing a good relationship with a wine merchant is a must for anyone seriously interested in wine. The supermarket may be fine for buying everyday drinking wine, but for fine wines it is best to go to

Closeout (Bin End) Sales

One can find occasional bargains from closeout sales at wine shops. Often when stocks of a particular wine are nearly exhausted, the merchant will make a special display or bin of wines at much reduced prices in order to clear the way for new merchandise.

a wine specialist. Let your wine merchant know what you like and how much you want to pay. If he or she is doing the job right, you'll get tips on good buys for the future, what sorts of wines to lay down, and which wines to drink now.

With the growth of the huge discount chain stores, the number of service-oriented wine merchants is shrinking. It is true, of course, that if you know exactly what you want, it is sometimes possible to get very good buys on wine from these giant stores. Just don't expect a high level of wine knowledge from the sales staff.

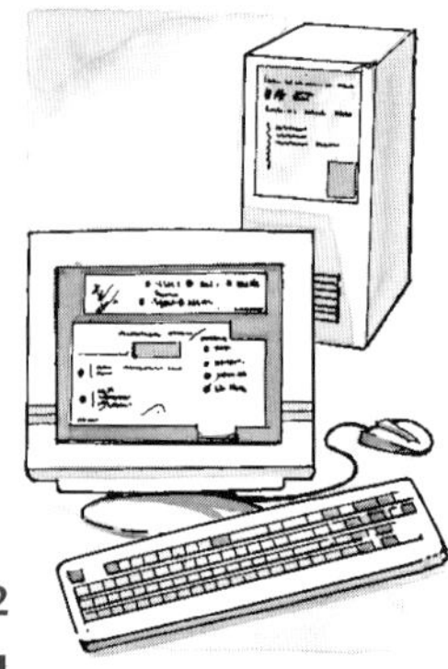

BUYING WINE ON THE INTERNET
One of the most convenient ways of purchasing wine these days is to order it on the Internet.

Buying wine on the Internet or by mail is increasingly popular. The one major disadvantage is that you cannot taste the wine in advance. If you live in a remote area, however, it may be the only way to get the wine you want. Find out before buying if the seller will accept returns. A major plus for buying this way is convenience as well as access to a large stock of wines, especially in the case of many Internet suppliers who can tap into huge supplies of wine without the expense of holding stock on hand. One hopes that these savings are passed on to the buyer.

At one time, buying wine at auctions was considered rather esoteric, something for those interested only in rare old vintages. As auctions become more common, knowledgeable buyers are finding them to be excellent sources of wine, not only for long-term cellaring but to drink in the short term. Many of the wines offered could be described as precellared, wines with some age that are ready to drink. You do pay a premium, but you have not had to worry about cellar facilities.

For the most part, wines bought at auction cannot be tasted in advance; nor can they be returned. If you wish to try your hand at auction buying, obtain a copy of the catalog in advance and decide what you are interested in buying and how much you want to pay. Wine auctions are not the place for impulse buying.

Buying wine as an investment is recommended only if you have researched the market and know it well. In the United States and England, there are several large commercial auction houses where you can purchase fine wine.

Futures (En Primeur)

Wines that are sold before bottling are said to be sold as "futures," or en primeur. *This practice, which originated in Bordeaux, in France, has been taken up in other winemaking regions, notably California. Futures are sold to the trade, or directly to the consumer, at a price anticipated to be below the wine's price when bottled and released. Besides the (potential) savings, a futures purchase gives the consumer a way to secure scarce wines before their release. There are risks involved. If economic conditions change, the price paid may actually be higher than the price at release. There is also the chance that, after the consumer pays the opening price, one of the middlemen in the deal could fail, leaving the consumer without any wine.*

Vintage Guide

Vintage guides such as this one offer a broad generalization to point you toward the best wines available. They apply only to the top wines.

The numerals 1–10 give a rating for each year (10 is best).
R = red wines W = white wines
Not ready · Just ready · At peak · Past best

	98	97	96	95	94	93	92	91	90	89	88
BORDEAUX											
Médoc and Pessac-Léognan (R)	7 Not ready	7 Not ready	8 Not ready	8 Not ready	7 Not ready	6 Just ready	4 At peak	4 Just ready	8 Just ready	8 Just ready	8 Just ready
Graves and Pessac-Léognan (W)	9 Not ready	5 Not ready	8 Not ready	8 Not ready	8 Just ready	5 At peak	4 At peak	4 At peak	9 At peak	8 At peak	9 At peak
Sauternes (W)	7 Not ready	9 Not ready	9 Not ready	7 Not ready	6 Not ready	4 Just ready	3 Just ready	3 At peak	10 Not ready	9 Not ready	9 Not ready
St-Émilion, Pomerol (R)	8 Not ready	7 Not ready	7 Not ready	8 Not ready	7 Not ready	6 Just ready	4 At peak	2 At peak	9 Just ready	9 Just ready	8 Just ready
BURGUNDY											
Côte d'Or (R)	8 Not ready	8 Not ready	9 Not ready	8 Not ready	5 Not ready	8 Not ready	6 At peak	7 At peak	10 Not ready	8 At peak	8 At peak
Côte d'Or (W)	7 Not ready	8 Not ready	9 Not ready	9 Not ready	6 Just ready	6 Just ready	9 Just ready	6 At peak	8 At peak	9 At peak	7 Past best
Chablis (W)	7 Not ready	8 Not ready	10 Not ready	8 Just ready	6 At peak	6 At peak	7 At peak	6 Past best	9 At peak	8 Past best	7 Past best
RHÔNE											
North (R)	8 Not ready	7 Not ready	7 Not ready	8 Not ready	7 Not ready	4 At peak	6 Just ready	9 At peak	7 At peak	8 Just ready	8 Just ready
South (R)	9 Not ready	6 Not ready	6 Not ready	8 Not ready	7 Just ready	6 Just ready	5 At peak	5 At peak	9 Just ready	10 Just ready	9 At peak
CHAMPAGNE Vintages usually only declared in the best years (several years after the harvest).											
Vintage Champagne	8 Not ready	7 Not ready	9 Not ready	7 Not ready	5 Not ready	5 Not ready	5 Not ready	5 Not ready	9 Not ready	8 At peak	8 Just ready

	98	97	96	95	94	93	92	91	90	89	88
UNITED STATES											
California Cabernet	8	8	7	8	8	7	8	9	8	6	7
California Chardonnay	6	7	6	8	8	7	7	9	8	7	7
Oregon Pinot Noir	9	5	7	5	9	7	9	8	9	8	7
Washington State Merlot/Cabernet	8	7	9	8	9	7	9	8	7	9	7
ITALY											
Piedmont (R)	9	10	8	8	6	7	4	5	10	9	8
Tuscany (R)	8	10	8	9	8	8	5	7	10	6	9
SPAIN											
Rioja and Ribera del Duero (R)	6	7	9	8	9	5	6	7	7	8	4
PORTUGAL For port, a vintage is generally declared only in the best years.											
Vintage port		7	8	8	10	2	9	8	6	6	5
GERMANY											
Mosel Riesling (W)	8	8	7	9	7	9	7	6	10	7	8
Rheingau Riesling (W)	8	9	8	7	6	7	8	5	9	7	8
AUSTRALIA											
Hunter Chardonnay	9	5	8	8	8	7	5	9	7	7	6
Barossa Shiraz	8	8	9	8	9	7	6	8	8	6	7

Index